R. Burman/*Vogue India*

KHULLAM KHULLA

KHULLAM KHULLA
Rishi Kapoor
Uncensored

With Meena Iyer

HarperCollins *Publishers* India

First published in hardback in India in 2017 by
HarperCollins *Publishers* India

Copyright © Rishi Kapoor 2017

P-ISBN: 978-93-5264-302-8
E-ISBN: 978-93-5264-307-3

2 4 6 8 10 9 7 5 3 1

Rishi Kapoor asserts the moral right to be identified
as the author of this work.

The views and opinions expressed in this book are the author's
own and the facts are as reported by him, and the publishers
are not in any way liable for the same.

HarperCollins *Publishers*
A-75, Sector 57, Noida, Uttar Pradesh 201301, India
1 London Bridge Street, London, SE1 9GF, United Kingdom
Hazelton Lanes, 55 Avenue Road, Suite 2900, Toronto, Ontario M5R 3L2
and 1995 Markham Road, Scarborough, Ontario M1B 5M8, Canada
25 Ryde Road, Pymble, Sydney, NSW 2073, Australia
195 Broadway, New York, NY 10007, USA

Typeset in 12/15 Cardo Regular at
SÜRYA, New Delhi

Printed and bound at
Thomson Press (India) Ltd

To my parents
Krishna & Raj Kapoor

CONTENTS

Contents

FOREWORD

RANBIR KAPOOR

I'm thirty-four now. As I sit down to analyse my relationship with my father, I would say that the most precious gift he has given my sister Riddhima and me is that we can love our mother unconditionally. He showed us by example that she was at the centre of all our lives and our home. With her as our bedrock, none of the ups and downs in our lives could really touch us.

The second gift is that he has been a good husband to my mother. My parents have had their fair share of intense fights. They have sulked with each other and all of that, but he truly loves my mother in a very solid way. He gave her and continues to give her tremendous respect, love and care. To my sister and me, this matters a lot. As children we have learnt a lot about love and human behaviour through observing our parents – how they are with each other, how they speak to each other.

I am not sure if I can adequately convey how much I admire the respect and deep caring they have for one another.

The third thing is that he taught me to respect my work. I became an actor in 2006–07. I was living with my parents at that point. And each morning I would observe my father getting ready for his shoot. I saw his enthusiasm even at that age, after all those years in the industry. He had it in him to better his craft, go shopping for his costumes or examine every minute aspect. He is that kind of man; very detail-driven. This is something I deeply admire. Looking back, he probably did the same kind of characters for the first twenty years of his life. However, in his second innings, he has worked hard to reinvent himself. He started experimenting with the characters given to him. He started having fun with his work. I sensed a child-like enthusiasm and a certain abandon when it came to his approach to roles. Again, this was done with a lot of respect – his ultimate goal was always to excel in what was offered to him. Perhaps this is what has stood him in good stead.

As far as my personal relationship with him goes, well, it is one of complete reverence. I am closer to my mother. I feel that Dad modelled his relationship with me on the one he shared with his own father. And it is true that I have never crossed a certain line with him. But there is no sense of loss or vacuum here. I do wish sometimes that I could be friendlier with him or even spend more time with him. Sometimes I wish I could just pick up the phone and ask him, 'Dad, how are you doing?' But we do not have that. We do not have a phone relationship. Of course, he does message me. He also takes care of the financial side of my work. So we are more connected now.

When I get married and have children, I would want to change that dynamic with them. I don't want my relationship with my children to be as formal as the one I have with my father. I want to be friendlier, be more connected, spend more time with them than he did with me. Having said that, I love my father dearly and have immense respect for him. I'm inspired by him and never want to let him down. I know he has only my best interests at heart. His confidence in me and my work makes me take pride in it. I persevere that much harder because of this. His belief and his encouragement are important to me.

I know my father appears boisterous and loud, but he is, in fact, a very reserved man. He never really 'exposes' himself to the world. Perhaps because he is an actor, he reserves a lot of emotions within. A lot of actors do that. They have a reserve bank of emotions because they need that to portray emotions on screen. My dad also does that.

I do not have a take on his Twitter personality, though that is usually the first question anyone asks me about my father. All I can say is, so long as he is being honest and having fun, it's his prerogative. Social media is something very personal. Of course, he gets himself into a spot sometimes with his frank speak, but I know he has no agenda and no hidden motive. My father is a straight arrow.

These are, however, personal things. I have a professional assessment of him too. I am an actor myself and I have a keen interest in movies and performances, and I can honestly say I do not see anyone on the same level as Rishi Kapoor. There is a certain naturalness about him, a certain spontaneity. And he was like this way before anyone else. Most actors of the earlier generation had a distinct style to their acting, but my father was very natural and effortless. The way he enacted his songs, the way he serenaded his heroines on screen was laudable. Here I must say that he was also an overweight actor. Even when actors started becoming conscious of their weight, he continued to remain the way he was. He never let this come in the way of his performances. You must remember that looking good, having a fabulous body are important aspects for an actor. After all, an actor has to entice an audience. My father managed to do that despite the fact that he wasn't exactly slim. In that way, he broke certain barriers. And he was so charming. See *Chandni*, *Deewana* or *Bol Radha Bol*, or for that matter any of his work in the 1980s and '90s, and you will see that, despite his weight, his charm remained infectious.

Now, with his second innings – *Agneepath*, *Do Dooni Chaar*, *Kapoor & Sons*, and others – my father is winning more accolades and awards than he ever did in his first stint. Nothing can keep a good actor down. A man who has withstood the test of time for forty-four years in showbiz must have something special in him – there's little else I need to say in summing up here.

1

INEVITABLY, A LIFETIME
IN FILMS

I was born lucky.

On 4 September 1952, the planets, I am told, were in perfect alignment. My father, Raj Kapoor, was twenty-eight years old and had already been hailed as the 'showman of Hindi cinema' four years before. He was an actor, a film-maker and the owner of a studio that had produced films such as *Aag* (1948), *Barsaat* (1949) and *Awara* (1951), heralding the arrival of a showbiz wunderkind.

He was also a man in love – at the time, unfortunately, with someone other than my mother. His girlfriend was the leading lady of some of his biggest hits of the time, including the ones I just mentioned, his in-house heroine, the lady immortalized in the RK Studios emblem. Their on-screen romantic pairing was not just the most sought-after of that era, but is still widely acknowledged as one of the most iconic. In short, he was in a great place with his work and in life.

On this day, he was at home in Matunga. Along with him were about as many Kapoors (and a smattering of other relatives) that you could possibly fit into one room. My mother, Krishna, was surrounded by her in-laws, her brothers, including my mama, actor Prem Nath, her older children and my father. My two older siblings, four-year-old Dabboo (Randhir Kapoor) and three-year-old Ritu, although not entirely sure what the excitement was about, were caught up in it nonetheless.

My father's nineteen-year-old brother, Shamsher Raj Kapoor (later popularly known as Shammi Kapoor), had swung home from nearby Khalsa College. His youngest brother, fourteen-year-old Balbir Raj Kapoor (who grew up to be the heart-throb Shashi Kapoor), had joined the group after finishing his day at Don Bosco School.

My grandfather, veteran thespian Prithviraj Kapoor, who was a legend in his own right and acclaimed for his performances in classics such as *Alam Ara* (1931) and *Vidyapati* (1937), had wrapped up work on *Anand Math* (1952), his seventeenth film, and hurried home.

My grandmother, Ramsarni, pushed the men out of the room. When I finally emerged hours later, a robust and rosy-cheeked baby, my relieved and joyous father popped open a bottle of champagne to celebrate the arrival of yet another boy. I could not have asked for a more boisterous or star-studded welcome.

I am Prithviraj Kapoor's grandson.

Raj Kapoor's son.

I am Neetu Kapoor's husband.

Riddhima and Ranbir Kapoor's father.

I am Rishi Kapoor.

I was born lucky and stayed lucky.

There is an image of me from the 1970s and '80s as a romantic star, a jersey-clad, tune-humming, cocky Casanova, with a guitar in one hand and a girl in the other. Fast forward thirty years, and that image has been replaced by more varied and mature on-screen personas, from the repentant, estranged husband of *Hum Tum* (2004), the gay dean in *Student of the Year* (2012), the don in *D-Day* (2013) to Rauf Lala, the pimp in *Agneepath* (2012) and the naughty ninety-year-old in *Kapoor & Sons* (2016). These continuing opportunities to perform and explore a range of characters is a rare blessing at the age of sixty-four.

The two phases of my career have mirrored the reality of my life as it was and is – the early, young and brash actor who had it all, and now the more grounded family man who wants to give it his all and is lucky to be able to do that.

Acting was in my blood and there was simply no escaping it. When I say this, I am thinking of not just the Kapoors but also the Malhotras, my mother's side of the family, who were just as volatile as my father and his relatives.

Stories about the Kapoor men abound, and my favourite story is about my father's grandfather, Basheshar Nath, who was a tehsildar and was fondly referred to as Diwan Sa'ab. He was suspended from active duty at the age of thirty-six after he was caught digging a tunnel to his girlfriend's house. There is another story about a friendly encounter between him and a British superior who said admiringly of his horse, '*Teri ghodi achchi hai*', to which he responded, '*Teri gori achchi hai*', referring to the white woman accompanying the superior.

My father loved the company of men like him, the sort that flirted with the forbidden. So it wasn't surprising that he got along splendidly with Basheshar Nath. Interestingly, for all the infamous flamboyance of the men in our family, we inherited our famous blue eyes and aristocracy from our grandmother, Ramsarni Kapoor. In her youth, my dadi was a stunning woman who made heads turn. My grandfather was more benevolent than badmaash. It was he who changed the family name from Nath to Raj, so that Prithvi Nath Kapoor became Prithviraj Kapoor. My father was named Shrishti Nath Kapoor at birth, but this was changed to Ranbir Raj Kapoor, which in turn became Raj Kapoor. Ramsarni's children inherited her vivaciousness, which took on a new form with my father's antics at the start of his career as an actor and film-maker. It was he who established the swashbuckling Kapoor image, not my stately grandfather, Prithviraj Kapoor.

Towards the end of his life, my grandfather lived in a cottage in Juhu, which he called a jhopdi. Juhu, the posh suburb of today, teeming with movie stars, was considered the back of beyond in those days. The well-heeled and the famous wouldn't dream of settling down there, but my grandfather adamantly spent his last days in a house built on the same plot of land that the vibrant Prithvi Theatre stands today.

I grew up in a joint family, with my grandparents, in a big house on R.P. Masani Road in Matunga, which at the time was regarded as the Beverly Hills of Bombay (now Mumbai).

As a child, I recall, I thought a gentleman called S.P. Kriparam, who lived with us, was a distant relative. It was only much later that I realized he was not. My large-hearted grandfather, a true Gandhian, had one day invited his friend Kriparam to dinner at our Matunga residence and he ended up staying there for the next twenty-five years. Unbelievably, even after Dadaji had moved to his new home in Juhu, the atithi stayed on.

My childhood was a dream, like an unending mela. People from the film fraternity constantly streamed in and out of our home, and I was weaned on a steady diet of cinema. I was enveloped by the Hindi film industry both inside the house and outside it, as the houses up and down the street were crammed with the stalwarts of Hindi cinema of that period, including K.L. Saigal, Jayant, K.N. Singh, Madan Puri, Jagirdar and Manmohan Krishna.

The Kapoors have always been proud of our profession; nobody has ever been apologetic about belonging to the entertainment industry. Unlike some of our friends, whose parents sought to shield them from the film world, we were never discouraged from visiting the studios as children. Nor were we stashed away in the attic, never to be aired publicly, like some celebrity children were. In fact my father delighted in letting the world see his brood and even famously filmed a line from a song on his three oldest children. It certainly didn't dent his romantic image or make a difference to his legion of fans – or, for that matter, to his leading ladies.

Thanks to my early induction into the film industry, I have had the privilege of witnessing some of the historic moments in Hindi cinema. One afternoon, when I was about six or seven years old, my grandfather had a special treat lined up for Dabboo, Ritu and me. He piled us all into a tiny Opel and drove us to the magnificent set of K. Asif's *Mughal-e-Azam* (1960), in which he played the great Mughal emperor, Akbar. While most actors are able to speak of this classic or count the number of times they've watched it until they have memorized every line and pause, I was taken by Emperor Akbar himself to spend an afternoon on that historic set.

It is one of my strongest memories – every detail etched into my mind. However, the strongest of these images, I must admit, has nothing to do with what was being filmed that day – the epic scene between Emperor Akbar and Prince Salim (Dilip Kumar), where the emperor tries to dissuade his son from fighting against him. It has nothing to do with the other mega stars present, the breathtakingly beautiful Madhubala or the charismatic Dilip Kumar.

All I remember is being mesmerized by the plaster of Paris swords, sabres and spears that had been made for the battle scene. I could not look at anything else. What I took home from my visit was a dagger that Asif sa'ab gave me as a present. I was so thrilled with it that I don't remember seeing even Madhubala during the shoot. She held no particular fascination for me at the time. Even when Madhubala came home for our Diwali parties, I was too busy with the colas, crackers and cigarette stubs strewn around the party area to register her grace or beauty.

By the time my grandfather played Emperor Akbar, he had put on a lot of weight and looked gigantic. As a young man, he had been a pehelwan but once he turned to acting, he had gradually given up the punishing regimen of exercises that his body had become used to. Given the Kapoor tendency to gain weight, the kilos speedily piled up and stayed on, much to my grandmother's consternation.

During the filming of *Mughal-e-Azam*, Dadiji put my grandfather on a strict diet that she personally monitored. He also dosed himself with a concoction that was very popular then, a powder called Limical (not to be confused with Limca, the lemon beverage), dissolved in water, which was believed to suppress one's appetite.

K. Asif was a regular visitor to our home, dropping by to discuss matters related to the film with my grandfather. One evening, Dadaji invited him over for dinner and laid out a fabulous Punjabi spread for him. For my grandfather, however, dinner was a glass of Limical along with a plate of salad. Asif sa'ab was aghast. He said, '*Papaji, main* Mughal-e-Azam *bana raha hoon,* Jodha Akbar *nahin.* (I'm making *Mughal-e-Azam*, not *Jodha Akbar*.) You don't have to go on a diet to play the emperor.' With that remark, he endeared himself to my grandfather forever.

Indian cinema is over a hundred years old now and the Kapoors have been an influential part of it for almost nine decades, spanning four generations, beginning in 1928 when my grandfather joined the Grant Anderson Theatre Company. He was, in fact, the last of the male Kapoors to graduate from college. He had started a course in law too, but the draw of theatre was too strong. He abandoned that degree for an acting career.

My grandfather was only fifteen or sixteen years old when he chose to become a stage actor. And his foray into the film industry was heralded by no less a figure than Rabindranath Tagore himself.

In his early days in theatre in Calcutta, my grandfather had played Ram to Durga Khote's Seeta, in the stage production of *Seeta*. Tagore had seen it and was tremendously impressed by his performance. So when his friend, B.N. Sircar, producer and founder of New Theatres, decided to turn *Seeta* into a motion picture, Tagore suggested that he cast Prithviraj and Durga in it. *Seeta*, the film, was a blockbuster. Thus began the Kapoor khandaan's tryst with the Hindi film industry.

While his stature grew by leaps and bounds, my grandfather remained a simple man who worshipped his craft above all else. One of his weaknesses was that he was painfully shy, and any discussion regarding his fee remained a challenge for him until the very end. If a producer paid him for his work, he accepted it gracefully. If he didn't get paid, he remained silent with equal grace. The nature of his remuneration never reflected in the work, which he would continue to execute with utmost sincerity.

Dadaji lived his life by an uncompromising set of principles. Those were the days when the Hindi film industry was flush with cash, unaccounted income that was hidden to evade tax. My grandfather was perhaps the only industry man who emphatically rejected black money; he never took cash payments and insisted on declaring all his income to the income-tax authorities. It was a unique act of probity in the 1950s and '60s. Despite being father to three superstar sons – Raj Kapoor, Shammi Kapoor and Shashi Kapoor – who earned handsomely, he was fastidious about living within his means and insisted on footing all his bills himself. Much later in life, when the offers he received were mostly for B- and C-grade films, my father and uncles urged him not to accept them. But my grandfather's pride in his ability to look after himself trumped all other considerations.

Strangely, despite Prithviraj Kapoor's stature in the film industry, my father didn't grow up dreaming of an acting career for himself. He in fact wanted to enrol at Dufferin, the naval training school, and join the Indian Navy. Fate willed otherwise and perhaps it was also the pull of his genes towards the world of cinema. After he failed his final exams at school, Papa started work as an assistant to film-maker Kedar Sharma.

It wasn't a long stint though, because he ended up stepping in front of the camera – and a star was born. His first role, at the age of twenty-three, was as lead actor in Sharma's own *Neel Kamal* (1946). After that there was no looking back. Just one year later, he launched his own film production company, RK Films, becoming the youngest studio owner ever in India. He made his first film, *Aag*, the same year. These achievements were early evidence that he would go on to be regarded as one of the most influential film-makers in the history of Indian cinema.

In his own way, my father retained much of the innocence of his youth: his staple reading throughout his life was restricted to *Amar Chitra Katha*, *Tintin* and *Archie* comics (a pile of comics was always stacked by his bedside). But unlike my almost pious grandfather, Papa – or Sa'ab as I called him – was worldly-wise, well-spoken and fearless.

Despite the family legacy, and very much like my father in his early years, I didn't grow up yearning to join the 'family business'. Forty-six years and about 150 films later, the truth is that I wanted to be a great many things but never an actor.

However, I had all the Kapoor family traits. Unlike Dadaji, neither my father nor my uncles or brothers were studious enough to earn a college degree. I followed in their wake. I was no good at sports or other extracurricular activities either. Many actors today talk of having excelled in either academics or sports but, apart from a little bit of elocution, I didn't do anything remotely spectacular in school.

It is ironic then that my first role as the male lead, and my character in many subsequent films, was that of a college student. In real life, I have never set foot on a university campus. I haven't even hung out in a college canteen. I had no time to do the things other teenagers did – at the age of sixteen, I was already working in *Mera Naam Joker* (1970).

Also ironic is the fact that, for all my disinterest in an acting career, I was the youngest of Raj Kapoor's children to face the camera for the first time. I was two years old, so I have no recollection of that acting 'debut', but it is captured on film and I have heard countless tales of the day when my father cast me in a passing shot in his film *Shree 420* (1955) with my two older siblings, Dabboo and Ritu. These are primarily scathing accounts of star-sized tantrums, grumpiness and even bribery. I guess certain traits show up early.

The song being filmed was '*Pyaar hua iqraar hua*'. As Nargis-ji, the leading lady of the film, mouthed '*Main na rahungi, tum na rahoge, phir bhi rahengi nishaaniyan*', the three of us had to walk through heavy rain. But the water kept getting in my eyes and hurt me, so I would cry and refuse to shoot. Finally, Nargis-ji figured out how to handle my tantrums. Every time I had to do a retake, she dangled a bar of Cadbury milk chocolate before me, promising to give it to me if I did exactly what my father wanted me to. In the end, that was all it took for me to cooperate.

While my acting debut as a toddler is well known, few know of a very early foray into Hindi theatre when I was about five years old, as a junior artiste at Prithvi Theatre. It was in a play called *Deewar* and I had to lie in my stage mother's lap during a wedding scene. That is the closest I have ever come to doing theatre, but I do have the distinction of having worked with my grandfather in that play. I have no other recollection of my theatre debut.

I may have been a reluctant two-year-old actor, but before I turned eighteen, my father had me hooked to the movie business for life. I was sixteen when he cast me as the young Raju, the film's protagonist, in his semi-autobiographical film, *Mera Naam Joker*, a celluloid narrative in three parts. By now I was old enough to know what I was doing, and it is crystal clear in my mind that *Joker* was when I began to enjoy the film-making process.

For something that would prove to be a pivotal moment in my life, even fetching me a National Award, it began rather undramatically. My father casually handed me the script across the dining table one evening. The whole family was having dinner together when he asked my mother for permission to let me play the young joker. My mother thought about it for a while and agreed, with the caveat that it shouldn't interfere with my studies or my attendance in school. Papa assured her that he would shoot my sequences only over weekends, so there would be no question of bunking school. I pictured us taking the Deccan Queen to Pune on Friday evening, filming for two days, and returning by Sunday evening to resume school on Monday.

As my head swung back and forth between my parents, listening to them discussing the matter so casually, I couldn't believe what I was hearing. I could feel the excitement steadily growing, until I could hold it back no longer. I rushed to my room, pulled out a pad from my drawer and furiously started practising my signature, for future autograph hunters!

I hadn't harboured any thoughts of becoming an actor until then, but I could feel the germ of ambition taking root. Shashi Uncle insists that he always knew I would become an actor, from the time I was four years old, because he would see me running to cry before a mirror every time my mother scolded me for being naughty. Perhaps there was some sort of subconscious desire to be an actor. In hindsight, I have to admit that whenever I visited my father on set, I could not stop playing with his makeup, using dark pencils to draw a beard or a moustache on my face and examining the effect in the mirror.

For me there could have been no film institute better than RK Studios. Since film sets were not out of bounds for us, we grew up comfortable in that ambience. The language, the stories and the discussions at home were almost entirely about films. Growing up, our lives revolved around cinema. The studio was like a temple for us, although we were not allowed to visit a set when a shoot was in progress.

From very early on, we were also exposed to another side of the acting profession, the seductive, heady and gratifying aspect of it. I am speaking of the fame and adulation that follows success. We saw it every time my father put a foot out of the door. While for us he was just 'Papa', we only had to step out to realize what a popular man he was. Any outing would have people gawking at him or rushing to do things for him or requesting him for an autograph. It was incredibly exciting and we grew up revelling in it. But for all the fame that my father brought into our lives, my mother worked hard to keep us grounded and did her best to bring us up like regular children.

My life as a student began after we shifted to our bungalow in Deonar, near Chembur, and became a nuclear family. My school life was fragmented as I went to four different schools and fared badly in all of them. The kindergarten years were spent at Don Bosco School in Matunga, followed by Walsingham in Walkeshwar. From there I was packed off for a brief stint at boarding school, to Mayo College in Ajmer, Rajasthan. I returned from Mayo and went to Campion School in Colaba, where I appeared for my Senior Cambridge exams and failed.

Joker was filmed during my Campion days. Despite the promise made to my mother, from the moment I started filming for the movie, attendance at school and studies receded into the background. My initial presumption that my part in *Joker* would be completed over a weekend in Pune was soon dispelled – my first shot was actually filmed on a skating rink in Shimla. Decades later, when I returned there to shoot for *Student of the Year*, I was flooded with memories of those first steps I had taken as an actor.

My father fine-tuned my performance by making me rehearse each shot to the last detail before the camera rolled. I can never forget a scene with Achla Sachdev, who played my mother, in which she had to slap me a few times. Papa instructed her to really get into character and execute the scene as realistically as she could. We ended up doing eight or nine takes of the scene, by the end of which I was red and blue in the face and weeping copiously. My father was unaffected. But that was him – film-maker first, father later.

Mera Naam Joker failed but my debut was applauded. I didn't understand the importance of a National Award in an actor's life at the time, but I was excited nonetheless when I won it. I loved the buzz around it and watching the reaction of my ecstatic family. I was a clueless teenager, so the credit for my performance must undoubtedly go to my father.

I distinctly remember wearing a suit and attending the stiff, formal function in Delhi to receive the award from V.V. Giri, the President of India at the time. Once I had received the award, I automatically gravitated towards Papa with it. He was overwhelmed. Back in Mumbai, he packed me off to visit my grandfather for his blessings. Dadaji was ailing then (he passed away the following year, in 1971). But he was visibly moved as he took the medal in his hand and kissed it. I was unnerved because I'd never before seen him in tears. He blessed me, kissed my forehead and tearfully said, 'Raj *ne mera karza utaar diya* (Raj has repaid my debt today).'

Thus Dadaji welcomed me into the industry with tears of pride and joy. He also warned me sagely that it was only the beginning of what would be a long and difficult trek, and to equip me for it, he narrated the story of a madari, a street acrobat, and his two-year-old son. The madari played the dholak while his wife, with her young son fastened securely to her waist, balanced on a high rope and carefully walked across it. The child, terribly pleased with what he was doing but with little understanding of the perilous nature of the act, looked down at his father and asked him enthusiastically, 'Father, how am I doing?' The madari replied, 'You're doing well, son, but you have a long way to go and many more difficulties to face.' Dadaji's words have stayed with me and guided me through my career.

In acting, as in life, you can never claim to have done it all and rest on your laurels. You are always a student, constantly learning and honing your craft. From my first tentative steps on the sets of *Mera Naam Joker* in 1970 to the more confident but ever-evolving actor of today, it's the fiery, burning passion for cinema that has kept me going through the dizzying highs and crushing lows. It is the same passion I saw in my father. Such was Raj Kapoor's passion for cinema that till the success of *Bobby*, he did not have a house of his own. He invested all his earnings from cinema in the films he made. It was only after *Mera Naam Joker* failed that this dawned. And only after the success of *Bobby* did he buy his own house.

Papa was driven by a zeal that simply could not be dampened. It was his one true and constant companion. The harder he fell, the stronger he bounced back. When *Aah* (1953) flopped, he made *Boot Polish* (1954) with two newcomers, and it became a massive hit. When *Mera Naam Joker* flopped, he responded with *Bobby* (1973), once again with newcomers. He took risks, and some paid off while others were epic disasters, but whatever the outcome, they were a testament to his indefatigable spirit. My father was also immensely gifted. His understanding of music and direction was phenomenal, and he was a brilliant actor too.

Though *Mera Naam Joker* failed at the box-office, it has, over time, become one of RK's highest-selling films in the home video segment and continues to be a perennial favourite with viewers. I feel that *Joker* is a much misunderstood film. When Papa announced it, I think people expected it to be a comedy, given the 'joker' in the title. We have a strange approach to comedy in our country, where physical deformities are played for laughs and people slipping on banana peels are a staple. *Mera Naam Joker* was anything but. It was a deeply philosophical meditation on the joker and what being one entails. No wonder the audience could not relate to it. Much later, J.P. Chowksey, a family friend, urged Papa to cut the film to three hours. Papa's first reaction was, '*Beti ghar se vidaa ho gayi, ab kya…* (The daughter has left the house, what's the point)', and it took months for Mr Chowksey to convince him. Eventually, a three-hour version was released to full houses in a number of places. Incidentally, all the cuts pertained to the second and third parts of the film; the first part was left intact. In fact, Satyajit Ray had initially asked Papa to release the first part (which starred me) as an independent film, saying that with its lyrical storytelling it would go down as one of the greatest films in the world.

The failure of *Mera Naam Joker* threw the family into a financial mess. RK Studios was mortgaged and my father faced a number of problems. To compound matters, *Joker* was followed by *Kal Aaj Aur Kal* (1971). The film, which was to launch my brother Randhir as a lead actor and on which I was an assistant director (AD), was grossly ill-timed. India and Pakistan went to war in December 1971 and all the evening shows of the film had to be cancelled. Unlike now, when a film has 1,500-plus shows, in the 1970s they had a limited release and it goes without saying that in times of war people didn't leave their homes to go to the movies. *Kal Aaj Aur Kal* crashed at the box-office.

It wasn't the best of times for us. My grandfather's health was failing and it was a struggle for him to film his scenes in *Kal Aaj Aur Kal*. But he survived long enough to see his grandson's film, which featured three generations of Kapoor men: my grandfather, my father and my brother. The lead actress was Babita, Dabboo's fiancée, so *Kal Aaj Aur Kal* turned out to be truly a family film.

My father had to think on his feet and quickly make another film to pull RK Studios out of the red. In the early 1970s, Rajesh Khanna was the superstar who ruled the box-office; the other reigning stars included actors such as Sharmila Tagore. Any one of them would have given their right arm to work with Raj Kapoor. Manoj Kumar and Dharmendra, who had worked in *Joker*, offered to work for free in any new film he announced. But my father wasn't interested. He told them, 'You are big stars, I will come to you when I am back on my feet.' A voracious reader of Archie comics all his life, he came up with the idea of a teenage love story about a very young boy, just out of school and ready for college. Love stories of that era were built around mature lead actors in their thirties. It hadn't yet occurred to anyone to make a film about teenagers falling in love.

My father's idea was transformed into a script by Khwaja Ahmed Abbas and V.P. Sathe, and once that was ready, the hunt began to find a girl for the title role. Contrary to popular belief, *Bobby* was never meant to launch me as a lead actor. The opening shot did not have me riding a motorcycle or a horse, nor were any scenes written to showcase me as an actor. For that matter, even the film's name, *Bobby*, belonged to the lead actress. For my father, a movie was about telling a story, and the story always came first. Personal relationships were never allowed to get in the way.

During the filming of *Bobby*, Dimple became like a part of my family. Despite all the ups and downs in my own personal equation with her, she is still close to the Kapoor family. When we started *Bobby*, I used to call my father 'Papa'. So Dimple began calling him 'Papa' too, and she continued to do so long after the shoot was over, right up to his dying day. In fact, even after I started addressing him as Sa'ab, she stubbornly continued to call him 'Papa'.

That I was cast in *Bobby*, one of the biggest box-office successes of 1973, was sheer chance – or destiny, perhaps. Nothing I had done until then had been a runaway success. *Mera Naam Joker* was a flop, *Kal Aaj Aur Kal*, which I had assisted in, also sank. I failed in my Senior Cambridge exams and then, despite this string of failures, I got the lead part in *Bobby*!

Had I fared well in academics, I may have ended up charting a very different course and gone to England to earn a degree in business administration. That's what all my non-film friends did at the time and I might have followed suit. But I also had a bunch of film-land buddies, including Rahul Rawail, Bittu Anand (who studied with me briefly at Mayo) and Junior (Prem Nath's son, Prem Krishen). So I had plenty of reasons to stay back too.

Everything fell into place when *Bobby* did stupendous business and the spotlight suddenly turned on me. Dimple had got married before the movie was released, so I ended up benefitting from the full blast of attention. Almost overnight, the demand for me soared so high that I started being paid the unimaginable sum of ₹500,000 for a film.

I didn't realize then that victory could be short-lived. I was just twenty years old and a real brat. I had the world at my feet and didn't give a damn for anything but my stardom. That reality hit me only a little later. I didn't have a film slated for release immediately after the extraordinary success of *Bobby* as I signed all my new films only after its release, and films those days were made at a leisurely pace.

It's true that I had an incredibly easy entry into the film world. I didn't have to struggle for fame and fortune. But not even my extraordinary family legacy could protect me from the realities of life. After my hugely successful debut as a leading man, there was no magic wand to gift me an unbroken string of blockbuster movies. Bitter disappointment and paralysing defeat awaited me and I could do nothing about it.

Bobby was followed by my first flop as a hero, *Zehreela Insaan* (1975). It prompted the question: was *Bobby* just a flash in the pan? Fortunately, I had begun work on a few other films, and before I could be completely written off, *Rafoo Chakkar* (1975), a semi-hit, came along and rescued me from certain oblivion. But since I was made up like a girl for a major part of the film, I could not be endorsed as a bona fide heart-throb whom female fans could swoon over. I had to wait a while longer before I could be emphatically hailed as a romantic lead. It finally happened with *Khel Khel Mein* (1975), whose phenomenal success ushered me once again into the limelight and established me as a singing, dancing romantic star. And the best was yet to come. What really swept me to major stardom was *Laila Majnu* (1979), a spectacular solo success.

With that I consolidated my position in the industry and settled down as an actor. Luckily, I was still too young and brimming with spirit to be felled by my setbacks. In fact, the silver lining to all those early failures was that they turned me into a fighter, prepared to stand up to anything that life might throw at me. If success gave me confidence, the screw-ups humbled me.

When I was cast in *Bobby*, one of my first tasks was to lose weight for the role. Before the film went on the floor and all through its making, my steady girlfriend was a drop-dead gorgeous Parsi girl called Yasmin Mehta. She was my first serious girlfriend. I adored her and used to see her every day. There was a popular slimming centre in Mumbai in the 1970s called Jussawala. Sanjeev Kumar had enrolled there to lose weight for *Love and God* (released only in 1986 after a long and troubled production history). I went there too, but it didn't work for me. I am a beef-eating Hindu, although my mother did not allow it at home. Yasmin made me change my Punjabi food habits. She whittled down my diet to a single lean beef steak with salad for every meal and that was what helped me lose weight and get into shape for my big break.

By the time *Bobby* was released in 1973, *Stardust*, which was the most popular magazine of its time, published a story about a budding romance between Dimple and me. Dimple, who by this time was already married to Rajesh Khanna, was not greatly affected by it. But it put paid to my relationship with Yasmin.

Yasmin was my support system for three years till 1973. She lived on Marine Drive in south Bombay while I stayed with my parents in Chembur, a faraway suburb. Her older sister was seeing a friend of my brother Dabboo, and that's how I met her. We grew immensely fond of each other and soon became inseparable. When I was shooting in Pune for *Bobby*, I would go to the post office and book lightning calls to talk to her every day. My father knew that Yasmin had a special place in my life but he didn't actively encourage it.

Admittedly, life changed for me after *Bobby*. I became a huge star and my attitude transformed into one of brash arrogance. Yasmin realized that somewhere along the way I had ceased to be the boy she had liked and dated. So she did what she thought was right – she dumped me. My friends tried to persuade her not to call it off but she was adamant. I thought her decision was unacceptable and tried everything I could to win her back.

Immediately after our break-up, I had gone for an outdoor shoot for *Zehreela Insaan*, to Chitradurga in Karnataka, where I used to get drunk and make my co-star Neetu Singh (whom I later married) telephone Yasmin and try to cajole her into talking to me. I would go to the post office and wait for lightning calls to come through. It was cold in Karnataka and the wait was often long. One evening, one of my calls went through at 10.30 p.m., and her mother answered. Very kindly she said to me, 'Rishi, my son, forget about Yasmin.' I was heartbroken and handled my grief exactly as a brash movie star might be expected to – with alcohol and cringe-making behaviour.

Soon after I returned to Bombay from the shoot, I headed to the Apollo Bar at the Taj Mahal hotel to drown my sorrows in alcohol with two of my close friends, Bittu Anand being one of them. As I entered the hotel I saw Yasmin with a friend of mine whom she was now dating. It completely threw me. The two of them went up to the restaurant, Rendezvous, and we followed and sat a few tables away.

After downing two drinks, I had a bottle of champagne delivered to her table, and she promptly sent me a message through Bittu, asking me to stop making a fool of myself. By this time I was devastated and was drinking heavily too. Towards the end of the binge, I wound up arguing with the manager of the restaurant. Years later, I met him at the Taj in New York and we reminisced about what had happened that night. We had argued because I had run up a bill of approximately ₹18,000 and I had only ₹2,000 with me. The manager threatened to call the cops when I threw my stardom in his face. He was not impressed.

Then my assistant Ghanshyam Rohera joined the group. As inebriated as I was, he announced, 'I want to buy this hotel, my hero has been insulted.' At some point, however, we finally settled the bill and left. It was all very unpleasant, but I was too drunk to realize it at the time.

The next morning, hung-over but sober, I had a vague

recollection of my shenanigans and fervently hoped that I had not misbehaved with Yasmin. But my friend Bittu brought me up to speed soon enough and I could only regret what I had done.

I met Yasmin on a few occasions after that, but by then I had come to terms with our break-up and handled myself with a lot more dignity. She later married a very dear friend of mine. Neetu was always very cordial with her and her untimely death a few years ago saddened me greatly.

Yasmin had presented me with a ring when we were dating, a simple one with a peace sign on it. When we were filming *Bobby*, Dimple would pull it off and wear it on her finger. She ended up keeping it. When Rajesh Khanna proposed to her, he saw the ring and flung it into the sea near her house in Juhu. Inevitably the headlines blazed: 'Rajesh Khanna throws Rishi Kapoor's ring into the sea'. The truth is that I was never in love with Dimple or even infatuated with her. I was probably a little possessive after working with her in *Bobby*. In any case, as a young lad of twenty, I don't think I knew what love was all about.

2

THE RAJ REIGN

The fourteenth of December. A day circled on the calendar of every prominent person in the city, and certainly those with ties to the film industry. My mother would be on the phone all week, reminding people about the event. Not that anyone needed reminding – it was an occasion they waited for all year.

Our bungalow in Deonar was always party-ready. Mom, dressed in her immaculate white sari, was also always prepared, a hostess extraordinaire, used to entertaining a dozen or more guests every other evening. But the famed Kapoor hospitality had as much to do with Papa as with Mom. He had a thumb rule. A guest should never have to repeat how he liked his drink – a good host would keep tabs on every individual's preference once the first drink was ordered. The staff would be instructed accordingly and it was they who'd be in a flurry all evening. Papa was the quintessential 'Showman' who heartily welcomed everyone and then drank and enjoyed himself as much as any of his guests did. But 14 December was the big one, the Showman's birthday. It was the biggest annual event in the city's social calendar. Celebrities old and new and all our parents' acquaintances and friends turned out in their finest for the glittering dinner party on our lawns. The attendance roster was a good gauge of who the rising stars of the day were. If you were someone to watch out for in the film industry, you'd be at Raj Kapoor's birthday party that year.

My parents would start planning the menu with the caterers months in advance, fine-tuning it until the very end. Mutton was among my father's favourite meats and always had pride of place on the table. Parathas and rotis hot off the grill were another speciality of the house. Black Label whisky, wines and champagnes were stocked. The directive from my father was clear: the bar was never to run out of liquor.

While my parents, especially my mother and elder sister, Ritu, bustled around to ensure that everything was flawless, I was busy too. Except it had nothing to do with helping out. Since this was one day when the adults had no time to pay attention to the kids, we had our own little party, away from the bright lights. Smoking on the sly was the high point of the evening. My buddies and I would collect all the leftover liquor and cigarette stubs, sip and blow smoke and have the time of our lives. On one occasion, just when our kiddie party had really got swinging, my maid caught us. She went straight to Mom and – *whack!* – I got slapped right across the cheek. My mother was not one to spare the rod. Another time that I really riled her was when I drank so much milk that I threw up. Every time I overstepped, I got a smack from her.

I grew up surrounded by fame and fortune, was exposed to things most ordinary kids were not. I was a ridiculously pampered child (much more than my siblings Dabboo and Ritu) – yet I had a more or less regular childhood, much like that of my other classmates. A big part of this was the treats and trips that my parents organized for us, which I looked forward to eagerly.

Among the most memorable outings of my school-going years was a drive through the city on Republic Day. More than fifty years ago, Republic Day was a very different affair in Mumbai. The city and all the major landmarks were beautifully lit up to mark the occasion. Driving around town on 26 January to see the lights was a special outing for most families. As with everything, the Kapoor khandaan did this too in style. The whole clan would get into a truck, along with our security personnel, and weave through Mumbai after sundown. It was a major thrill for us. Invariably, the Esso building and Mantralaya would be the best-lit monuments. After the 1971 war and subsequent curbs on extravagance, this unique celebration of Republic Day was significantly toned down.

I remember my early school years as being extremely happy and carefree. We would travel from Chembur to Matunga by BEST bus with Dwarka, an elderly family chaperone who had been with us since Dadaji's time. He had even chaperoned my uncle Shashi Kapoor when he was a schoolboy. After school, I used to have lunch at my grandmother's house in Matunga, play for a while with my friends, mostly boys belonging to families from the film fraternity who lived in the neighbourhood, and then come home with Dwarka in the evening.

We were sent to school by public transport because my parents didn't want us to grow up with a sense of entitlement. But we were always aware that Papa was a very important man, largely because of the way people reacted to him wherever we went. During my school years I was too young to fully grasp what it meant to be a 'star'. It was only when I was a little older that I began to take advantage of my father's clout.

Our bus journeys stopped when we started attending Campion School in Colaba, where we were taken by car. I recall with some chagrin that I was the reason why one of our chauffeurs quit his job. I used to while away the time on the long journey every day from Chembur to Colaba and back by terrorizing my siblings. Dabboo, the eldest, was the calm and collected one, while Ritu was always a mild lamb. I had a favourite window seat and I bullied everyone else to get it. When my younger sister, Rima, joined us, I found one more hapless victim. I browbeat both my sisters, pulling their braids. Each day, the car turned into a battlefield with constant fights between my sisters and me and sometimes between my two sisters too. Then, one day, the driver had enough. He announced to my mother that he wouldn't drive us to school anymore. 'It's impossible to drive with them in the car. Chintu, in particular, fights all the time.'

Being Raj Kapoor's children meant all sorts of privileges

for us. My father used to have a running tab at the Sun-n-Sand Hotel in Juhu, the only five-star hotel in the suburbs in the 1960s and '70s, and one at Nanking restaurant in south Mumbai. I loved going to Nanking and putting my bill on Papa's account. I would take my friends there often. Our usual order was a coke float (a huge glass of cola with a dollop of ice cream on top) and something to eat. The norm was to split the bill, which usually worked out to ₹10 or 12 per person. I would collect their share in cash, charge the entire bill to my father's account and pocket the money. Not only was I a brat, I was a cheapskate too.

I also started smoking when I was in my last year of school at Campion – on the sly, of course. There was a Coca-Cola stand close to the school, run by a man called Ahmed. We called him 'Cokevala'. Only we were not interested in his Coca-Cola, we wanted cigarettes. We would sneak behind the stand to smoke them. Often, I did not pay him but put it on a running tab, and very quickly it had run up to ₹300, pretty high for a school kid in the 1960s. Ahmed would threaten to go to RK Studios and tell my father if I didn't settle his dues. I was petrified of this happening but the poor man never did. I don't remember what happened to his bill because I failed my exams in 1969 and became a movie star soon after. In 1973, when I went back to school for an event, Ahmed, who was still there, gave me a big salaam and I hugged him.

One day, I remember, my dad's makeup man lit up while we were waiting for him and I took a few drags of the cigarette. My dad caught me at it and the result was a stinging slap.

Although that slap put the fear of Papa in me, it didn't really stop me from becoming a smoker.

I was always on the verge of being thrown out of school and fared miserably in exams. I rarely showed my report card to Papa or Mom. My father attended a PTA meeting only once in his life, when Campion wanted to rusticate me. This was because I had started acting in *Mera Naam Joker* and the school had a policy not to allow children to work. Papa pleaded with them to reinstate me and even donated a swimming trophy to the school.

Growing up, my father was never around because he was always working. It was my mother we went to for everything and it was she who made the decisions in the family. We mostly met Papa late at night, at whatever late hour he chose to come home. There was a point in time, when I was a young boy, when his arrival was anything but pleasant. Those midnight moments haunted me for a long time, although I steadfastly refused to share my feelings with anyone, until now.

My father would not only come home very late, but also very drunk. He would rave and rant loudly in his stupor. Our house in Deonar was huge, but haphazardly planned. It didn't have too many rooms, despite its size. There were one or two rooms upstairs and a couple on the ground floor. At night, my mother and all the children would sleep in a common room. From the moment my father staggered home, I would hide under my razai, shivering but alert, my eyes wide open, straining to hear what he was saying or doing. It was only when I heard his voice growing faint, as he moved towards his room, that I would relax and breathe easy.

Every day I would wonder what mood or condition he would turn up in at night, dreading the thought of him being drunk and picking a fight with my mother. For a very long time I remained terrified of my father, and I am convinced that this fear sprang from those early drunken scenes. Although I was just a little boy then, I made a promise to myself that, when I grew up, I would never drink and frighten my kids like that.

As I grew older, I began to understand and accept that my father was an exceptionally creative and eccentric man. Some nights, after drinking, he would go to a buffalo shed to hear the bhaiyas sing. Often, he joined in and even played the drum or the harmonium with them. During Dussehra he would go to Shivaji Park to listen to Bangla songs.

My father's behaviour became easier to deal with as we grew older and moved into our own rooms, but somewhere deep inside, the fear remained. Although I like my drink too, I have kept my promise of never frightening my children in a drunken rage, at least not intentionally. I have never had my father's capacity for liquor anyway – I simply cannot drink all night. My norm has always been to drink, eat and fall asleep.

I am not entirely sure when I stopped fearing my father. It may have happened with my own rising stardom. My father and I had a strange relationship. One day, I remember, soon after I had become a star in my own right, we inadvertently shared a bedroom. I was quite high and wanted to go to the bathroom. On my way back, in my drunken stupor, I turned right instead of left. Without realizing it, I ended up sleeping next to my father. When I woke up I was in the tiger's den.

After all those years of fearing him, I ended up sharing a bed with him!

When I finally got over the fear of my father, it was replaced by an indescribable love and respect that just kept growing, especially after I had the opportunity to work closely with him. For me, Raj Kapoor was both father and guru, the person who taught me everything I know about my craft. I worked with him in three movies (*Mera Naam Joker, Bobby* and *Prem Rog*), the most for any actor after Nargis-ji.

As an adult, I shared a few drinks with Papa, but I never smoked in front of him. It was just something that came from a deep sense of respect – he knew by then that I smoked. Papa was also a smoker and even after he was told to kick the habit, he'd cheat. He even smoked on the sly in the hospital when he was seriously ill with chronic asthma.

I was very young when my father had an affair with Nargis-ji, and so was not affected by it. I don't remember feeling anything was amiss at home either. But I do remember moving into the Natraj Hotel on Marine Drive with my mom during the time Papa was involved with Vyjayanthimala. My mother had decided to put her foot down this time. From the hotel, we shifted for two months into an apartment in Chitrakoot (the building still stands on the curve of Altamount Road). My father had bought the apartment for Mom and us. He did all he could to woo her back, but my mother wouldn't give in until he had ended that chapter of his life.

In an interview published a few years ago, Vyjayanthimala denied ever having an affair with my father. She claimed that he had manufactured the romance because of his hunger for publicity. I was livid. How could she be so blasé and pretend the affair never happened? She had no right to distort facts just because he was no longer around to defend the truth. When her book hit the stands, several friends in the media contacted me for my reaction and I told them exactly what I thought. With time though, my anger has ebbed. I've come to accept that people tend to gloss over uncomfortable facts for reasons of their own. But I can say with absolute certainty that if Papa had been alive, she wouldn't have denied the affair so blatantly or called him publicity hungry.

My father lived large and, most of the time, on his own terms. Apart from his birthday celebration, the Ganesh Chaturthi and Holi parties in Raj Kapoor's house were well known. The family started bringing Ganpati home in 1952, the year I was born, and it's a tradition that we follow with great reverence to this day. Holi, too, was a spirited annual affair. Sadly, we had to discontinue it after Papa passed away because we couldn't control the gate crashers. In so many ways, with Papa's passing, a lot of the revelry stopped too.

My father loved his cinema, his booze, his leading ladies and his work. But for a man legendary for his hospitality, he was very possessive of his whisky. When we started drinking together, for him it was always Johnny Walker Black Label bought in London, while we were served locally procured whisky. When he passed away, we found heaps of unopened Black Label bottles stashed away in his cupboards.

With time, I find that I have acquired some of my father's

quirks and habits. After a shower in the evening, Papa would light an agarbatti. I do that too. My favourite fragrance is Naag Champa and I carry it everywhere I go. Neetu points out that whenever we stay at a hotel, the entire corridor smells good, courtesy my agarbattis. It is a dead giveaway to where Rishi Kapoor's suite is in a hotel!

My father was a devotee of Lord Shiva, and performed Shiv aarti every day. I continue the practice. Many years ago, the legendary singer Asha Bhosle had given my father a pendant of Lord Shiva on one of his birthdays because he was such a great believer. When my father passed away, my mother gave me the pendant. In fact, my mom gave away all his little things. Someone got a watch, another got a pen. My father loved piggy banks, and all the loose change collected from different parts of the world would go into them. There was one that he had with him all through the making of *Bobby*. After his death, Dimple started chasing me for it, which I thought was rather sweet and sentimental. But I said, 'No way.' In the end, Dabboo trumped both of us and said that it belonged to him.

I don't remember who got Papa's hip flask. He always carried one, though he never drank from it. He also had several high-end watches. Dabboo and Chimpu (my brother Rajeev) got one each. He also had two or three very rare guns. My mother had one too, bought during the making of *Jis Desh Mein Ganga Behti Hai* (1960). Today, each of those guns must be worth a fortune. I inherited one of them and it needs special care and cleaning. During every election, the local police take it away and keep it in their custody. The law of the land says you can't keep weapons at home during an election.

One major difference between Papa and me is in our attitude towards America. I have always loved the US. Ranbir, like me, loves America too. I need only the slightest of excuses to go there. The fascination goes far beyond the shopping. It is the whole American experience. I can't wait to go to Broadway to watch a play, to walk the streets of Manhattan, to go restaurant-hopping. Papa, on the other hand, was never very fond of America. For him, it was always Russia.

And Russia loved him back. He was a huge star in India but he was a demigod there. I witnessed this craze for him when I accompanied him to the Tashkent and Moscow film festivals in 1974, '76, '78 and '80. The Russians treated him like royalty. Elderly women were so overwhelmed to see him in flesh and blood that they wept and kissed his hand. Young men emulated the Raj Kapoor look. Thousands of people lined the street outside his hotel, waiting for a glimpse of him.

My father himself seemed unaware of how widespread his fame was. When diplomatic relations and protocol were established between India and China in the mid-1970s, we learnt to our great surprise that his films, which had been officially sent to Russia, were being shown in China for free. The Chinese government requested the Indian authorities to send Raj Kapoor to their country on an official visit. Although he was excited to begin with, Papa eventually decided against making the trip. A huge believer in a star's responsibility in preserving his image, my father, who was old and overweight by then, knew he was not the same Raj Kapoor that the Chinese had seen and admired. He said to my mother, 'Krishna, I don't think I will go because I'm not the way I used to be.' So he never visited China or enjoyed the adulation that most certainly awaited him there.

Papa was extremely fond of Chinese food and so is the rest of the family. After we'd all grown up and started having families of our own, he would try and get everybody together for a meal at China Garden. My uncle Shammi Kapoor would always lament that 'Chintu slips out and settles the tab before anyone can'. I did, but I also know that my father felt very proud that I did. I loved to see him enjoy a good meal with his family around him. We're all foodies, so many of our best family moments happen around meals.

Some of the happiest memories of my youth are from the time when I started earning both money and a name for myself and could indulge my parents in a little treat every now and then. I was shooting in Las Vegas for Pramod Chakraborty's *Barood* (1976) when my parents and my sister Rima came along for a vacation. My father was well-pleased that his son was working there while all of them were holidaying. In the evenings, I'd take them all out for dinner and it thrilled me no end to be able to do that.

There was one particular trip to New York, after I married Neetu, which turned out to be unforgettable for many reasons. It was 1982. Mr and Mrs Raj Kapoor and Mr and Mrs Rishi Kapoor were flying by Concorde from London to New York. I was going there for a stage show while my parents were on holiday. The organizers had booked certain seats especially for me and Neetu but once onboard, my dad insisted on appropriating them. He told the airline staff, 'He's not that Kapoor, I am.' I was only too happy to let him have the seats. Flying Concorde was an amazing experience, sitting anywhere. Imagine flying from London to New York in three-and-a-half hours!

To welcome us in New York, the organizers of the show had arranged a grand reception. The press were waiting for me with their cameras (video cameras had only recently been launched). When we walked out, all the cameras were trained on me and flashlights started popping everywhere. I was embarrassed to see my father being sidelined and insisted that they focus the attention on him instead of me.

My father did everything with great pomp and show and that included our wedding ceremonies. He flew in the maestro Ustad Nusrat Fateh Ali Khan from Pakistan for my sangeet. It was a typical Raj Kapoor event that started at 11.30 p.m. and continued till 6 a.m. J.P. Chowksey later told me that something unexpected had happened on my wedding day too. Nargis-ji had not set foot in RK Studios after she completed *Jagte Raho* in 1956. However, that day, she came with Sunil Dutt to attend the ceremony. She was apparently very nervous about attending a Kapoor event after twenty-four years. My mother, sensing her hesitation, reportedly took her aside and said, 'My husband is a handsome man. He is also a romantic. I can understand the attraction. I know what you are thinking, but please don't beat yourself up over the past. You have come to my home on a happy occasion and we are here today as friends.'

Papa had bought the rights to the Pakistani song '*Aaja re*

mahi' around this time. We used it years later in the film *Henna* (1991), which Dabboo eventually directed. However, the film had been entirely conceptualized by my father, who had even started screen-testing girls for the title role. In *Henna*, like *Bobby*, I was once again cast in a film that was named for the lead actress. Dimple had also auditioned for it but couldn't be cast because she was not the right age. My father had always wanted a Pakistani girl to play the role and he had even screen-tested an actress from a popular Pakistani television series. But she too had not fit the bill. We found the perfect fit in Zeba Bakhtiar much later, after Papa had passed away, and it turned out just as he had wanted it – a girl from Pakistan played Henna.

When my father died on 2 June 1988, due to complications related to asthma, Farouq Rattonsey, a friend of mine and a film producer, was informed of his passing by a cab driver in Tel Aviv. It was a revelation to us that my father was a celebrity even in Israel and that *Sangam* (1964) had run in theatres there for two-and-a-half years.

Papa had been in a coma for a month. As he battled for his life at the All India Institute of Medical Sciences in Delhi, we could only pray for a miracle. It did not happen. What did materialize, though, was a very touching episode when my father's best friend, Dilip Kumar, visited him at the hospital.

Dilip Kumar had been visiting his ancestral home in Pakistan when he was informed that Papa was critically ill. He immediately flew to Delhi to see him. Visitors were not allowed into the ICU but an exception was made for him. He sat on a chair beside Papa's bed, staring at him pensively for a while. Then he said, 'Raj, get up, stop clowning. You've always been the scene stealer. You've made headlines all over. *Ab uth ja*, Raj (You've got to get up, Raj).' Tears welled up in my eyes as I watched him hold my father's hand and urge him to open his eyes. He continued, '*Main abhi* Peshawar *se aaya hoon* (I've just come from Peshawar) and I had those delicious chapli kebabs. You and I used to eat them when we were kids. Now get up and we'll both go and have those chapli kebabs.' He sat there talking to Papa in this vein for about twenty minutes. It was heart-breaking to watch and I remember telling my mother about it later.

Papa and Dilip Kumar were rivals at work but the best of friends in life. That is a rare and precious thing. I don't think that kind of friendship exists between two rival contemporaries in any film industry. They were so close that my father had actually offered him the lead role in *Sangam*. Although Dilip sa'ab didn't accept it, they remained friends and wished each other well all their lives.

Sunil Dutt and my father also shared a good relationship despite the awkwardness of Dutt sa'ab being married to Nargis-ji. When Papa was taken ill and flown to Sloane Kettering in New York for a check-up, Dutt sa'ab, who had made good contacts during Nargis-ji's cancer treatment there, referred my father to Dr Manjit S. Bains, who headed the oncology team.

After my father's untimely demise, I was in a daze. The

shock was too great for me to react for the first few days. He passed away in Delhi, we brought him to Mumbai, cremated him, and took his ashes to Haridwar. Rajiv Gandhi, the prime minister at the time, had graciously granted us permission to use a chartered aircraft to bring his body to Mumbai. I was on autopilot through all of this, the enormity of the loss yet to sink in.

After the chautha in Mumbai, we went to our farm in Loni to make a samadhi for him next to my grandfather's. I was with my uncle, Shashi Kapoor, and brothers Dabboo and Chimpu the day it finally hit me that my father was no more. We were sitting in the dining room where he had once presided over the table so exuberantly, when the grief came crashing down. Loni was also where a number of movies, including *Joker*, *Bobby*, *Satyam Shivam Sundaram* (1978) and *Prem Rog* (1982), were filmed and the memories were overwhelming.

Towards the end of his life, my father sold two stages of RK Studios for a paltry sum. As his sons and heirs, Dabboo, Chimpu and I may not have succeeded in making many films but we have not sold any part of the property. We hang on to our father's legacy for dear life.

A question I am frequently asked is why none of us has resurrected the RK banner. My answer is simple: times have changed. My father often told us, 'When I became a lead actor, it was much easier for us because there were so many stories to tell, so many problems. India had just got its independence, it was a budding nation, there was so much happening.'

There are times when I think there is nothing new left to

be said, not just in India but anywhere in the world. Can you name one good story that has emerged in the last twenty years in world cinema? We still talk of Shakespeare and George Bernard Shaw, of Keats's poetry, of Picasso and Michelangelo's paintings. We go and see the *Pietà* in Rome. We gawk at stuff that's 500 years old. But there is nothing to wonder at today, no great writers, sculptors or artists, because there is nothing new to narrate or portray. The West has offered us new ideas in animation and futuristic films but there is little else. There is a void everywhere, not just in RK.

I have seen my father lament about the lack of talent in his own time. He would get exasperated and say, 'Thank God Mehboob and Shantaram are not around. If they'd seen the kind of films we're making, they'd have committed suicide.' I think my father may have wanted to do the same today. Towards the end of his life, he was horrified by how busy actors had become and how wages had shot up, and how little actors were involved in a film as a whole.

Once, when he was making *Shree 420*, Papa told my mother that he'd be away for two nights to Thane and Lonavala to picturize the song '*Mera joota hai Japani*'. He was the only actor required for the sequence and since he was also the director, he took off with his cameraman, Radhu Karmakar, with a studio van and a hired truck. But when he arrived there, he didn't like the visuals. He couldn't see the clouds in the black-and-white frame. He began to chase the clouds and reached Kolhapur. From there he landed in Belgaum and finally found himself in Ooty. So what was to be two days of shooting in Thane ended several days later in Ooty, all in search of the perfect shot.

We did that during *Bobby* too. We had originally gone to Kashmir to film just one part of the film. We ended up staying there for a month and a half. There was no problem of dates. It was one big RK family. Everybody was there only for *Bobby* and nothing else. By staying on without any constraints, we got the winter and the snow, we got spring with its flowers, and we got the meadows. We got Kashmir in full bloom. Films are just not made like that anymore.

After that kind of relaxed film-making, when Papa had to work with actors who doled out a precise number of dates, he found it maddening. One can only imagine how disheartened a man of his creativity would have been if he saw the way we make films today, with actors wanting the lion's share of everything. For my dad and his contemporaries, the film-maker was supreme. The film was his baby, his project. My father and Dilip Kumar were both huge stars, but they were petrified when they shot for *Andaz*. My father would tell me, '*Hum* Mehboob Khan *sa'ab se aankh se aankh nahin milate thhe*. (We didn't dare look Mehboob Khan sa'ab in the eye).' That was the kind of reverence they had for their directors.

Let me illustrate this with a little example. All his life, my father had a small pit on his face that was caused by a pimple which was badly treated by a doctor. The pimple had popped up during the shooting of *Andaz* and it was removed so carelessly that he couldn't shoot until it had healed. When that happened, Mehboob Khan actually came to the hospital to see whether Papa was shamming or whether he was really taking time to heal.

Papa was sixty-one years old when he made his last film,

Ram Teri Ganga Maili, which became a super hit. He passed away at sixty-four. I know how sensitive he was to changing trends and times, and I'd like to believe that Indian cinema would have been the richer for it had he lived a while longer, but perhaps it was best for him to go when he did. Somehow I don't see him fitting comfortably into the changed film industry. It's certainly more about the money now, less about content. Today, we are businessmen more than film-makers. Papa was never a nafa-tula businessman who looked only at the profit line. If he'd been around, he would have squandered all his money on his films, like he did during *Joker*. People like him wouldn't have survived in the film industry of the twenty-first century.

Over the years, the sprawling RK bungalow in Deonar, with its badly planned rooms, has been rebuilt completely. Spread over two acres of land, it has a separate wing for each of us. Everybody is welcome to treat it as home at any time.

Mom often calls us over to visit her in Deonar. When I was nursing a bad leg a couple of years ago and Neetu was in London, she asked me to stay with her for a couple of days. I love the laad, the affection, she still showers on all of us. I have, of course, stayed over with her on a number of occasions. On 26 July 2005, when there was a cloudburst in Mumbai and the suburbs were flooded, I had to spend the night in Deonar. But I have to confess that 'home' for me means our bungalow 'Krishna Raj' in Pali Hill, Bandra. Although I was born and brought up in Deonar, I've spent more than half my life in Krishna Raj. I can't ever think of moving anywhere else. Dabboo and Chimpu have homes in Pune. Chimpu lives there most of the time but they are constantly in and out of Mom's house.

The sibling I've been closest to is Dabboo, who is five years older than me. Chimpu, who is the youngest, and I share an uneasy relationship. There is a distance between us that we've been unable to bridge even over time. My sister Ritu was married by the time I was seventeen. Dabboo and I grew up more as friends than as brothers, and grew closer after my father's passing. We're comfortable sharing confidences. We may not meet often, given the distance between Deonar and Bandra, but we do talk at least once a day. One of the reasons I starred in a wacky comedy like *Housefull 2* (2012) was because I got a chance to act with Dabboo for the first time. To be able to spend time with him in London, where it was filmed, was a huge incentive. We had come together earlier to make *Henna* as a tribute to Papa, to give shape to his last dream. We again joined forces on *Prem Granth* (1996) in which Chimpu made his debut as director, and then *Aa Ab Laut Chalen* (1999), which I directed. All those experiences cemented our bond and made it even stronger.

It is Dabboo who holds the family and the banner together. I worry a lot about Chimpu and feel sad that he has never been able to realize his true potential. He is the most talented of us and has an uncanny ear for music. He plays the piano superbly without ever learning it. He did a commendable job as editor on my film *Aa Ab Laut Chalen* (1999) and could have been the best in the field, if only he had applied himself better. My sister Rima continues to be the life and soul of all family get-togethers. She is vivacious, has a great sense of humour and is great company when any of us falls sick. I have mentioned how she and I used to fight in the car on our way to and from school, and we continue to fight even now. I am amazed at how she connects to people – she knows more people than all of us put together.

I speak to my mother in Chembur every morning and Facetime my sisters if they're travelling. All through 2013–14, we huddled together as a family to see Ritu through a major illness. My younger sister Rima Jain left her husband and kids to look after Ritu in the US. Although Ritu had her retinue of staff from Mumbai and Delhi, and brilliant doctors taking care of her, nothing could be a substitute for family. I love Ritu but I couldn't leave my work and be with her. It requires a lot of inner strength to dedicate yourself to looking after an ailing family member. Rima has it in abundance. Ritu's husband Rajan and her son Nikhil constantly travelled between Delhi and New York to be with her. She was in the US for over a year, which was not easy on anybody. It was even tougher on my mother because she was not well enough to travel to the US and couldn't see her older daughter for a year. She was only able to see her after she returned to Delhi.

During the two years that Ritu was gravely ill, I realized what a brave person my sister is. She stoically bore the many days and nights of excruciating pain, the endless procedures. It was a time of terrible upheaval – physical and emotional – but she handled it with a rare courage. Seeing her deal with her illness has been an inspiration to us all. Ritu ultimately won the battle and returned to Delhi. It was our strength as a family that saw us through that devastating time, and it is reassuring to know that even without Papa, our bond remains intact.

3

A FAMILY TREE OF CELEBS

I count myself among the wealthiest actors in Hindi cinema, not in terms of money but because of my incredible legacy. I have a vault filled with priceless memories, and a unique vantage point since birth. I have seen four generations of Kapoors at work – from my grandfather, my father, uncles and brothers, to Karisma, Kareena and Ranbir.

My inheritance does not include only the Kapoor legacy but also the great privilege of knowing huge marquee names, across several eras, stars most people have only admired from a distance. Dilip Kumar, Dev Anand, Rajendra Kumar and Manoj Kumar were all 'uncles' for me. They were followed by Dharmendra, Amitabh Bachchan and Jeetendra, all of whom I have known closely. I've also had the pleasure of being good friends with contemporaries such as Rakesh Roshan, whom I address by his nickname, Guddu.

Then, on my mother's side, there were her brothers Prem Nath, Rajendra Nath and Narendra Nath, and her brother-in-law Prem Chopra. Even some of the actors linked to Prithvi Theatre, like Trilok Kapoor and Sapru, were distantly related to us. There were many more including actor Sajjan sa'ab (actor Sajjan), celebrated music composers Shankar–Jaikishan and a host of talented technicians who were so close to the family that we grew up calling them 'uncle'. Each one of them has enriched my life in untold ways.

Families are of many kinds. The Kapoor and Nath khandaans are my families of course, but I am blessed to have also been part of the extended Hindi film family, which included my father's colleagues and Hindi cinema royalty, Dilip Kumar, Dev Anand and Pran.

Raj Kapoor, Dilip Kumar and Dev Anand were considered the holy trinity, the Big Three, of the box-office in the 1950s and '60s. Each had his unique style of acting and a distinct appeal, and all three had equally fanatical fan followings. Although they reigned concurrently, they shared an easy camaraderie. Their professional rivalry never spilled over into their personal lives.

Dilip Kumar, whose real name is Muhammad Yusuf Khan, has been like a father figure to me. There was always a lot of coming and going – aana jaana, as we say – between our homes. I had seen him work with my grandfather on the sets of *Mughal-e-Azam*. He was one of my father's best friends and I had grown up watching his films. But beyond the personal, I have always been in awe of him. He was and remains a legend of Hindi cinema.

So when I was offered my first chance to work in a film with Dilip Kumar, I was ecstatic. The film was *Duniya* (1984), directed by Ramesh Talwar, written by Javed Akhtar and produced by Yash Johar. I have an awkward, disconcerting story from our days on the set of *Duniya*.

Dilip Kumar had got embroiled in a scandal during this time. His secret marriage to a lady named Asma was the talk of the town. On the day in question, the entire cast – Dilip Kumar, Pran, Ashok Kumar, Amrish Puri, Prem Chopra, Dingy (Amrita Singh) and I – was present to film an intense scene. Dilip Kumar, who was an exponent of method acting, was totally prepared to deliver a dramatic dialogue when suddenly Ashok Kumar asked him, 'Yusuf, *mujhe yeh batao, humse ek biwi sambhali nahin jati, tum kaise do biwiyon ko sambhalte ho?* (We can't handle one wife, how are you managing two of them?)' We were all stunned and I braced myself for an outburst. Unbelievably, Dilip Kumar, completely unruffled, replied calmly, 'Ashok bhaiya, let me finish this scene and then we can talk about it.' The two stalwarts had a long-standing camaraderie – Ashok Kumar could say literally anything to Dilip Kumar and get away with it.

When Chimpu got married in 1999, my mother insisted that Dabboo and I personally carry the invitations to Yusuf sa'ab and Dev Anand, both of whom lived in Pali Hill like us. What a study in contrasts they made.

We met Yusuf sa'ab at his house and ended up spending over two hours there, as he regaled us with stories of my father and the good times they'd had together. He spoke of 'Kardar sa'ab', 'Mehboob sa'ab', 'Modi sa'ab', of my grandfather 'Prithvi-ji', and of 'Raj', my father. He was very eloquent. Saira-ji fussed over us, plying us with chai and cheese toast, saying, 'Raj liked this.' After what seemed like an eternity of khatirnawazi, when we finally took our leave, Yusuf sa'ab promised to come to the wedding and said, 'Raj will be so happy that his youngest son is also getting married.'

From there we went straight to Dev sa'ab's room at Anand recording studio, a stone's throw from Dilip Kumar's bungalow. While we waited for him, Dabboo and I couldn't help remarking on the stark difference in ambience. We had just stepped out of a place steeped in old-world culture and hospitality and landed straight into a room full of books on Hollywood and everything American. Suddenly, Dev sa'ab burst in, wearing yellow pants, an orange shirt, a green sweater and a muffler. He was warm and jovial, welcoming us with a cheery, 'Hi boys, how are you? You guys are looking damn good.' When he heard why we had come to meet him, he perked up even more. 'Oh, Chimpu is getting married, good, good, good, good, *achchi baat hai, shaadi karo*, have girlfriends. You guys have girlfriends?' He cut such a dashing figure, so full of joie de vivre, that you couldn't help but be swept away by his energy.

My mother later met Saira-ji and Yusuf sa'ab on his ninetieth birthday. Unfortunately, by then, he was ailing and thoroughly disoriented. He kept asking for my father, saying, 'Raj *nahin aaya* (Raj hasn't come),' before bursting into tears. Mom had to console him. Tears welled up in my eyes when she told us about it, thinking back to that time in the hospital as my father lay dying.

Pran sa'ab is another veteran actor I have a deep and abiding respect for. In 1997, Dabboo and I approached him to play the role of the grandfather in *Aa Ab Laut Chalen*, a home production that I directed. I practically pleaded with, telling him that I wanted to begin my career as a director with him in my film, just as I had started my acting career working with him in *Bobby*. He would be required to film for only six or seven days in Delhi and the weather would be lovely too. I reminded him of his long association with the RK banner and urged him to agree to the role. But he steadfastly refused. He said that if anything happened to him during the filming, he would not be able to face Raj Kapoor. I didn't understand. Then he explained that his health was failing and if he succumbed to his illnesses midway through the shoot, the continuity would suffer and I would be left stranded. He said, 'I don't want to do any more films because I don't want them to suffer because of me. I am getting on in years. Anything can happen to me anytime.' Dabboo and I were bowled over by his integrity. Alok Nath played that role eventually.

I have been privileged to live in the time of legends such as Pran and of having worked alongside them. I am constantly reminded of stories about their commitment, dedication and sense of honour – qualities that are generally not associated with those in the movie business. We do not all lead false and empty lives. Under all the tinsel and sparkle, there is heart and soul.

My 'bank balance' burgeoned with the arrival of the 'star sons', including Sanjay Dutt, Kumar Gaurav and Sunny Deol. Soon, Anil Kapoor, Shah Rukh Khan, Aamir Khan and Salman

Khan appeared on the horizon, and a whole new generation began to address me as 'uncle'. Life has come full circle. I have seen my nieces, Lolo (Karisma Kapoor) and Bebo (Kareena Kapoor), grow up before my eyes. So have many other actresses, including Raveena Tandon, whose father, Ravi Tandon, directed one of my biggest hits, *Khel Khel Mein* (1975). Then there are Pooja Bhatt and Alia Bhatt, whom I have known from birth and whom the entire film fraternity feels avuncular about.

It's humbling to think about my association with such legends, across such a wide expanse of time. I can't think of any other actor who has interacted with so many actors across so many generations. And then I have a family tree that's as festive as an X-mas tree, decorated and lit up with bright stars everywhere.

I have very fond memories of my aunt Jennifer (Jennifer Kendal), the British actor Shashi uncle married. Christmas was earmarked every year as a special day to spend with the half-British Kapoors. We would go to their house for a delicious Christmas lunch and Jennifer aunty would organize a treasure hunt for us, to find our presents. After she succumbed to cancer in 1984 and Shashi uncle withdrew into a shell, their son and my cousin, Kunal, has taken over the responsibility of organizing the Christmas get-togethers. It's the one time we get to meet the whole family, especially Shashi uncle. I have worked with him as an actor, I have interacted with him as a nephew, and now that he's unwell and wheelchair-bound, I feel sad to see my uncle reduced to a shadow of his old, handsome self. Kunal and I continue to have a great relationship. We get together for dinner occasionally and always have lots to talk about.

There was a sizeable age difference between my father, the eldest of six children, and his brother Shammi Kapoor. There were two more children in between, Devi and Bindi, both of whom died in infancy. One died of measles and the other ingested rat poison by accident. So, Papa, who had so many brothers, grew up with only one sister, Urmila Sial, née Kapoor, who also passed away many years ago. We were close to all our mamas and chachas, each of whom influenced us, especially Dabboo and me, in their own ways.

Shammi uncle was our absolute favourite. He lived close to us in Deonar. He was not only a dynamic hero and a rebel star, but also vivacious in person. My father was just Papa to us, we couldn't relate to him as a star. However, we got all the stardust we wanted from watching Shammi uncle. He had such flamboyance, it was exhilarating. If I remember right, he once had two tiger cubs in a cage as pets. They had to be handed over to the zoo when they grew into adults, I think. And what a treat it was to visit him! He had a projector at home and would show us his films when we went over. Shammi uncle's wife, Geeta Bali, was an affectionate and beautiful woman and we had a great time with her too. She regularly planned interesting picnics for all her nieces and nephews.

Today, Chembur and Deonar are a concrete jungle. But there was a time when our house was surrounded by marsh and jungle. It was an isolated area and there were only three bungalows in that wilderness. We lived in one and Shammi uncle in another. The third belonged to another family. I remember my father had to get a proper road constructed to our bungalow for Ritu's wedding.

Shammi uncle had this unbeatable aura, one that we were totally in awe of as children. There were so many interesting things he did – like driving his jeep while holding a bottle of beer in both hands. Here was a real-life super hero who could drive a jeep with his feet! He also had a gun and I would feel most important whenever he allowed me to hold it. Once, he took us along with him on a shikaar. Dabboo sat in front with him and I was in the backseat. Although he didn't shoot anything significant, much to our disappointment, it was still a thrilling experience.

There is another episode that's etched into my memory. Returning late from a shoot one day, Shammi uncle met with an accident at Chembur naka. It was about 4 or 5 a.m. Geeta aunty called us, panic-stricken, and we rushed over to see him. We found him with blood soaking through his white outfit. But in his hand was his beloved bottle of beer, which he held on to while he waited for the doctor to arrive. You couldn't help but be floored by his verve and zest for life.

When Geeta aunty passed away, Shammi uncle moved in with us for three months. He was shooting for *Teesri Manzil* (1966) at the time and had to watch his weight. Not easy, given Mom's penchant for lavish spreads and the fact that he could never resist good food. He would literally salivate at the table.

Shammi uncle is the only lead actor I know who gave up a flourishing acting career when still a young man in his late thirties. He hung up his boots when he started putting on weight during the filming of *Andaz* (1971). Let me put that in perspective: the Khans today are over fifty years old and are still going strong, while I continued to be a lead actor until my forty-fifth birthday. Shammi uncle was on the verge of retirement when I started my career with *Bobby*. Randhir Kapoor had already become a hero and Shashi Kapoor was having a very successful run at the box-office.

I can recall any number of amusing incidents involving Shammi uncle. This was the period after Geeta aunty had passed away and for a while Shammi uncle seemed to have gone berserk. Every year on 14 December, my father's birthday, he would make an appearance late in the night, quite drunk, and create chaos. He would try to impress some woman or the other and pending a response would proceed to break glasses or threaten to put his fingers into electrical sockets. Another one occurred just as we had started out making *Bobby*. Papa had recorded the song '*Main shayar toh nahin*' at a studio in Lower Parel, right after which he threw a party to celebrate the start of his new film. Among the invitees were Shammi uncle and Feroz Khan, who had just returned from Canada after shooting for *International Crook* (1974). The Khans and Kapoors, all flamboyant, fiery, colourful people, had always been great friends.

Shammi uncle had put on a lot of weight by then and had also grown a beard. Feroz Khan, his contemporary, dressed all in black, looked handsome and fit. He was about to start his film *Dharmatma* (1975), the Indian version of Marlon Brando's *The Godfather*. Feroz bluntly told Shammi uncle that he looked like he could play his father in *Dharmatma* (a role that eventually went to Prem Nath). The remark led to a heated exchange of abuses followed by full-blown fisticuffs. Soon enough, Randhir was pulling Shammi uncle away while Sanjay Khan was doing the same with Feroz. It took a while for us to separate them. Papa was livid that his celebratory party had come to this. They were then put into their respective cars. However, it turned out that they drove to Haji Ali where they proceeded to drink some more and cry on each other's shoulders!

When we were shooting *Bobby* in Pahalgam, we received a telegram from Shammi uncle seeking my father's blessings before he embarked on a new role as director, with *Manoranjan* (1974). They loved and respected each other tremendously – he always touched my dad's feet when they met; in fact, touching the feet of elders in the family is a tradition that all of us, including the current generation, follow – and Papa was moved by his younger brother's gesture.

Shammi uncle and I have been co-stars as well. The first time we worked together was in a film called *Aan Aur Shaan* (1984) which was directed by Ravi Tandon. It was an insignificant film, one of many I was part of in that period, severely delayed in production and released so many years later that no one has probably heard of it. But a piece of advice that he gave me during the very first scene we filmed together, a church sequence, has stayed with me forever: he told me to forget that we were relatives and to focus on my job as an actor.

We went on to star in a number of films together. *Prem Rog* (1982) was a landmark movie on women's emancipation, while *Yeh Vaada Raha* (also in 1982) was just a big let-down. *Prem Rog* was the first time Shammi uncle worked with my father. We also co-starred in *Ajooba* (1991), which Shashi uncle directed.

Even after his swashbuckling days were behind him, Shammi uncle continued to be spirited and great company, always up for an adventure. He was fifty years old, married to Neela aunty and an incorrigible gastronome when I went on a world tour in 1982 and invited him to join me on the American leg of the trip. He agreed to come. Neetu was pregnant with Ranbir and Riddhima was a toddler, barely two years old. Shammi uncle grew very close to my daughter on that trip. There is one incident I remember vividly from that time. It was evening, I was drunk and wanted to take a cab to Harlem. Neetu, Neela aunty, everyone was scared to go to a ghetto in the night but Shammi uncle was game, and he came along with me.

As with Shashi uncle, I have watched Shammi uncle through all the phases of his life. From the spectacular 'Yahoo' days to his final moments, when he was ailing and finally slipped away.

Another uncle I was close to was Prem Nath, my mother's brother. Not to be confused with Prem Chopra, who is also an uncle to me. Prem Chopra is married to my mother's sister, Uma maasi, so he's also Prem Nath's brother-in-law. In *Bobby*, Pran and Prem Chopra were cast as the villains. In the climax, they are the two baddies chasing Dimple and me, with Prem Nath single-handedly fighting them off. So there was Prem Nath fighting his brother-in-law in front of the camera, with his other brother-in-law, my father, behind the camera. Like *Kal Aaj Aur Kal*, *Bobby* too was something of a family project.

I think of Prem Nath as a god who later became a devil. In his later years, co-stars and other people on the set were wary of working with him. He became unpredictable and eccentric, and my father had to constantly restrain him. We made three films together, *Bobby*, *Karz* (1980) and *Dhan Daulat* (1980), but I never really feared him. He loved us dearly. Bina aunty (Bina Rai), his wife, a leading actress of the black-and-white era, was a sweet, gentle lady but I don't have many memories of her.

When we were children, we spent our holidays in Jabalpur, Madhya Pradesh, with my maternal grandfather, Rai Sahab Kartar Nath Malhotra, Inspector General of Police, and Prem (Nath) uncle. The big high for us was going to Empire theatre, which was owned by Prem Nath, to watch adult films, such as *V.I.P.s*, starring Richard Burton and Elizabeth Taylor, which we saw fourteen or fifteen times. The long kisses in that film amused us no end. The other highlight of those outings was the mutton chops, which we bought for four annas a piece.

Prem uncle cut a dashing figure in the films of the late 1940s and the '50s and was a much-in-demand hero. In fact, he was cast in a parallel role to Raj Kapoor in *Barsaat*. After his run as a lead actor was over, Prem uncle returned to acting in supporting roles in films such as *Teesri Manzil* and *Johny Mera Naam* (1970), both of which were huge hits. These films marked the beginning of his phase as a character artiste and he went on to play many memorable roles, both as villain and Good Samaritan in several films, including *Roti Kapada Aur Makaan* (1974), *Bobby, Shor* (1972) and *Dharmatma*.

Prem uncle may have been eccentric, but he was also very effective as an actor. He routinely improvised his costumes and, I still remember, wore his own suit in *Bobby*. There was a scene in *Bobby*, which we filmed at RK Studios, in which his performance was so realistic that I was momentarily terrified. After the shot, my father went over and hugged and complimented him. Papa and he were good friends. Another film-maker who was very fond of Prem uncle was Subhash Ghai, who directed him in a memorable role in *Karz* as the mute villain who drummed his orders to his minions on a tumbler.

Uncle was a remarkable man, large-hearted and generous. He regularly supported young actors who did not have the means to survive in the industry. He had made a lot of money – he lived in Darshan Apartments, the most prestigious address in south Bombay at the time, with its own swimming pool – but gave away large chunks of it to charity.

Mom's other brother, Rajendra Nath uncle, used to treat me like a son. He married late in life, so I suppose I really did fill that space for him then. He started out wanting to be a lead actor but ended up becoming a comedian. Uncle introduced his own unique style of acting, which became very popular, and acted in over 250 films. He was one of the top comedians of the 1960s, mastering the art of playing the sidekick in films starring Shammi Kapoor, Rajendra Kumar, etc. His role as Popat Lal became a landmark comic one, he wore maxis and night shirts in the typical comic persona he established on screen. We worked together in a couple of them, including successes like *Prem Rog* and *Rafoo Chakkar*. In real life, he was very different from his screen persona. He was a quiet, reserved man who loved to daydream and kept to himself. One of the odd but vivid memories I have of him is from the time he had a bad accident, on the same day that his sister Uma married Prem Chopra.

With Prem-ji I had a whole other equation – he was always more than an uncle to me, and is a part of my inner circle of friends along with Jeetendra and Rakesh Roshan. He is a fine actor, a wonderful human being, has a terrific sense of humour and is great company. We have had a lot of fun together. There is this little game that we play whenever we speak to each other on the phone, in which we give ourselves different celebrity names. For instance, he will call me and say, 'Brando speaking', or I'll tell his staff when they answer the phone, 'Tell Prem sa'ab that Sonia Gandhi wants to speak with him.'

Prem-ji came from a non-film background and established himself by dint of sheer perseverance and hard work, as well as commitment to his craft. At eighty-one, he is still an impressive personality. At the height of Rajesh Khanna's superstardom in the 1970s, Prem-ji was among the few people to give him a run for his money in *Do Raaste* (1969), as he had done in *Upkar* (1967), in which he was pitted against Manoj Kumar. For a man so affable and good-natured, Prem Chopra made a very effective villain. After Pran sa'ab, my vote for the best villain of all time in Hindi cinema would go to him; I place him even higher than Amjad Khan.

Prem-ji has had a long and distinguished career, resulting in a phenomenal body of work. Lately, we haven't worked together as much as we once did, but he's always the first to congratulate me on a good performance. If it is a bad performance, he is kind enough to make a joke of it. I was touched by his lavish praise of Ranbir's performance in *Rocket Singh* (2009) in which he worked alongside Ranbir. If I am not mistaken, he is the only actor who has worked with all the Kapoors – Prithviraj Kapoor, Raj Kapoor, Shammi Kapoor, Shashi Kapoor, Randhir Kapoor, Rajeev Kapoor, Rishi Kapoor, Karisma Kapoor, Kareena Kapoor Khan, Ranbir Kapoor, not to mention the Kapoor wives, Neetu and Babita.

Our family tree was enriched exponentially when Amitabh Bachchan was added to it by marriage, after his daughter Shweta married my nephew, my sister Ritu's son, Nikhil Nanda. Amitabh, I have discovered over the years, is a cut above everyone else in everything he does. He is just so proper. Every year on 2 June, my father's death anniversary, every member of his family calls to pay their tribute to Raj Kapoor. He religiously remembers every birthday and anniversary, and is among the first to wish us on every festival. He does this because he's bound by tradition in many ways and believes that he must follow the custom as a 'betiwala', being from the girl's family. Sometimes I wonder if I could be like him, so meticulous and thoughtful, but I know that's just wishful thinking.

4

MISSES, MULTI-STARRERS AND MUSICAL CHAIRS

There is a saying in the film industry: '*Jiske liye* film *hoti hai, woh us hi ke liye hoti hai*' and I've seen it come true over and over again. Irrespective of whether I initially rejected a role or if it got shelved at some stage, if a film was destined for me, I ended up working in it.

Amjad Khan was destined to play Gabbar in *Sholay*. The role had first been offered to Prem Nath and then to Danny Denzongpa, but ultimately it was immortalized by Amjad Khan. It was in his kismet. Similarly, if Raaj Kumar or Dev Anand had said yes to Salim–Javed, Amitabh Bachchan would not have got his big break with *Zanjeer* (1973). But *Zanjeer* was destined for Amitabh.

K.C. Bokadia pursued me for a month to star in a film he

was producing, called *Pyar Jhukta Nahin* (1985). He used every bit of influence he could find to get me to agree. He tried to reach me through Neetu, who had worked in one of his films, and via my mother-in-law too. But I didn't want to do the film because the role required me to play father to a six-year-old. At that point I was a Nasir Husain hero, my film *Zamaane Ko Dikhana Hai* (1981) was due to release soon. So I refused *Pyar Jhukta Nahin* in spite of how much I liked the Pakistani film *Aiyna* (1977) on which it was based. And the film ended up catapulting Mithun Chakraborty into the big league.

Hrishikesh Mukherjee's award-winning *Anand* (1971), which was a feather in Rajesh Khanna's cap and helped consolidate his superstardom, had originally been designed for my father. Papa used to affectionately call Hrishikesh Mukherjee babumoshai. But he couldn't do *Anand*. He also didn't do *Milan* (1967), even after Laxmikant–Pyarelal had recorded all the songs with Mukesh for it. The composers had been thrilled to finally get a chance to work with Raj Kapoor. But *Sangam* (1964) was delayed, and the film's producer, L.V. Prasad, had already waited for three months. My father didn't want to keep him hanging any longer. So he called Mr Prasad and requested him to cast someone else. That's when Sunil Dutt entered *Milan*. And the chartbuster '*Sawan ka mahina*', which was composed by Laxmikant–Pyarelal for my father, became one of the biggest hit songs of Dutt sa'ab's career.

Such musical chairs are an intrinsic part of our film industry. *Daane daane pe likha hota hai khaanewale ka naam* (Every grain has its destiny inscribed on it). Some roles slipped through my hands while others fell into my lap. But I like to believe that in the overall scheme of things, luck has favoured me.

Somebody once asked me if Raj Kapoor paid me, like a film-maker pays an actor, to act in his films. And the answer was: never. Working with my father was its own reward. Everything he taught me and did for me is still worth its weight in gold. I have been paid a million times over in the acclaim I have received as an actor only because of the films that he made with me.

Everything I ever did for my father has been a milestone in my career. My grooming in the film industry started at RK Studios from the day I began work as an AD on *Kal Aaj Aur Kal*. It was an inconceivable high for me to be picked from among Rahul Rawail, Prem Nath's son Prem Krishen and J.P. Dutta, all of whom were assistants on the film, to give the mahurat clap for a sequence that featured my grandfather, my father and brother, Randhir Kapoor, in the same frame.

But there was also a downside to being Raj Kapoor's son. When we were filming *Bobby*, I became my father's favourite scapegoat for everything that went wrong in a scene. Dimple was new, while I was family. She was a fine actor, but she was raw. If I was in a shot with Dimple, Prem Nath and Pran sa'ab, and if, even after two or three retakes, Papa wanted another because one of them hadn't got it right, he would always blame it on me. He didn't know how to tell the others to do it again, so I had to take the rap. He did this so that whoever had actually muffed the shot was not made self-conscious by their mistake.

If it became obvious that Chintu was being scolded too

often, Papa had a back-up plan. He had a secret code with his technicians. When he was dissatisfied with a shot, he would ask Allauddin Khan, his sound recordist, 'Khan sa'ab, shot *kaisa tha* (How was the shot)?' On cue, the soundman would answer, 'Sir, *ek aur lete hain* (Sir, let's try it one more time).' My father handled his actors with kid gloves, building their confidence and coaxing a better shot out of them.

When Papa was filming *Mera Naam Joker* and Simi (Garewal) couldn't get a particular shot right, he said to her, 'Simi, imagine if this shot turns out perfect, the whole world will be watching it on premiere night. Imagine everybody watching and saying, *kya* shot *hai* (what a shot).' Simi was so charged that she just had to get it right.

Papa wooed his actors and treated them tenderly, like fragile china. He was never harsh or rigid. There were none of the horror stories you hear today about directors who are hard on their actors, even abusive. He modified his approach depending on the actor and the situation, but was always kind and courteous.

Although it didn't start out that way, acting soon became a passion for me, and to be able to make a career doing something you love is a great blessing. I'm not sure if I'm a born actor but I'm certain that I'm a natural actor. I am instinctive and spontaneous, I feel emotions rise from deep within me and am able to convey them convincingly on camera. I am also able to switch off quickly, pack those emotions back in once the cameras have stopped rolling. I rarely carry home any baggage from the set.

I am also a director's actor, always striving to fulfil the director's vision of a character and a story. During *Joker*, I was a teenager without focus, unsure if I even wanted to become an actor. But when we made *Bobby*, the confusion was replaced with clarity, and I transformed into an excited novice, sure that this was what I wanted and this was where I wanted to be.

By the time *Prem Rog* (1982) came along and I got to work with my father again, for the third time in my career, ten years had elapsed. During that period, I had worked with a lot of other directors and that exposure made me appreciate and understand Raj Kapoor's true worth. *Prem Rog* was great fun to make but also a lot of hard work. I loved the story, the music, and every character in it. Even today, directors like Karan Johar and his contemporaries profess to have been inspired by *Prem Rog*.

By now I was bonding really well with my father. Few know that Papa also tried to groom me as a director. Perhaps because he had become a director so early on in his career, he wanted it for me too. He wanted me to direct *Prem Rog*, to be the captain of the ship. But I had become so busy as an actor that there was no way I could fit direction into my plans. So Papa handed the reins to Jainendra Jain, who was our writer. But Radhu Karmakar, the renowned RK cameraman, protested, complaining to Papa that Jainendra-ji didn't know the basics of direction. That's when my father stepped in and became the official director of *Prem Rog*.

Papa had his unique way of drawing out a performance from his actors, and the brief I received on how to play the besotted lover, Devdhar, was also unique. He said to me, 'I want Yusuf in your eyes. I want that serious, intense look on your face which I've seen in no other actor but Dilip Kumar.' He believed Dilip Kumar to be the greatest onscreen lover, unmatched in his intensity. I remember recounting this story to Yusuf sa'ab later and how happy it made him.

In the 1970s, audiences were extremely forgiving, allowing film-makers to rehash the lost-and-found formula endlessly. The plot pretty much boiled down to children being separated at the start, only to reunite in the end, once the villain had been killed. Viewers would rejoice and clap and watch these stories ad nauseam. Today, nobody would accept such tiresome clichés, but in the '70s, they worked like magic. Blockbuster film-makers like Manmohan Desai and Nasir Husain were masters of the lost-and-found formula, and I was lucky to have worked with both of them.

In fact, I worked with almost every top-ranking director of the 1970s and '80s, in the biggest films that were made. One of the major multi-starrers that I worked in was *Amar Akbar Anthony* (1977) but the story of how I came to accept the role is a rather wacky one.

To understand why I reacted the way I did when I was initially offered the film, one needs to know what an eccentric director Manmohan Desai was. He filmed the most preposterous, illogical sequences but got away with it in film after film. He did the most implausible things with such conviction and panache that people swallowed it whole. Before I got to know him, my impression of him was that he was a master of the ludicrous.

I was shooting for *Laila Majnu* in Bikaner when I first heard from him, via a telephone call. Mobile phones hadn't been invented then and when people wanted to make an urgent call, they would book a lightning call, which sometimes matured after a day or two. You couldn't even dream of having a call put through to your room, let alone walk around with a phone in your pocket. One had to go to the reception for everything, to make or receive a call.

One evening, Danny, Ranjeet, Asrani, Ranjeeta and I were playing snooker when around 7.30 p.m. a waiter announced, 'There's a lightning call for Rishi Kapoor.' I wasn't expecting to hear from anyone, so I was rattled as I walked to the reception to take the call. It was my secretary Ghanshyam. The connection was terrible. His voice was unclear, there was a lot of static and we could barely hear each other. In the distance I could hear him repeat, 'Hello, hello, hello,' to which I screamed back my 'Hello'. As I strained to hear what he was saying, I picked up the words, 'Manmohan sa'ab wants to talk to you, he has a film to offer you.' The very next moment I found myself speaking to the man himself. It was just the beginning of my career and we were still pretty formal with each other. He greeted me and then offered me a role in *Amar Akbar Anthony*. He wanted me to play Akbar in the film.

Except I didn't hear all of that. All I heard, standing at the reception and hollering over a really bad telephone connection, was that he wanted me to play Akbar. So I bellowed back, 'Thank you very much, Mr Desai, but how can I play Akbar? My grandfather played Akbar [in *Mughal-e-Azam*]!'

On the other end of the line, Man-ji, as he was popularly

called, was baffled by my response. I heard him say in Gujarati, 'What's wrong with this stupid man?' We left it at that for the moment and since I was returning to Mumbai soon, I promised to meet him on my return. By the time I put the phone down, the others, who had heard me screaming, came running to find out if everything was okay. I said, 'Yeah, it's okay. Manmohan Desai called to offer me a role in a film called *Amar Akbar Anthony* in which he wants me to play Akbar. But how can I look like Akbar? I don't look like my grandfather. How can I play that immortal role my grandfather played?'

In my mind I pictured a bizarre plot featuring Amar, the eternal lover, with a flute and all, Antony (Marc Antony) of Caesar and Cleopatra fame, and Akbar from *Mughal-e-Azam*. I did not put anything past Manmohan Desai. At the time, Man-ji was making *Dharam Veer* (1977) in which he had Dharmendra and Jeetendra wearing skirts, so none of this was far-fetched.

When I returned to Mumbai, I forgot all about speaking with him. So Man-ji came to RK Studios to meet me and once again I pleaded with him, 'How can I play my grandfather's role?' He had had enough. 'Akbar is the name of the character, you dolt, and you're not playing Prithviraj Kapoor.'

I, of course, accepted the role and we went on to do six films together, three with him as the director (*Amar Akbar Anthony*, *Naseeb* [1981], *Coolie* [1983]) and three more under his banner. He was a wonderful man to work with. Although much older than me, he behaved like a peer. He was a spontaneous director, a man with conviction, and extremely focused. He was unfazed by an actor's stardom. Dharmendra, Amitabh Bachchan or myself, we all did exactly what he wanted. We also became family when his son, Ketan, married my first cousin Kanchan, daughter of my uncle Shammi Kapoor and Geeta Bali.

Another interesting story is how I came to join the cast of *Kabhi Kabhie* (1976), a landmark film in my career. I had rejected it outright. Early in my career, a megastar was on the rise in Hindi cinema. A tall man had appeared on the scene, with a breakout performance in a film called *Zanjeer* that had many of my friends, including Bittu Anand, Tinnu Anand and cameraman Sudarshan Nag, raving. They all advised me to steer clear of him. But I was never afraid of being overshadowed by anybody.

So it had nothing to do with Amitabh Bachchan being in it – I was just not interested in *Kabhi Kabhie*. I didn't even like my role in it. But there was a strong buzz about me working in the film. Dharmendra and Rajesh Khanna's names were also being mentioned. When Yash Chopra offered it to me, I refused it saying, 'Give me Neetu's part in the film,' and went away to Paris where I was shooting for Pramod Chakraborty's *Barood*. He was perplexed. I didn't know that his financier, Gulshan Rai, had asked specifically for me, the new youth icon, to attract the younger audience. It seemed the movie could not be made without me, though by now Amitabh Bachchan and Shashi Kapoor had signed on.

I returned to Mumbai from Paris to celebrate the one-year run of *Bobby* at Metro. Pramod Chakraborty had given me a few days off on my father's personal request. After the celebration, I went to Delhi to watch a cricket match. The film unit of

Kabhi Kabhie was then shooting in Kashmir. Shashi uncle did something unprecedented: he flew down to Delhi with Yash Chopra to talk to me again. At no point so far had he intervened in my career. I respect him a great deal, as I do all my elders, so I succumbed to the pressure and that's how I finally agreed to be a part of *Kabhi Kabhie*. Even then, I told myself that I would work on the film for a day or two and walk away as I had to be in Madrid in two days' time. Between the time I reached Srinagar and my next flight from Delhi to Mumbai and on to Madrid, Yash Chopra made me work non-stop. We filmed twelve or thirteen scenes in a row. The fitful start notwithstanding, I went on to have a long and affectionate association with Yash-ji.

The filming of *Kabhi Kabhie* in Kashmir was eventful in many ways. It was the first film after *Bobby* that I was shooting there. I was no longer an unknown newcomer but a star, and I stayed at the Oberoi in Srinagar. *Kabhi Kabhie* was planned as a two-month, start-to-finish schedule but because I had not given a straightforward 'yes', it took a little longer. My work in it was completed over seven different trips.

This period also marked the beginning of political unrest and anti-India feelings in Kashmir. An ugly incident happened on the last day of filming for the song featuring Naseem, Neetu and me in Pahalgam, on my birthday at that. Yash Chopra had organized a party for me that evening. The entire unit, including a lot of young kids who had come in as junior artistes from Delhi, was invited.

While our party was swinging inside, a number of horse

owners and taxi drivers waited outside the hotel. One of the drivers got drunk and picked a fight with a horse owner. Yash Chopra's assistant, Deepak Sareen, went out to resolve it but the situation rapidly spun out of control. There was chaos with a thousand-strong mob flinging stones and fireballs at the hotel. The crowds were baying for Deepak Sareen's blood and mine too.

Inside the hotel, we were all herded off to our rooms for safety and asked to lie down under our beds. Our rooms were locked from the outside and the curtains were drawn. But the windows were soon smashed to smithereens and the hotel was gutted. Those were by far the scariest moments of my life. Nazir Bakshi, our local liaison, had to contact Chief Minister Sheikh Abdullah, who had us evacuated with the help of the military. It was an unfortunate incident and the horse owners' union apologized to me later on. But three years had to pass before I could bring myself to visit Pahalgam again.

That incident notwithstanding, Kashmir was truly heaven on earth those days. I have shot seventeen or eighteen films there, but can never get enough of its splendour. Donga boat parties (parties aboard houseboats) used to be the order of the day. All the stars filming in Kashmir organized such parties. Sadly, Kashmir has become a paradise lost for decades now.

Kabhi Kabhie was one of the numerous films in which I wore my famous jerseys. That was the phase when I was known as the 'Jersey Man'. I wore a jersey in most of my films in the 1970s and '80s, and they were all from my personal collection. Jerseys were not available in India at the time. I used to travel extensively and would buy them everywhere I went. At one point of time I had nearly 600 jerseys. People used to quietly send word to find out where I got them from and whether they were being specially made for me somewhere. They were in vogue those days and everyone wanted to wear them. The sad part is that all of them had to be thrown away because they were put on hangers and went limp.

Today, it's unimaginable to think of my repertoire without *Kabhi Kabhie* in it, a film I had so reluctantly accepted. Looking back, I wonder how I could not have done the film. We shot for it in 1974–75 and that was the time my romance with Neetu started budding. Even otherwise, it was an extremely satisfying experience.

I must admit that in those days there was an unspoken undercurrent of tension between Amitabh Bachchan and me. We never sat down to sort it out and luckily the strain evaporated on its own. It was only after we did *Amar Akbar Anthony* that the two of us got friendly with each other.

Incidentally, my conviction that I could perform alongside any other actor even in those early days did not stem from an exaggerated sense of my own talent or from arrogance. I was simply confident. It wasn't only in multi-starrers that I worked with self-assurance and stood my ground. I also did many heroine-oriented films where the spotlight was not on me. Even *Prem Rog* was a heroine-oriented film. But there, too, I know I acquitted myself well. My father used to tell me that the hero is usually the saviour of such films, which was a different way of saying how vital it was to have the right actor balance what was essentially a girl's story.

To go back to Amitabh, I must confess there is still a lingering issue I have with Amitabh Bachchan. A big disadvantage of working in an all-star movie in those days was that everybody only wanted to make action films, which automatically meant that the star who could carry off action with the most flair would get the meatiest part. That's how, with the exception of *Kabhi Kabhie*, which was a romantic film, none of the multi-starrers I featured in had an author-backed role for me. Directors and writers unfailingly reserved their strongest, pivotal roles for Amitabh Bachchan. And it wasn't just me. Shashi Kapoor, Shatrughan Sinha, Dharmendra, Vinod Khanna faced it too.

Amitabh is undeniably a superb actor, immensely talented and, at the time, the number one star who ruled the box-office. He was an action hero, the angry young man. So roles were written for him. Although we may have been smaller stars, we were not lesser actors. Yet, the rest of us had to constantly measure up to him. We had to work hard, really exert ourselves to match up. In my time, the musical/romantic hero had no place. Amitabh was an action hero in an era of action films. As such, writers gave him the lion's share and he had the author-backed roles in almost all his films. This gave him an advantage over the rest of us who had to make our presence felt with whatever we got.

But this is something that Amitabh has never ever admitted to, in any interview or book. He has never given due credit to the actors who have worked with him. He has always credited his writers and directors, Salim–Javed, Manmohan Desai,

Prakash Mehra, Yash Chopra and Ramesh Sippy. But it is also true that his co-stars had an undeniable role in his success. Shashi Kapoor in *Deewaar* (1975), Rishi Kapoor in *Amar Akbar Anthony* and *Coolie* or Vinod Khanna, Shatrughan Sinha and Dharmendra all contributed to the success of his films where they shared credit with him, even if in secondary roles. This is something no one has realized or acknowledged.

But it was the way things were and we accepted it gracefully. Not because we considered ourselves inferior actors but because *tedha sikka chal raha tha* (that was the coin of the day). It cannot happen today. No Khan works with another Khan. Nobody is willing to work with any other hero on such unequal terms. Today, if Shah Rukh Khan is ruling the roost, Salman, Aamir or Hrithik will not accept a secondary role. Vinod Khanna was damn good in *Khoon Pasina*, Shatrughan Sinha shone in *Kaala Patthar*, Shashi uncle was superb in *Kabhi Kabhie*. But if they remained unappreciated, it was because they were working at a disadvantage. But still we worked together amicably.

While Amitabh and I got over it all, there was always an unresolved tension between him and Rajesh Khanna. After they had worked together in *Anand* and *Namak Haraam* (1973), when Rajesh was the reigning superstar and Amitabh the newcomer, the equation changed. Rajesh, or 'Kaka' as he was called, was dethroned by Amitabh and they never worked together again.

Although I cannot think of a valid reason for it now, I never got along with Kaka-ji either. He did me no harm and I can see today that it was all my doing. So why did I dislike him? The only reason I can think of is that he stole my first leading lady

(Dimple) before our film was even released and I was probably possessive of her. However, I was always open to working with Kaka-ji and, in fact, co-starred in three films with him.

Having said that, I did get involved in one of the biggest controversies of the era, during the casting of the male lead in my father's film *Satyam Shivam Sundaram* (1978). Papa was fond of Kaka-ji and he was one of the main contenders for the role. But soon stories began to circulate that the rest of the Kapoor clan had ganged up against him and made its displeasure clear. Ultimately, the part went to my uncle, Shashi Kapoor.

The stories were true. I was one of those who objected to Kaka-ji being cast in the film. It is not something I am proud of and later admitted as much to Kaka-ji before he died. We talked about it during the making of *Aa Ab Laut Chalen*, the film I directed, in which I had cast him in an important role.

I am not sure how far our war cry against Rajesh Khanna had any impact on my father. He was not the kind of man to keel over and succumb to emotional pressure. Yet, it's also true that Shashi uncle was very busy during that period. In fact, Papa used to call him 'taxi' because, as he said, anybody who paid the fare could hire Shashi Kapoor. At the same time, Rajesh Khanna was ready to give his left arm to do a Raj Kapoor film. In such a scenario, I wonder if Papa's decision to cast a Kapoor had something to do with our 'tandav' committee.

I don't think my objections to Kaka-ji had to do with Dimple alone. No one really liked Rajesh Khanna in those days. I had seen him ridicule my father during an outdoor shoot of *Bobby*. Dimple was married to him by then and my father had to seek his permission to film the remaining scenes with her. I had to see my father fawn over him. That unpleasant memory stayed with me and I feared a repeat of such scenes if Kaka-ji joined the cast. Still, I have to concede that he was genuinely fond of Papa and would have given anything to have a Raj Kapoor film on his resume.

In fact, barring the initial tension with Amitabh Bachchan and my illogical dislike of Kaka-ji, I did not have any rivalry with any actor or co-star. The number and variety of actors I have worked with, I am pretty certain, is unmatched by any other actor. I don't think even Amitabh Bachchan and Jeetendra have worked with the range of people I have. Apart from the innumerable co-stars in my films of the '70s, my roster of co-actors includes all the Khans, Akshay Kumar, Ajay Devgn, Saif Ali Khan, Irrfan Khan, Arjun Rampal, Naseeruddin Shah, Paresh Rawal and Om Puri. I've worked with the young generation of stars too, with the exception of Ranveer Singh, Bobby Deol, Emraan Hashmi and Imran Khan. Imran is the grandson of one of my favourite film-makers Nasir Husain, and Ranbir's contemporary. Nobody has offered me a film with him so far.

People credit me with introducing a record number of heroines in my films. Interestingly, my record with the leading men who have made their debuts in films with me is quite impressive too. The roster includes Shah Rukh Khan (*Deewana*), Emraan Khan (*Inteha Pyar Ki*), Arbaaz Khan (*Daraar*), Luv Sinha (*Sadiyaan*), Jackky Bhagnani (*Kal Kissne Dekha*) and Varun Dhawan and Siddharth Malhotra (*Student of the Year*). Malayalam superstar and legend Mammootty too made his Hindi film debut in *Dhartiputra*, a film that I starred in.

A quirky fact that may even be a strange record of sorts is that although I have worked with Jackie Shroff in three films, we have never been in a frame together. We've both worked in *Azad Desh Ke Ghulam* (1990), which also starred Rekha, *Aurangzeb* (2013) with Arjun Kapoor and *Palay Khan*, in which I had a guest appearance. It was Jackie himself who pointed this out to me at Amitabh Bachchan's Diwali party in 2015.

Despite having worked with the likes of Raj Kapoor, Manmohan Desai, Nasir Husain and H.S. Rawail, I do regret wholeheartedly the major omissions in this list. Hrishikesh Mukherjee, Shakti Samanta, Gulzar and Basu Chatterjee made my kind of cinema but we never got to work together. It perplexes me, in fact, that I have never socially met a man who is practically my next-door neighbour in Pali Hill. Gulzar and I have never even had a drink together. He has never written a song, a dialogue or a single line for me in any film. An overwhelming majority of my songs were written by Gulshan Bawra or Anand Bakshi. Considering my image as a romantic hero, it remains a mystery why Gulzar and I have never worked together.

We also have much in common. R.D. Burman was Gulzar's favourite person. They enjoyed working together and were close friends. In fact, Gulzar did some of his best work with Pancham, as Burman was called. And I loved working with Pancham too. Gulzar was married to Rakhee, with whom I acted in films like *Doosra Aadmi* (1977), *Kabhi Kabhie* and *Yeh Vaada Raha*. And yet, Gulzar and I never came together for a film.

Unlike in the case of Gulzar, I know why I never made a film with Shakti Samanta, Hrishikesh Mukherjee and Basu Chatterjee. Shakti Samanta wanted to work with me but he offered me a Bengali film which I didn't want to do. Hrishi-da called me twice. Once, he wanted to remake *Anari* (a 1959 movie starring my father), which I didn't think was a good idea. Unfortunately, he took my 'no' rather personally. Later, he wanted me to work with his son in a film called *Lathi*, which was predominantly a Dharmendra film. But I was absolutely sure that I didn't want to do a *Lathi* type of film and after that I never heard from Hrishi-da again. Basu Chatterjee also offered me a film very early in my career, with Moushumi Chatterjee as the heroine. However, Vinod Mehra ended up playing that role.

I never made a film with the other well-known film-maker of that era, Mohan Kumar. He shot a few scenes with Rameshwari and me for a remake of *The Lost Weekend* (1945) and then scrapped the film. When a film gets shelved, you just have to shrug and move on. Another eternal regret I have is that I never got to work with Vijay Anand. Some associations are unfathomable and my professional equation with Vijay (Goldie) Anand was among them. I actually did three mahurats with him. There was one that featured Amitabh Bachchan, Randhir Kapoor, Vinod Khanna and myself. There was another with Jeetendra and me, and a third mahurat with just me. None of these got made despite many sittings and photo sessions.

I also had a sitting with his older brother, Chetan Anand. He wanted to make *Salim Anarkali* with Padmini Kolhapure and me in the lead roles, and was keen to cast Raaj Kumar as Emperor Akbar. Chetan sa'ab even gave me five gold guineas (British gold coins) as shagun. He had grand visions of making another *Mughal-e-Azam*, but the film was never made and he passed away soon after.

It was a different era then, when producers would sometimes give actors a valuable gift before starting a film, as a token of good luck. Chinnappa Devar gave me a gold locket to mark the start of *Raaja* (1975), a film with Sulakshana Pandit, and gave an identical one to my assistant Ghanshyam, because a secretary was key to a star's dates. A small bribe of sorts.

Although I missed out on working with some very worthy directors, I got lucky with the legendary Chopra brothers, B.R. Chopra and Yash Chopra. The only film that B.R. Chopra ever directed outside his own banner was *Tawaif* (1985). Rati Agnihotri and I led the cast of the film, which turned out to be very successful. Yash Chopra, of course, gave me some of my most memorable roles in films like *Kabhi Kabhie* and *Chandni* (1989), apart from films such as *Doosra Aadmi* and others made under his banner.

5

DREAM RUN, DEFEAT AND DEPRESSION

Sometime in September 2010, when Shabana Azmi invited me to her sixtieth birthday party, I sent her my best wishes along with a message that I'd be away. I chuckled to myself as I added in the note, 'I'm entering your territory because, for the first time in my career, there's going to be a retrospective of my films in South Africa.' Then again in August 2016, I was invited to the Melbourne Film Festival, where they honoured me with a Lifetime Achievement Award and also screened *Kapoor & Sons*.

That retrospective was a novel experience for me – a heartening acknowledgement of a career spanning over forty years. In all that time, I had performed consistently, given my best, often going above and beyond what a role called for. Unlike Shabana and others of her ilk, recognition and state accolades have always eluded me as an actor. I was branded a commercial film star and perhaps that's why I was never considered worthy of any national awards.

But sandwiched between the mighty Raj Kapoor and the youthful Ranbir Kapoor, I can safely say that I have stood tall (figuratively speaking, of course), never losing ground to any actor. And that is no accident. It is because I built my resume with great care. I always wanted to work with the finest of film-makers and actively sought them out. Sometimes I even made a film with a director past his prime, only because I wanted his name in my filmography, a document that will live on long after me.

I considered it a privilege to work with directors like Raj Khosla and veteran actor-turned-director Manoj Kumar even when their careers were on the ebb. It was disappointing but not surprising when my films with them didn't resonate with an audience that had moved on to a different kind of cinema. But working with great directors who were also great teachers was its own reward.

Raj Khosla was perhaps the suavest of the directors I worked with. He was very British in how he spoke and dressed, and was a true gentleman. Impeccable style, fine manners and exceptionally articulate – everything about him was top drawer. One day he asked me in his flawless English, 'What is acting all about?' 'Like a sponge yearning to learn and absorb,' I replied without hesitation. To which he said, 'Acting is all about style. It's all about how you do things in your own style.' He first offered Dev Anand as an example, how he stood, spoke, sang.

He then noted how different his style was from that of Raj Kapoor and Dilip Kumar and finally concluded, 'Every actor has his own style. Otherwise every Tom, Dick and Harry could have become actors. A signature style is what captures the attention of the audience.'

My own views on acting are very different, believing as I do that it is all about spontaneity. But Raj Khosla wasn't off the mark either. In Hindi cinema, stylized performances were the norm for the longest time. Think Raaj Kumar. Today it is frowned upon and everybody tries to be effortless and natural in their performances. Raj Khosla was speaking for his times.

I worked on two films with Raj Khosla: *Do Premee* (1980) and *Naqaab* (1989). The latter was meant to be Vinod Khanna's comeback vehicle after his return from Oregon (where he had spent time at Bhagwan Rajneesh's ashram) but he was erratic and finally walked out of the film. So Raj Khosla approached me to take his place and I didn't have the heart to say no to him.

When Manoj Kumar cast me in *Jai Hind* (1999), the patriotic fervour that was the cornerstone of his movies had long become passé. His strong suit was his ability to write dialogue overflowing with patriotism, but deshbhakti and naarebaazi were no longer box-office draws. Films have to mirror contemporary society to connect with the audience, and Hindi cinema in the 1990s was centred on action, corruption and the underworld. The film, therefore, didn't garner even a decent release. But I have no regrets about doing it. Although I had already worked alongside him in *Mera Naam Joker*, it was an honour to be directed by Manoj Kumar.

Like a collector who cherishes his treasures, I count the directors I have worked with as being among the most precious gifts of my life, for the value and sparkle they have added to my career.

Manmohan Desai was one of them. For a pint-sized man, he had the persona of a Goliath. He'd tell a man to his face what he really thought of him; he feared no one and spared nobody. And he had a very colourful vocabulary. I was aware that at one time he used to speak disparagingly about me and say things like, '*Char* foot *ki* height *se jaise saat* foot *ka* actor *hai sala* (a 4-foot-nothing actor strutting around like he was 7 feet tall).' When we were shooting *Bobby* at RK Studios, he was filming *Raampur Ka Lakshman* (1972) with Dabboo in the same studio, on a different stage. He used to watch us shoot and exclaim, 'Raj *sa'ab bhi sathiya gaye hain* (Raj sa'ab has gone senile).' The reason: 'After *Joker,* he needed a huge set-up and he's gone for a 4-foot actor.' His disdain extended beyond my height. He would ask wryly, 'Is a guy like Rishi Kapoor hero material?' Man-ji, as we called him, also described Amitabh Bachchan as '*Tange tange* [all legs and legs] Amitabh Bachchan'. The irony is that when Manmohan Desai launched his production company, he signed '*Tange tange*' and '*Char futiya*' along with Vinod Khanna as the all-star cast of *Amar Akbar Anthony.*

I have always relied on my ability as an actor to help me weather the naysayers and any ridicule that came my way. There have been times when I was unceremoniously written off, especially when a new star arrived on the scene, but I have always taken it on the chin. When Kamal Haasan strayed into

Hindi films with *Ek Duuje Ke Liye* (1981), which was a huge hit, he was already a major force at the box-office in Madras (now Chennai). Many other actors made their presence felt around the same time: Jackie Shroff, Sunny Deol, Anil Kapoor, to name a few. Each had his place under the sun and, yet, every time a young actor succeeded, the alarm bells would sound and the headlines screamed, 'Move over, Rishi Kapoor'. Everyone would be convinced that my time was up. I don't know how many times they wrote my obit. But I was sure I was in the right place. I was rarely insecure because that's the sign of a man who doesn't know his craft. I don't claim to be the ultimate actor but I am a good learner and constantly work on my skills. I am no stranger to hardship and have learned how to beat it. I will never forget the battle I fought for *Laila Majnu*. I don't know why the film didn't receive due critical acclaim, but it was a huge hit in its time; it was the crane that lifted me out of the dumps in which I found myself after *Bobby*.

Today, I admit that my second film *Zehreela Insaan* was a mistake. After the bubbly *Bobby*, I should have stuck to something similar and not gone for a film so drastically different. It was a remake of the much feted and immensely successful 1973 Kannada film *Naagarahavu*, and was directed by Puttanna Kanagal, who directed the original. However, the subject matter was not something the Hindi film audience of the time was used to. The one enduring memory of the *Zehreela Insaan* shoot was the black trouser I had bought from Beirut. I was in the habit of shopping for my costumes and this tight-fitting beauty with flares caught my fancy. It was only later, when I wore it in the song '*O hansini*', that the dress man pointed out that its zip was to the side and not in front. I had made a fashion boo-boo, picking up a ladies' trouser. My third, *Rafoo Chakkar*, should have run for fifty weeks because it was well made. But it ran for only hundred days because the audience wanted the Rishi Kapoor of *Bobby*. The fourth, *Zinda Dil* (1975), was hopeless. Though *Khel Khel Mein* was a very successful film, the film that resurrected me as the love-struck boy of *Bobby* was H.S. Rawail's *Laila Majnu*.

Karz was another film that was important to my career. Subhash Ghai had so far made only *Kalicharan* (1976) and *Vishwanath* (1978), two successful action films, and now wanted to make a reincarnation-themed love story. He narrated the story to me at the Sun-n-Sand hotel. I was excited to be working on the remake of *The Reincarnation of Peter Proud* (1975). Ghai wanted a suitable lead actress and he found the perfect one in Tina Munim. I was also comfortable with her; we were working together in a number of films around that time, including *Aap Ke Deewane* (1980) and *Katilon Ke Kaatil* (1981).

Subhash Ghai's production company, Mukta Arts, took off with *Karz*. I was also the lead actor in the maiden films of a few other newly established production houses including Rakesh Roshan's Filmkraft, Rahul Rawail's and Manmohan Desai's MKD.

Subhash Ghai, a trained actor from the Film and Television Institute of India (FTII), Pune, is a visionary and full of ideas. He had a lot of spunk and creative vision and I would have loved to work on more films with him. Unfortunately, Subhash-ji never offered me the lead role again after *Karz*, I don't know why. But we stayed in touch and have kept our friendship alive to this day. Many years after *Karz*, he cast me in *Kaanchi* in 2014 as a character actor.

We had great fun filming for *Karz*. Subhash Ghai is a very lively man with a fabulous sense of rhythm. Often we'd sit in the parking lot of the set, with him singing and drumming on the bonnet of his car. The very first sequence we shot for the film was the song '*Dard-e-dil dard-e-jigar*'. When I asked him for a choreographer, he told me that he wanted to do it himself. He offered to bring in a choreographer and reshoot it if I did not like his effort. But just two days into shooting I realized the man really knew what he was doing. He had done his homework. He had all his ideas clearly worked out in his head, much like how Nasir Husain sa'ab planned his sequences.

On the third day of filming, I fell ill with jaundice. The set had to be dismantled, I was advised bed rest and we couldn't shoot for the next three months. By the time we returned to the studio, I had lost a lot of weight and looked weak. But we picked up right where we'd left off. Subhash-ji played back the dance sequence we had shot in the first two days and I was truly bowled over by his creativity. To our regret, *Karz* wasn't the huge hit we'd expected it to be, though it did decent business.

The reason: Feroz Khan's lavishly made *Qurbani* (1980), which released just a week after *Karz*. Both films had great music. *Qurbani* boasted the cult '*Aap jaisa koi meri zindagi mein aaye*' by Pakistani pop singer Nazia Hassan and we had '*Om shanti om*'. But *Karz* had only one star, Rishi Kapoor, and was a small film in comparison. Tina Munim was a promising newcomer and the director had not yet become 'The Subhash Ghai'. *Karz* had a strong supporting cast in Prem Nath, Pran, Durga Khote and Simi Garewal but we didn't really stand a chance against *Qurbani*, a stylish, action-oriented film that also starred Vinod Khanna and Zeenat Aman. Shot in London, it had sex, music and slick cinematography, and all the trappings of a blockbuster.

These days a film can recover its investment in the first three days but the movie business was very different in the 1980s. A film grew slowly and collected its money over several weeks. By the time word of mouth could fan interest in our film, *Qurbani* came along and swept everything in its wake.

And I lost my nerve, sinking into a deep depression. I was so demoralized that I couldn't face the camera anymore. I would tremble on the sets and feel faint. I'd sink into my chair, go to the makeup room and ask for water. The *Karz* vs *Qurbani* stand-off at the box-office happened in June 1980, five months after Neetu and I had got married. I now began to blame my marriage for my diminishing fan base. I believed that my acting days were numbered, that I had hit rock bottom. I felt every ounce of confidence drain out of me. *Karz* had held great promise, I had thought it would do wonders for my career. It had wonderful music, and some great work by the cast and crew. I believed it would be a resounding success and earn rave reviews. When that didn't happen, I was shattered.

At that time I was shooting simultaneously for four films: *Naseeb*, *Deedar-e-Yaar*, *Zamaane Ko Dikhana Hai* and *Prem Rog*.

But I couldn't bring myself to go to work. The entire cast and crew of these films would wait for me to turn up. Directors H.S. Rawail, Nasir Husain, Manmohan Desai, as well as my father, watched and wondered what had happened to Chintu. Big stars like Amitabh Bachchan, Hema Malini and Shatrughan Sinha were on standby because one last day of filming was left for *Naseeb*. But I wouldn't turn up. At one point I turned up on the set of *Prem Rog*, but I might as well not have. I just couldn't get up and look at the camera. My father was a worried man. Doctors were called in to analyse my condition, psychiatrists were consulted. Meanwhile, four film crews were considerate enough to hold everything and wait for me to get well.

My father took me to our farmhouse in Loni. He thought a change of scene would do me good and give him the chance to have a heart-to-heart chat with me. H.S. Rawail stood by me like a parent would. Nasir Husain thought I was in financial difficulties, so he sent me Vitamin M (money). He actually sent across one lakh rupees, hoping to ease my troubles.

Manmohan Desai was in a fix. He only had a final day of shooting left on *Naseeb*. He called me to the Sea Rock Hotel to film just two shots, which I think he was perfectly justified in doing. I was forced to go and complete the film, but you can tell from my vacant expression in the shots that my mind was elsewhere. A qawwali was being shot at RK Studios for *Deedar-e-Yaar* with Reena Roy making a special appearance. She moved around her dates because I was indisposed. It was truly a kindness; she is reported to have said, 'Whatever dates I have to adjust with Chintu, I will. Just let him recover.'

It dawned on me much later that my breakdown was the direct result of *Karz's* unfortunate fate at the box-office. I would regain some of my lost confidence when I had a drink in the evening with my friends. But on set the next morning, I would tremble with fear. I became paranoid and kept fearing that one of the big set lights was going to fall on me. But in my brief moments of clarity I also knew that I had to pick myself up and get back to normal. And although the process was slow, I managed to climb out of it and regain normalcy.

Many months later, Amitabh confessed to me that he had faced something similar. My father also recalled a time when Yusuf sa'ab had suffered a similar trauma and had torn off his own shirt while shooting for *Dil Diya Dard Liya* (1966). I had no idea that actors were prone to depression until I went through it myself.

As harrowing as it was for everyone concerned at the time, I realized that the situation was largely a product of my own imagination. In reality, my life was in perfectly good shape, I was working in the biggest projects of the day with the best-known directors of the time, and marriage had not dented my career in any way. My biggest learning from the experience was that problems are often created in one's mind and are usually less overwhelming than they appear to be, although the fear and trauma are all too real and crippling while you are going through it.

Things soon sorted themselves out and the films I was working on released with mixed results, the usual package of hits and flops. *Prem Rog* was a big hit and so was *Naseeb*.

Zamaane Ko Dikhana Hai did not do well and *Deedar-e-Yaar* was a flop. Then *Coolie* came along and managed a really good run, although of course I wasn't the hero of the film, Amitabh was. It was finally Harmesh Malhotra's *Nagina* (1986), which gave me a thumping solo hit even though it was a woman-oriented subject, brilliantly performed by Sridevi. Harmesh may have been an average director but he was a very nice person. Sometimes he would come to me in the evening and request me to call for pack-up, saying he was feeling sleepy! In the normal course, directors invariably keep asking for an extension of the shift to finish work. He was the opposite – asking for pack-up ahead of schedule.

It was in the late 1970s that a particularly satisfying relationship came to fruition for me. It quickly went from being strictly professional to warmly personal, and was marked by a great deal of mutual affection and respect. And it has remained one of my biggest regrets that it ended the way it did.

I had grown up on the romantic capers that Nasir Husain had made with my uncles, Shammi and Shashi Kapoor. So when he called me to top-line his *Hum Kisise Kum Naheen* (1977), in which a new girl called Kaajal Kiran was to be cast opposite me, I was thrilled to tick his name off my wish list.

Apart from coming up with racy scripts, Nasir sa'ab had a great ear for music and was meticulous about detailing every frame of a song picturization. He would put all the music, every line and interlude on paper, and he knew exactly what the actor would be doing at any moment, the complete flow of the sequence. Pancham would write scores for his films according to Nasir sa'ab's notes.

I have vivid memories of the incredibly lively music sittings for *Hum Kisise Kum Naheen* during which Nasir sa'ab would describe the scene to Pancham with exceptional clarity. 'Chintu is now on the cycle and Kaajal is running. Kaajal's shawl has been left behind on the cycle and a buffalo sees it ... Chintu is now wooing Kaajal, she's in her PT class and she starts dancing to the beat. The class goes haywire...' Pancham would compose the music to sync with the visuals described to him. It certainly made life much easier for everybody.

Nasir sa'ab made unpretentious, breezy films and had no qualms about declaring that all his films were based on two or three standard templates. With admirable candour, he would say, 'I just rehash the same stories by breaking and joining them differently.' In his college days, he won an award for a story he had written. He later turned that story into a black-and-white film with Rajesh Khanna and Asha Parekh, called *Baharon Ke Sapne*. Almost simultaneously, he made another film, *Teesri Manzil*, in colour and on a more lavish scale. Intriguingly, instead of directing the bigger (in terms of the stars and scale) project himself, he entrusted it to Vijay (Goldie) Anand.

The story goes, and I have it from the horse's mouth, that Nasir sa'ab had the means and the intent to make two films, both of which he had written. But his idea was to direct one and ask Vijay Anand to helm the other. Since they were both his productions, it went without saying that he would direct the one with the bigger stars. But Goldie took offence to being offered a film with a newcomer, and refused the assignment. So Nasir sa'ab very generously swapped the projects, giving

Teesri Manzil to Goldie, and took on a newcomer called Rajesh Khanna, who had won the Filmfare–United Producers' contest in the 1960s.

There was an age difference of only about twenty years between us but Nasir sa'ab treated me like a friend, and I, in turn, respected him immensely and was always careful not to overstep any boundaries. He was one of those who saw me right through my courtship with Neetu. Pancham, Majnu uncle (lyricist Majrooh Sultanpuri), Nasir sa'ab and I shared a close bond, despite the difference in age. Nasir sa'ab would lay out fantastic Lucknowi spreads at home and I was frequently invited to those meals. It suited me well because he lived in Pali Hill and so did Neetu. I'd have a drink or two with him and watch him have another one with his dinner. Then I'd amble over to Neetu's apartment.

After *Hum Kisise Kum Naheen*, which was one of the biggest hits of my career, Nasir sa'ab made *Zamaane Ko Dikhana Hai* with Padmini Kolhapure and me which, once again, had great music. But the film didn't live up to the expectations of a Nasir Husain–Rishi Kapoor–R.D. Burman blockbuster. While it was still being made, Nasir sa'ab had already lined up another all-star cast for a film that was tentatively titled *Zabardast*. It included Dilip Kumar, Dharmendra, Sharda, Tina Munim, Zeenat Aman and myself, and there was feverish anticipation all around. There were so many people keen to be a part of such a massive collaboration that Nasir Husain sold the overseas rights for an unheard-of sum of over ₹10,000,000. But after all that hype, the film couldn't be completed because Nasir sa'ab and Yusuf uncle had a major falling out. The project had to be shelved.

I couldn't believe it when I heard about it. Nasir sa'ab was constantly pulling my leg over something or the other, so when he called me to say he had scrapped *Zabardast*, I thought he was joking. But then I realized he was serious, and that it was true. He even told me I was free to give my dates to other producers. Soon after, *Zamaane Ko Dikhana Hai* was released and declared a flop. It was a hard blow and I was still vulnerable. I had just come out of my post-*Karz* depression and this failure, I believed, was all my fault.

By now I was married and had shifted to Pali Hill. Nasir sa'ab reached out to me several times, asking to meet him, but I was so guilt-ridden after the debacle of *Zamaane Ko Dikhana Hai* that I avoided all contact with him. I couldn't face making another film with him. He took my behaviour as an indication that I did not want to work with him again. So he moved on and made *Manzil Manzil* (1984) with Sunny Deol and Dimple, although he had written it with me and Dimple in mind. Both his nephew Aamir Khan, who was his assistant at that time, and his son Mansoor, confirmed this to me.

Around the same time, I was starting a new film, *Saagar* (1985), with director Ramesh Sippy and co-stars Dimple and Kamal Haasan. I admit that I was perhaps distracted by the idea of working with the more successful director. Nasir sa'ab was a Pathan and he refused to wait around for a response. He went ahead and cast Sunny Deol instead. Pancham would ask me many times why I wasn't meeting Nasir sa'ab but I'd always use my busy schedule as an excuse and wriggle out of an honest answer. That effectively ended our professional relationship and I guess I have to take the rap for it.

Of the many jewels who studded my career, Yash Chopra shines bright. He was an avid Raj Kapoor fan and I had a deep connect with him. I loved Yash-ji's style of film-making. I've mentioned earlier that I was reluctant to do *Kabhi Kabhie* in the beginning because I had been warned against working with Amitabh Bachchan. The second reason was that I felt Neetu had a more prominent role than I did. That's why I had said to Yash Chopra, if you want me to do the film, give me Neetu's role. Naturally, Yash-ji was confused. After Shashi uncle intervened, and I relented and shot for the film for one-and-a-half days, I finally got drawn into it. *Kabhi Kabhie* turned out to be one of my landmark films. It may have been a multi-star cast but I still believe that it was one of the loveliest, warmest films I have been associated with.

I had an amicable association with Yash-ji, with us pooling our talents and making some very memorable films. I made *Doosra Aadmi* with him in the 1970s, which was directed by Ramesh Talwar, and then *Vijay* (1988), a decade or so later, directed by Yash Chopra himself, which didn't turn out well. During *Vijay*, Yash-ji was in a bit of trouble financially and his career had hit a rough patch. The film was a poor rehash of his earlier hit *Trishul*, with none of the latter's dramatic highs.

After that, we made the epic romance, *Chandni* (1989), together. He said to me, 'Chintu, I have this idea about a girl dressed in white. White is very Raj Kapoorish, but you know I have this urge to call the film *Chandni*. I had a girl by this name in *Silsila* (1981) but now I want to call the film that.' At that point it was just a thought, an image, far from a complete story. He only said, 'I want you to work in it.' I listened to him and pointed him towards a film called *Whose Life Is It Anyway* (1981) with Richard Dreyfuss. 'Watch it and incorporate the track from that film,' I said to him. 'That would make it really exciting for me as an actor.' Yash-ji did as I suggested. He saw the film and liked it enough to add the part about the hero being paralysed and unwilling to ruin his fiancée's life. And that's how *Chandni* got made.

Papa passed away when *Chandni* was under production. During our chats at this time, Yash Chopra, the quintessential RK fan, would marvel at the fact that my dad had set up a studio by the time he was twenty-five years old, and would speak ecstatically about his film-making skills.

Yash-ji was under a lot of stress during the making of *Chandni*. I was very friendly with his brother-in-law Gurdip Singh (Gava) and he confided to me that if *Chandni* didn't do well, they would probably have to shut shop and make short films for T-Series. They had already worked out the modalities with Gulshan Kumar. Gava said that Yash-ji would not be producing mainstream cinema anymore because the times had changed. In an era marked by action-oriented and violence-ridden films, there was no space for romance. In fact, I remember a day when I visited him at his office just prior to the release of *Chandni*. The pre-release buzz about the film wasn't positive and pundits were predicting it would flop. I saw him bent over a diary, scribbling something. After a while he excused himself to go to the washroom and I couldn't help peering into the diary he had left open on the desk. I saw that he had written the words 'Help Me O God' again and again, on page after page! I was dumbstruck by what he must have been going through.

After the super success of *Chandni*, Yash-ji came back to me for the Firoz Nadiadwala-produced *Parampara* (1993), which he was directing, but I didn't want to do it. He asked me, 'Why aren't you doing any films with me?' I said, 'I don't like the role and I don't want to play an old father. Why should I play a father?' Despite the film starring Aamir Khan, Saif Ali Khan, Sunil Dutt and Vinod Khanna, it bombed at the box-office. It was quite unlike a typical Yash Chopra film and the audience rejected it.

He was back again a little later, this time with the script of *Darr* (1993), which he was making for his own banner. He wanted me to play the negative lead in the film. But I wasn't convinced that I was the right actor for it. I countered, 'I don't think I can pass myself off as a villain. I have done *Chandni* for you and now you want me to do this film? I did do a negative role in *Khoj* (1989) and it didn't work, so I'm not sure whether this film will do well.' We had such a great working relationship that Yash-ji wanted me to feature in *Darr*, irrespective of the role. So he offered me the other lead role, the one that Sunny Deol eventually did. But I was unwilling to take that either, because it meant playing second fiddle to the villain, who was clearly the pivotal character in the film.

Yash-ji was at his wits' end now. That was when I suggested he consider Shah Rukh Khan for *Darr*. I had worked with Shah Rukh in *Deewana* (1992), and knew that he was smart and capable. I don't know what happened thereafter because I heard that Yash-ji offered the role to Aamir Khan and Ajay Devgn. But ultimately he did go to Shah Rukh and the rest is history.

My career as a lead actor and 'hero' packed up after this and I became a character actor. But my association with Yash Raj Films remained as strong as ever. I did *Hum Tum* as Saif Ali Khan's estranged father and played Kajol's father in *Fanaa* (2006). By then, it was Yash-ji's elder son, Aditya Chopra, who was at the helm.

Such was the depth of my bond with Yash Chopra that when his dream to establish his own studio finally came true, with the setting up of the sprawling YRF (Yash Raj Films) Studios in Mumbai, they ensured that the inaugural movie to be shot at the studio was one that had me in it. The film was *Fanaa*, and the first shot ever to be filmed at YRF Studios was a train sequence featuring Kirron Kher and myself. There was naturally a lot of excitement around that first day, with Yash-ji and his wife coming for the mahurat.

When Yash-ji and I looked at each other, there were tears in his eyes. He had always marvelled at the fact that my father had started his own studio at such a tender age, and had yearned to have one of his own. That dream was now realized. And I cannot describe how happy I was for him that day. I hugged and congratulated him and said, 'You have come such a long way. At one time you were on the verge of closing shop and today you have your own studio.' I believe that I was among the very few who knew how close he had come to calling it quits, and was able to appreciate the full extent of his achievement.

I couldn't help remember the words he had been scribbling in his diary that day, so long ago, when the future looked so uncertain for him. Today, Adi runs YRF with great efficiency. But I will always cherish the deep connect I had with his father.

As I mentioned earlier, I also had the pleasure of making one film with Yash-ji's elder brother, B.R. Chopra. *Tawaif* was the easiest film I ever did in my life. As a director, B.R. Chopra did all his homework in great detail. He was the most competent and 'prepared' film-maker I have ever worked with. He was crystal clear about what he was going to do, how much work he would do in a day and when he would pack up. He would ask me, 'Son, what time do you want to come for the shoot?' I'd say 10 a.m. was good for me and he'd reply, 'Ten is fine, no problem.' He would start work at 9.30 a.m. and by 1.15 p.m. he'd break for lunch, then resume at 2 p.m. There would be a proper tea break at 4 p.m. He was the only director in the Hindi film industry to take this break, where a formal tea would be served complete with a table groaning with snacks. His friend and writer Rahi Masoom Raza used to make it a point to drop in for tea. All the set lights would be turned off to mark teatime and the table would be laid with a table cloth and napkins. Tea would be poured out of a lovely teapot with matching cups and saucers. It was all very proper and British. We'd sip tea leisurely, eat a sandwich or a biscuit, chitchat, and twenty minutes later it was time to get back to work again until we packed up at 6.30 p.m.

Tawaif was made in the shortest time possible. It was one of the rare films of my career that required no patchwork.

Patchwork, or cut work, implies shooting a close-up or a link shot required for a smooth narrative after the main shooting is completed. But B.R. Chopra was totally in sync with his editing department and had every shot worked out precisely in his mind. His brother Dharam Chopra was the cameraman, and between them they knew exactly what they wanted. BR and Yash were also very cerebral people, with a vast knowledge of literature. It was an honour for me to work with such creative and literary people.

No rundown of my resume would be complete unless I spoke of my work with celebrated film-maker H.S. Rawail. I worked with him in two films, *Laila Majnu* and *Deedar-e-Yaar*. *Laila Majnu* was my first major hit after *Bobby*. Rawail sa'ab's son, Rahul, and I grew up together as childhood friends and I used to often play in their house. So Rawail sa'ab treated me like one of his kids. Rahul became my father's assistant in *Mera Naam Joker* and then in *Bobby*. Rawail sa'ab had mastered the art of making movies on Muslim social themes like *Mere Mehboob* (1963) but faltered after films like *Mehboob Ki Mehndi* (1971) failed at the box-office. However, he was, and is, respected for his undeniable creativity. When he came up with the idea of a film that was an amalgamation of *Romeo and Juliet* and *Laila Majnu*, it was unique. Nobody had so far thought of putting a sword instead of a rose in Majnu's hand, even though in the original story Majnu was first known as Qais and he did wield a sword. It was only after he ceased to be Qais that he became Majnu. The idea was revolutionary in 1973–74. Rawail sa'ab took the legendary Majnu and transformed him into a

Romeo-esque character but with a lot of fencing and fighting. The film was a huge success. I had taken up distributorship of the film in a small territory of Rajasthan and made a lot of money from it.

For the role of Laila, Rawail sa'ab had wanted a new face, so a massive all-India hunt was launched and a lot of money was spent on finding her. There were full-page ads in newspapers in Chandigarh and many other cities, including Lucknow and Kolkata, announcing that we were looking for someone to play Laila and the auditions would be with Rishi Kapoor. But it was a quest in vain because we couldn't find her anywhere. Finally we found our Laila right under our nose, at FTII, Pune. Ranjeeta Kaur was perfect for the role, except that she was a little plump and would have to lose weight. She eventually managed to do it but took her time shedding the kilos. When she was almost there, they grabbed my dates and started shooting. So initially you'll find Laila looking a bit heavy!

Rawail sa'ab was a fastidious director and quite consumed by details. If he was checking an actor's costume just before a close-up, it would take about ten minutes. If the shot required the focus to be on a lead actor, with camels in the background, he would check the animals too. I would say, 'Focus on the girl, who is going to see the camels anyway?' But my suggestion fell on deaf ears. Every detail had to be checked and rechecked. It may have been a little annoying at the time, but when we saw the final results on screen, we couldn't deny that every minute had been well spent. He had created something dreamy and beyond our imagination.

The sets of *Laila Majnu* were unlike any other I had worked on. We had sand and tents, and every detail of a desert was painstakingly recreated at RK Studios. The sand consumed a lot of light, so the cameraman had to increase the number of lights. This, of course, added to our woes, which were already plenty since we were wearing wigs and ornate silk and brocade clothes in the heat and humidity of Mumbai. When Rawail sa'ab took his own sweet time with each shot, we would get really fidgety. Our annoyance was compounded by his habit of asking for 'one more, one more, one more', seemingly endless takes, however perfect a shot seemed to be. But in the end it was all worth it and I shall be ever grateful to him for giving me the role of a lifetime.

Laila Majnu was shot over a year and took up to 130 days. A period film takes a lot of time and with the elaborate sets, it becomes an expensive proposition. There was also the uncertainty of undertaking such a project without a bankable actress. *Laila Majnu*'s selling points were H.S. Rawail, Rishi Kapoor and phenomenal music by Madan Mohan. But our financier–producer Shankar B.C. was absolutely confident. He was certain that the combination would work. I didn't have a major hit to my credit after *Bobby* and Rawail sa'ab was going through a bad patch after *Mehboob Ki Mehndi* had failed to live up to expectations, despite featuring the superstar of the era, Rajesh Khanna. So the whole thing was a bit of a gamble.

However, as the shooting progressed, we saw the rushes and began to feel good about the content. The distributors were also upbeat. The music, the dances, the emotions, the presentation were all spectacular. The addition of action sequences made the film a milestone in my career. *Laila Majnu* did phenomenal business, especially in the north. Those were the days when the Amitabh craze had taken the country by storm and it swept everything away in its wake. Fans just couldn't get enough of him. Survival in the face of the Amitabh hurricane was tough, especially for a romantic hero. He was uprooting everybody else. Rajesh Khanna, the reigning superstar, was dethroned. People only wanted Amitabh Bachchan. If not Amitabh, Dharmendra, if not Dharmendra, Vinod Khanna or Shatrughan Sinha, it was 'all hail the action heroes'. A social-film hero like Jeetendra too jumped onto the action bandwagon. All the newcomers fell in line as well: Mithun Chakraborty, Sunny Deol, Jackie Shroff, Sanjay Dutt. I was one of the few who managed to stand apart.

Along with *Laila Majnu*, I had *Hum Kisise Kum Naheen, Khel Khel Mein, Sargam, Kabhi Kabhie, Amar Akbar Anthony, Katilon Ke Kaatil* and *Naseeb*. The list was long and studded with runaway solo hits as well as blockbuster multi-starrers.

Some roles, like the one in *Prem Rog*, were particularly difficult. *Damini* (1993) was another such. I was shooting at Filmalaya Studio in Mumbai when the Moranis (film producers) and Rajkumar Santoshi came to meet me and offered me a part in the film. It was an amazing story and my role sounded really challenging. I was to play a protective husband whose wife witnesses a rape and is determined to expose everyone involved. The husband is then caught between his family and his wife. But after the film was made and I saw it, I felt that

Sunny Deol, who played the lawyer, took away all the credit. Í must say here that Rajkumar Santoshi is definitely among the directors I admire. A gifted man, a good writer and director. Years later, he made a successful film with my son too, called *Ajab Prem Ki Ghazab Kahani* (2009).

When the story of *Damini* was first narrated to me, there were two male protagonists. One was a lawyer and another a drunkard. The two roles were later merged into one and played by Sunny Deol. Sunny at that time was obviously a more bankable actor than I was. Additionally, he was a friend of the Moranis and of Raj, who had started his career with Sunny in *Ghayal* (1990). Although I was supposed to be the hero of the film and Sunny had a guest appearance in it, in the end he walked away with the accolades and the applause. Audiences identify easily with loud characters. Underplaying a character and still standing out is a tough act to pull off. Perhaps Sunny was better than me, perhaps his role resonated more with the audience, but my character was more difficult to essay. I still maintain that my role in *Damini* was one of the most complex that came my way, and it was one of my better performances.

In fact, if you think about it, the other characters in the film had clearer motivations. Damini had a cause to fight for, a cause so strong that she didn't think twice before putting her loving husband through trauma. The alcoholic lawyer had the author-backed, audience-pleasing role. But I enjoyed the difficult shades of my character, the dilemma and the tortured anxieties of a husband torn between his family and love for his wife. Between the crusading wife and the lawyer looking to redeem himself in his own eyes, my character's lifelike quandary was difficult to execute.

The world is fraught with highs and lows, and this is certainly true of the world of movies. But one can't be selfish and align with only those who are successful. If I ever fall upon hard times, I would certainly appreciate a helping hand from my friends and I would do the same for them. My friend Bittu Anand produced two films with me as an actor, *Duniya Meri Jeb Mein* (1979) and *Yeh Ishq Nahi Aasaan* (1984). Both were non-starters at the box-office.

Bittu's brother, Tinnu Anand, got his break as director with these films. But once Tinnu got to direct a film with Amitabh Bachchan (*Kaalia*), Rishi Kapoor was a forgotten chapter and it was only Amitabh thereafter. Nothing succeeds like success. What Tinnu didn't realize was that with Amitabh Bachchan at his peak, even if you used a white negative, it would have worked. The success of the film was Amitabh's alone.

I also did two very successful solo movies with my friend, producer Ravi Malhotra: *Khel Khel Mein*, which was directed by Ravi Tandon, and another hit film, *Jhoota Kahin Ka* (1979). We did a third film together, *Rahi Badal Gaye* (1985), which failed. And then a fourth, *Hum Dono* (1995), with Nana Patekar and Shafi Inamdar. Every time I worked with friends, it was because of a sense of loyalty and a desire to help and support them in any way I could. Having found my place in the world, I wanted to help them find theirs.

Setbacks and successes are an intrinsic part of the movie business. I saw my father experience both. And I went through them myself. If I had a very successful *Laila Majnu*, I delivered a super dud too. High on the success of *Laila Majnu*, H.S. Rawail and I did another film together called *Deedar-e-Yaar*, which was produced by my close friend Jeetendra. Tina Munim was cast as the lead actress. On the very first day of the shoot, Jeetendra had a problem with Rawail sa'ab who, meticulous as always, kept asking for retakes. There was a particular shot where he asked for so many retakes that Jeetendra got fed up and growled, 'This is the best I can do. If you can make do with this, fair enough. If you can't, I suggest that you stop the picture right here because I can't do anything beyond this.'

I had to work on Jeetu and urge him to have a little patience. I spoke of Rawail sa'ab's talents and how well he knew his craft. Jeetendra's query was, 'How can I improve on my best? Rawail sa'ab will have to make do with that.' An uneasy truce was reached after which nothing untoward happened, at least not overtly. Despite our best efforts, the film turned out to be a debacle. The bad blood and constant sniping between the director and his producer–actor vitiated the atmosphere. The failure of the film prompted Jeetendra to find his fortune in the south Indian film industry. He told me that he made sixty films in five years in the south and wiped out the losses his company had incurred when *Deedar-e-Yaar* failed. It turned out to be the golden period of his career, just as destiny had preordained.

That's how destiny works: you get the work that's foretold for you. Like it was in my destiny to work in *Kabhi Kabhie*, however much I tried to push it away. But it wasn't in my destiny to go to England and study business management or become a chartered accountant. It was in my destiny to stay here and do *Bobby*. Similarly, Jeetendra was destined to make huge losses with *Deedar-e-Yaar*, which propelled him to the south to recover what he'd lost. When he and I talked about it, we realized that his dark cloud was *Deedar-e-Yaar* and the silver lining was his southern sojourn. And the former had driven him towards the latter.

6

MELODIES AND MAESTROS

It is hard to overstate the importance of music and songs in a Hindi film. Very often, the soundtrack of a film becomes far more popular than the film itself, and the songs become classics that transcend time. Music can also drive a film's success. As a romantic hero whose films relied heavily on song-and-dance sequences, it was imperative for me to have foot-tapping music with mass appeal. Happily (and fortunately), I have had an amazing repertoire of songs to perform to, which include some of the biggest chartbusters of my time. These memorable melodies played a big part in my successful innings as a young film star.

I'm the ultimate radio junkie and must listen to it at all times; in my bedroom, bathroom, and even my library. Radio stations in India, especially those based in Mumbai, frequently play half-hour slots of my solo hits or those I had with Neetu as my co-star, and each time the songs come on, I am filled with warmth and nostalgia. And I feel blessed, truly blessed.

However, I must admit that I was often hopelessly wrong in my initial reactions to some of these chartbusters. I remember Boney Kapoor coming to meet me, brimming with excitement, with a recording of '*Om shanti om*' in *Karz*. The composers Laxmikant–Pyarelal and director Subhash Ghai, obviously ecstatic with the results, had sent him to Panchgani where I was shooting. I gave Boney an earful, saying what a lousy number it was and wondering how Laxmikant–Pyarelal could come up with such a number for me. The same went for Pancham when he played the title track of *Yeh Vaada Raha* for me. I asked him, 'How can you give something like this to me?' I was equally dismissive when I first listened to the songs '*Dafli waale*' and '*Parbat ke us paar*' in *Sargam*, uncharitably ridiculing the former as '*kya dafli baja, dafli baja*'. Of course, over multiple sittings I came to realize how awesome these numbers were.

The music of *Bobby*, my very first film as a hero, was youthfully energetic. The score was composed by Laxmikant–Pyarelal and written by veteran lyricist Anand Bakshi, in their first collaboration with my father. All my songs were recorded in the voice of newcomer Shailendra Singh (Shailu), who was introduced as a playback singer in *Bobby*. The film marked the beginning of a long and rewarding association with Laxmikant–Pyarelal, with them composing music for over thirty of my movies, including musically rich ones like *Karz* and *Sargam*.

I also had the incredible honour of working with that

gifted genius, R.D. Burman, very early in my career. Virendra Sinha's *Zehreela Insaan* was one of the few films I'd signed before the release of *Bobby* and, to my delight, the music for it was composed by R.D. Burman. I didn't know him well at the time but in the course of working together on seventeen or eighteen films, we became close. Since the music of *Bobby* had caught on in a big way, I was keen that Shailu be the playback voice in all my other films as well. Film-makers and music composers went along with my request initially, so most of my earlier songs were sung by him. Pancham also acquiesced and recorded a couple of songs in *Zehreela Insaan* and *Khel Khel Mein* (including the chartbuster '*Humne tumko dekha*') with Shailu. But he soon put his foot down and announced that he would only record the three main songs, '*O hansini*' (*Zehreela Insaan*), '*Ek mein aur ek tu*' and '*Khullam khulla pyaar karenge hum dono*' (*Khel Khel Mein*) in Kishore Kumar's voice. He said, 'If these songs are not sung by Kishore, I won't record them.' When the director and producer informed me that Pancham had dug his heels in, I gave in and let the composer call the shots on his music. Later, I realized why Pancham had been so adamant. Those songs did merit a singer of Kishore Kumar's extraordinary calibre, his finesse and versatility that Shailu was yet to acquire.

Pancham scored the music for seventeen or eighteen films for me and most of these had memorable music, with songs which are favourites with radio channels even today. Unfortunately, towards the end of his life, we never got to work together. Sometime in late 1993, Pancham called me and, after exchanging pleasantries, told me how he was no longer composing for my films. He asked me to look into it and see if there was any possibility of him doing so for any of my forthcoming films. He added that it was not money he was worried about, that he was quite well placed financially, but that the lack of work was troubling him. As we went back a long way, he asked me if I could put in a word with the producers I was working with. In the early 1990s, the films I was working in had a new crop of composers, like Nadeem–Shravan, Anand–Milind and others. Film-makers who came to me had already decided on these composers and I had no say in the matter. Even as I was mulling over his request, wondering what I could do, extremely sad to see such a great composer come to this pass, came the news of his untimely death soon after. It remains an abiding regret that I could not do anything to help him when he probably needed it most.

Then there are music directors with whom I had the opportunity to work with only once, but their scores left a mark on my career. Incredibly talented individuals like Madan Mohan and Jaidev, who shared the credit for *Laila Majnu*, S.D. Burman (*Barood*), Khayyam (*Kabhi Kabhie*) and Ravi (*Tawaif*). I also worked with Rajesh Roshan, or Raju as we called him, in films such as *Doosra Aadmi* and *Aap Ke Deewane*, which again had wonderful music, with Kalyanji–Anandji in *Katilon Ke Kaatil* and *Rafoo Chakkar*, and with Anand–Milind in *Bol Radha Bol* (1992), *Eena Meena Deeka* (1994) and *Hum Dono*. The inspired compositions of such an array of creative men resulted in an extremely varied range of songs.

An everlasting regret I have is that I did not ever work with O.P. Nayyar. He scored the music for a number of my uncle Shammi Kapoor's hit films, but by the time I arrived on the scene, his career was almost over. I also rue the fact that I didn't get to do a full-length feature film as a romantic hero with Shankar–Jaikishan after starting my career with them in *Mera Naam Joker*, which turned out to be their last major film. In fact, it's interesting that my arrival as a star also marked a passing of the baton from older masters like Nayyar sa'ab, Shankar–Jaikishan and S.D. Burman to a new generation of composers.

Nadeem (of music director duo Nadeem–Shravan) once told me that they were such great fans of mine that when they started their career, they made all their music with either Rajesh Khanna or me in mind. He said to me, 'All our music was made by visualizing you. We'd ask ourselves, how would this sound if Rishi Kapoor were to sing it, *vaadiyon mein gaate hue, apni* jersey *pehne hue* (singing in a beautiful valley, wearing his famous jersey). *Humne har gana aapko madde nazar rakhte hue banaya* (We made all our music with you in mind).'

Nadeem–Shravan joined forces with RK Films to compose the music for my directorial debut, *Aa Ab Laut Chalen*. They told me they were particularly happy because, with Rajesh Khanna playing a cameo in it, they had the opportunity to work with their two greatest inspirations in one film. Kaka-ji was another lead actor who received the gift of some wonderful music in his films, and despite the fact that many believe that chartbusting music eluded Amitabh Bachchan, I count him too among the lucky few to have benefitted from some truly scintillating compositions. But yes, I have been luckier than most. I am hard pressed to find anybody else in my age group, or younger, with as many chartbusters, or someone who has worked with such a range of great composers. Not Amitabh, not Shah Rukh Khan, not Jeetendra. From having sung '*Teeter ke do aage teeter*' for yesteryear legends Shankar–Jaikishan in my first film *Mera Naam Joker* to working with current maestro A.R. Rahman in *Delhi-6* (2009), and the odd song in films like *Agneepath* and *Kaanchi*, no one else can claim to have had such a long and unbroken run.

And for this, I credit my directors. One cannot overemphasize the importance of a director in creating a musical blockbuster. The history of Hindi cinema is replete with great songs and musical scores languishing for lack of vision on the part of the film-maker. My own record is so rich because I worked with directors like Raj Kapoor, Manmohan Desai, Nasir Husain and Subhash Ghai, who were musically inclined people and got the best out of their music directors. They unerringly picked the most fantastic music for their films, which in turn added to my repertoire of chartbusters.

My performances led many to believe that I could actually play several musical instruments. But it was my passion for acting that made me work hard and perform like I knew how to play a guitar, a piano, or a dafli. I can't play any of these instruments. But as an actor it was my job to make viewers believe I was a dafli player in *Sargam* or a guitar player in *Saagar*, *Khel Khel Mein* and *Bade Dil Wala* (1983). I played the guitar in so many films that many people thought I could play it in real life. It gave me a lot of pleasure to tell them, 'I fooled you. I am an actor, I don't know how to play it but I made you believe that I could.' For that I can take credit, for my job as an actor is to make the make-believe look credible.

Legendary singer Mohammed Rafi paid me the biggest compliment of my life when he said that it was a pleasure to see me sing in his voice. He had noticed the effort I put into my songs and appreciated what he saw on screen. Before he passed away in 1980, most of my major films – *Laila Majnu, Amar Akbar Anthony, Katilon Ke Kaatil, Zamaane Ko Dikhana Hai, Karz, Sargam, Naseeb* – had songs sung by Rafi. In fact, many people who credit Kishore Kumar for a lot of my musical hits do a great injustice to Rafi sa'ab's contribution. Of course, by the time I arrived as a hero, Rafi sa'ab was no longer the first preference for composers. Kishore Kumar was the preferred playback for a youthful hero like me. I have been told how he came into the picture as my voice for *Laila Majnu*. It was during the last schedule of *Heer Ranjha* (1970), and *Laila Majnu* was being planned. H.S. Rawail approached Madan Mohan for the film as he was the composer for *Heer Ranjha*. 'I will do the picture, but all songs will have to be sung by Rafi and written by Sahir,' Madan Mohan sa'ab is supposed to have said. Rawail sa'ab was taken aback. Sahir was okay, but how could Rafi sing for Rishi? But Madan Mohan was insistent. That is how Rafi came to sing for me and indeed, became my voice in a number of films.

Together, he and I had some very popular hits like '*Tere*

dar pe aaya hoon' (*Laila Majnu*), '*Chal chal mere bhai, tere haath jodta hoon*' (*Naseeb*), '*Dard-e-dil*' (*Karz*), '*Dafli waale*' (*Sargam*) and '*Parda hai parda*' (*Amar Akbar Anthony*). He sang '*Parda hai parda*' with such zest and vigour that it doubled my energy on the screen. In fact, it is as much a tribute to his rendition of this and the title song of *Hum Kisise Kum Naheen* that I came to be known as the qawwali king of Hindi cinema. Of course, I prepared well for these songs, studying the postures of people like Babu Jani qawwal, even though I could never manage to sit on my haunches like qawwals do. His voice did half the work for me. I distinctly remember the day he recorded '*Parda hai parda*'. I was so excited that I stood near the door and watched him rehearse the number. Suddenly our eyes met. He interrupted the rehearsal and excitedly called out to me in Punjabi, '*Arre laale, puttar, ki haal hai? O yaar, bada mazaa anda hai tu jado ganda hai na. Ek thhe laale,* Shammi Kapoor. *Ek thhe* Dilip Kumar, *ek thhe* Johnny Walker, *aur ek tu hai. Kamaal kar diyo meri awaz. Lagta hain ke* hero *hi gaa raha hain.* (My boy, how are you? What a pleasure it is when you sing. There was Shammi Kapoor. There was Dilip Kumar and Johnny Walker, and there is you. You make magic with my voice. It really looks like the hero himself is singing.)'

Mohammed Rafi's special gift was his versatility, being able to sing convincingly for so many different actors from different generations. Unfortunately, much like the older composers who were on their way out by the time I arrived on the scene, Rafi sa'ab too was past his heyday. Fortunately for me, there was another legend still around, who gave voice to a number of my songs.

What a pleasure it was to record a number with Kishore Kumar for *Jhoota Kahin Ka*. It was a sort of repartee song where I spoke and he sang. In the recording room, Kishore-da told me, 'Your timing is so good that I can pick up exactly where you leave off, and sing my part.' It's not easy to time one's dialogue and I didn't know I had it in me until I actually did it. I also didn't know I was doing it well until he complimented me for it. He was very encouraging and we were so completely in sync that it spurred me on to improvise. I guess I enacted the numbers with the same passion with which he sang them, which is why the songs connected with listeners.

Such encounters did wonders for my self-esteem. I had dialogues in another famous song 'Chal mere bhai' from *Naseeb*, where Amitabh Bachchan and I spoke our lines while Rafi sa'ab sang.

Mukesh, Mahendra Kapoor and Kumar Sanu are also among the acclaimed playback singers who have sung for me. Unfortunately, music directors were not terribly enthusiastic about supporting Shailu, the voice I started my career with. I tried to get my way but had to finally relent. Still, I managed to get Shailu to sing some very big hits, including 'Hoga tumse pyara kaun' (*Zamaane Ko Dikhana Hai*), for me. The one stalwart who never sang for me was Manna Dey. In fact, after he had retired from active playback singing, Manna Dey remarked upon this in a book. He said that he'd had a wonderful career where he had the good fortune of being the voice for all the popular leading men of Hindi cinema except Rishi Kapoor. He didn't know why. And neither do I. That he mentioned it humbled and saddened me at the same time, more so because he sang some evergreen classics for my dad.

The only singer whose style made me uncomfortable and I found it difficult to lip-sync to was Kumar Sanu. He would take unnecessary twists and turns and throw out the rhythm. I found it very difficult to go along with the way he sang the song '*Sochenge tumhe pyaar karein ke nahin*' in *Deewana*. I would complain to the music director too. Kumar Sanu was not a recognized singer at the time. He was usually called in to sing a track that would later be dubbed by another singer in the final version. '*Sochenge tumhe pyaar*' was among the first songs where his voice was retained. If I am not mistaken, he even won a Filmfare award for the film!

Even as I express my heartfelt gratitude to the music composers, directors and playback singers who embellished my career, I also send out a huge vote of appreciation to the choreographers who helped bring the songs to life with the brilliant dance sequences that made me popular as a dancing star. Master Kamal, Suresh Bhatt and P.L. Raj were behind the well-orchestrated dance moves that the audience saw me perform on screen. It was quite a feat that they accomplished, turning me into a dancing star, because I believe I have two left feet. But I was very hard-working and had my facial expressions under control. In fact, Neetu was the one who noticed this and remarked to me, 'You were just an average dancer but nobody could replicate your expressions.' Perhaps that is why the dance numbers in films like *Karz* and *Hum Kisise Kum Naheen* have attained cult status.

Despite my hard work and abilities as an actor, I found the making of *Sargam* extremely challenging. It was a musical where I was required to dance, sing and play the dafli, and it was quite a task to synchronize all three. But director K. Viswanath helped me pull it off, with P.L. Raj doing some tremendous work in it.

Neetu and I were considered a terrific pair of dancers but that's because there was no one else on the scene. Jeetendra and Sridevi came much later. Jeetendra and Babita had danced well in *Farz* (1967) but when Neetu and I came on the scene, we started a new trend of young lovers who romanced, danced and sang songs. *Khel Khel Mein* established us as a dancing duo and I am eternally grateful to director Ravi Tandon, R.D. Burman and P.L. Raj for creating that image. It was youthful and Hindi cinema had not seen such abandon on the part of the hero and heroine in dance numbers. The trend we set caught on with Jeetendra and other actors. But Rajesh Khanna never danced, nor did Dharmendra, Shatrughan Sinha, Vinod Khanna, or my brother Randhir Kapoor. They may have done a number here or there but they did not become popular for their dance routines.

For all his fame as a dancing star, my uncle Shammi Kapoor didn't actually know how to dance. If you watch his song sequences carefully, you'll see that he had similar movements in all of them and they didn't make much sense. But he had great style and a flamboyance so enduring that no one has been able to quite match up.

Working hard and diligently following my choreographer's instructions, I was able to carve a niche for myself in the dance department. Thankfully, I was not at my peak at the same time as Govinda. I could never have done what he did. My forte was romantic and peppy numbers, and I had a particular knack for qawwali-style movements. Two of the greatest qawwalis ever picturized in Hindi film were filmed on me: '*Hai agar dushman dushman*' in *Hum Kisise Kum Naheen* and '*Parda hai parda*' in *Amar Akbar Anthony*. There was also '*Pari ho aasmani tum*' in *Zamaane Ko Dikhana Hai*.

But the music and the dance would have been hollow without the contribution of lyricists such as Gulshan Bawra and Anand Bakshi. Gulshan Bawra thought like a young man and that is why his words were peppy and appealed to the youth. Bakshi sa'ab wrote sublime poetry like '*Chingari koi bhadke*' for Rajesh Khanna in *Amar Prem* (1972) and youthful lyrics like '*Parda hai parda*' for me. So did Majrooh sa'ab with his foot-tapping songs in *Hum Kisise Kum Naheen, Zamaane Ko Dikhana Hai* and many others. All the music directors and lyricists had a ball working for my films because I was the quintessential flamboyant young lover, usually from an urban milieu. There was no heavy-duty stuff or Urdu poetry when they wrote for me because I did not play serious characters. So Gulshan Bawra came up with playful lyrics in songs such as '*Khullam khulla pyaar karenge*' and '*Ek main aur ek tu*' in *Khel Khel Mein* and '*Kisi pe dil agar*' and '*Tumko mere dil ne*' in *Rafoo Chakkar*. When I did play a substantially different character in a film like *Laila Majnu*, Sahir Ludhianvi wrote suitably beautiful lyrics for me like '*Tere dar pe aaya hoon*'.

It overwhelms me to look back and see the many legends and gifted talents who helped build an illustrious career for me. I don't see anybody else – none of my seniors, Papa's contemporaries or mine – who was similarly and uniquely blessed. I can't thank God and all these people enough for giving me the special honour of working with all of them.

I worked at a time when actors took an active interest in music sittings. Raj Kapoor, Shammi Kapoor, Rajendra Kumar, Dilip Kumar and Dev Anand gave as much attention to the song they were going to sing on screen as they did to a scene. They did this because they understood the critical part music played in enhancing their on-screen appeal. And the close interaction between actors and the music team brought out the best in everybody.

Whenever Shammi uncle had a sitting with Shankar–Jaikishan or went to a recording with Rafi sa'ab, they would invest a lot of time and energy in discussing the way the song would be picturized. Shammi uncle would tell Rafi sa'ab, '*Main aisa karoonga, toh aap usko tarannum mein laiyye, idhar giroonga neeche, aisa karoonga...* (I'll do this and I'll do that, when you sing this...).'

Those were the days when songs would be created on a harmonium, before traditional instruments gave way to synthesizers. I loved going for music sittings; it was fascinating to watch the birth of a song. Every music director had his own style of creating a new tune. When I had sittings with Nadeem–Shravan during the making of *Aa Ab Laut Chalen*,

Nadeem would play a percussion instrument, something like a bongo, to keep the rhythm.

Sittings with Pancham for movies made by friends like Ravi Malhotra or Ramesh Behl were fun-filled events. Every once in a while, strange things would happen. One day, Dev sa'ab, who had a sitting with Pancham after mine, turned up a little early. Pancham was in the midst of composing a peppy, vibrant number which Dev sa'ab happened to hear. He immediately said to Pancham, '*Gana bahut achcha hai, kiske liye banaya?* (It's a lovely song. Who have you composed it for)?' Pancham didn't tell him that he had created it for me, he only shrugged and said, 'I just made it.' Dev sa'ab promptly bagged it for himself. He told Pancham, 'I like it a lot. Please give it to me.' Pancham, not one to argue with a senior artiste, quietly handed it over. The song was '*Ruk jaana o jaana...*', which Dev Anand used in *Warrant* (1975).

Similarly, it was a pleasure to watch Nasir Husain interact with Pancham during the music sittings. He would explain each and every frame and nuance of the situation and Pancham would come up with tune after tune, till Nasir sa'ab was satisfied. Even the tunes they discarded were worth their weight in gold, but true to their craft, they would not rest till they had the best.

One of the defining traits of Hindi film music was how a singer's voice came to be associated with a star's. You could close your eyes and listen to a Mohammed Rafi song and be able to say which actor he was singing it for. Rafi sa'ab's voice was totally in sync with stars like Shammi Kapoor and Dilip Kumar. Mukesh-ji was, of course, the voice of my dad. For

Rajesh Khanna and Amitabh Bachchan, you cannot imagine anyone but Kishore Kumar. I had Kishore-da primarily, but also Rafi sa'ab. Today singers and musicians don't know which actor will portray their song in a film. But in those days, actors would inspire the singer to sing the song in a certain way. Shailendra Singh always spoke to me before a song and I would tell him, 'Sing it like this, *aisa karna*, Bobby *mein jo tuney kiya, waisa karna, woh achchha lagta hai, mujhe aisa karne mein maaza aata hai* (Do it the way you did it in *Bobby*, I like that and I enjoy performing to it).' At the peak of his stardom, Rajesh Khanna would go to all the music sittings. Laxmi-ji (of Laxmikant–Pyarelal fame) would also call me to their recordings, especially of the lively songs. I was at the sitting of '*Parda hai parda*' for *Amar Akbar Anthony* and for '*Mannubhai motor chali pum pum pum*' for *Phool Khile Hain Gulshan Gulshan* (1978). The songs were the product of a lot of teamwork.

One cannot be casual with a music director and say to him, '*Kuchh bana do* (Make something).' It's like telling a comedian, '*Kuchh* comedy *karo* (Do something funny).' It doesn't work that way. You must give them a frame of reference, a context. When you want R.D. Burman's music for your film, you have to collaborate and appreciate what he creates for you. I could not attend any of the sittings for *Laila Majnu*, but Madan Mohan sa'ab had me in mind when he composed every one of those musical gems. I often went to Rajesh Roshan's music sittings for films like *Doosra Aadmi* and *Duniya Meri Jeb Mein*, and he made some catchy music in those films. *Aap Ke Deewane* was his brother Rakesh Roshan's film, so Raju was on home ground there.

An actor can make a tremendous difference when he connects with his team and inspires fellow artistes, but much to my dismay I see that the connection is getting lost today. I don't see Ranbir interacting in the same way with his music directors. In any case, the way songs are shot, recorded and used in films has changed beyond recognition. Fewer songs are being lip-synced. A film these days often has a number of composers working on different songs. Gone are the days when one music director composed all the songs and one singer gave voice to the film's star. Also, film-makers seem to be apologetic about having songs as part of the narrative. In the search for authenticity and realism, we are losing out on an important aspect of Hindi cinema.

Hindi films are known and enjoyed worldwide for their songs and dances. These days it is fashionable to battle tradition by using a Western format of telling stories, where music stays in the background. I can't wrap my head around it. I don't think it helps the story move forward. I also believe that a film gets a lot of repeat value when an actor is wooing an actress with a popular song. We represent a dream world and our audiences love it. It may seem old-fashioned but I firmly believe that lip-syncing (by an actor) is the best way to picturize a song, to maximize its appeal. It simply does not have the same magic when the song is played in the background.

Ranbir once told me that he found it very difficult to lip-sync to a song. I was so aghast that I spluttered, '*Tu* Rishi Kapoor *ka beta hai* (You are Rishi Kapoor's son and this is how you feel about playback)?' To help my son with his problem I shared a tip with him. '*Tum kitne bhi besure ho* (However off-key you may be), when the camera is on, sing your lines out aloud. Let the heroine go deaf, it doesn't matter. You should sing along with the playback because the camera must see every muscle straining. Match the playback singer's pitch and heed the tempo of the music and the instruments. That will make it seem like you are the one singing.'

This is the technique I used when I was required to play an instrument on screen, the way I made my audience believe that I actually knew how to. It was thanks to my training as a kid, the years spent soaking up the conversations and discussions among great actors about their craft. I'd hear senior actors talk about the pitch of the piano or a guitar. I'd hear them criticize a performance with observations like, '*Kaisa bajata tha* piano', '*Woh* guitar *kaise pakda tha aur gana gaa raha tha*', '*Kaisa woh* drum *baja raha hai, na taal mein, na kuchh mein*'. I filed these away in my mind, to be recalled and applied when the time was right. If Pancham or Rafi sa'ab had rendered a song in a particular way, it paid to emulate those nuances on screen. A song deserves that kind of respect and it helps give the scene authenticity.

I rehearsed my songs with great sincerity. If you watch the song '*Meri kismet mein tu nahin shayad*', which Suresh Wadkar sang for me in *Prem Rog*, I believe you'll think that it was I who actually sang it. I know that I lived every song that I filmed for *Laila Majnu*. With a taskmaster like H.S. Rawail, there were fifteen to twenty retakes for every shot. He was never satisfied, and always wanted three or four 'okay takes', unlike most other directors who were content with one good take.

Song recordings for RK Films were like a big party, with contemporaries and friends pooling their talents to create magic. They were marathon sessions that would go on for over forty-eight hours at a stretch. Twelve hours of work followed by twelve hours of rest. Shankar–Jaikishan, Lata-ji, Shailendra, Mukesh, Raj Kapoor were all driven by passion and creativity. You could see it in the way they worked and in what they ultimately created together. I don't know why that atmosphere doesn't prevail today, why we can't make music the way it used to be made. These days, you often have instances of a director in Egypt, a composer in the US and a lyricist in Mumbai, composing a song over Skype! Perhaps that's the reason why old songs are still relished. Whenever anyone is playing antakshri, it's the old songs that are sung. Joyful songs like '*Mera naam chin chin chu*' still make you want to get up and dance. They have lyrical value, musical value and everlasting appeal. Do you realize that *Khel Khel Mein* and *Hum Kisise Kum Naheen* are over forty years old? Yet, songs from these films hog airtime today. Even a song from a film that flopped, like '*Hoga tumse pyara kaun*' from *Zamaane Ko Dikhana Hai*, has endured for close to forty years. Can you imagine anybody wanting to sing '*Baby Doll*' forty years from now?

Dabboo and I often recall the 1960s, when creativity was at its peak and every music director was in his or her prime. And I'm not just talking of the popular maestros, such as Roshan, Madan Mohan, O.P. Nayyar, Shankar–Jaikishan, Naushad, S.D. or R.D. Burman. There were other, lesser known but no less talented music directors, including Usha Khanna (the only female composer in an otherwise male-dominated industry), S.N. Tripathi and Iqbal Qureshi, who composed many memorable songs. Even a small film like *Mahua* (1969) had super-hit songs by composer duo Sonik–Omi. Films would be studded with seven or eight songs each, one more beautiful than the other, and at least six would become super hits. Consider, for example, a film like *Guide* (1965) or *Abhimaan* (1973). Eight songs in each and each better than the other. Fifty years later, every single song from these films still resonates with listeners.

People normally deride the music of the 1970s but I personally feel that we had some great music even in that era, music that has endured over the years. Yes, the language and style changed, classical music and Urdu gave way to Western sounds and more colloquial, everyday words. However, in the 1970s too, when Laxmikant–Pyarelal, R.D. Burman and Rajesh Roshan were ruling the roost, making music was a wonderful experience. During the filming of *Doosra Aadmi*, Neetu and I were dating and she used to call me 'Baba'. Ramesh Talwar, who was directing *Doosra Aadmi*, was very close to both of us, and he took that word and inserted it in the song, '*Nazron se keh do pyaar mein milne ka mausam aa gaya*'. It lent a personal touch to the music. Listen to the song '*Chal kahin duur nikal jaaye*' and you will immediately be able to visualize the picturization. Which song today does that?

It was in the 1980s that film music took a beating, with cacophony and vulgarity coming into play. There was a resurgence of sorts in the 1990s, with composers like Anand–Milind (*Qayamat Se Qayamat Tak*), Nadeem–Shravan (*Dil Hai*

Ke Maanta Nahin, Deewana) bringing melody back to films. I do not know what the future holds, but what we have lost, I feel, is that collaborative effort and those true-blue musicals with multiple chartbusters we could all hum together. Nowadays, the emphasis is on having one chart-topping item number which will ensure a good opening, even if it is not integral to the film's narrative.

During the making of *Prem Rog*, there was some friction between Raj Kapoor and Laxmikant–Pyarelal, primarily over the song, '*Meri kismet mein tu nahin shayad*'. My father briefed both the composers and asked each of them to come up with their version of the song. One of them came up with a tune (the one finally used) which the other didn't like one bit and rejected it, saying, '*Nahin, ye gaana nahin rakhenge. Ye nahin chalega*. (No, we won't use this version. It won't work.)' But my father thought otherwise and insisted that it would work splendidly for the film.

The song was recorded and Pyarelal-ji did a wonderful job of the recording and my father picturized it magnificently. We had a set in Mysore and we'd shoot till midnight every day. They had to release millions of litres of water for the fog machines around the palace. In those days the machines were very noisy and we could barely hear the song through the din. It was very cold too. Luckily, I had a shawl in the scene but Padmini had only her sari to keep her warm. We also used arc lights, like those used in Hollywood films, in one or two shots. It felt indulgent, like a treat. Lighting had to be doubled and tripled for night shoots. We shot under a lot of limitations back then but enjoyed every second of it. Actors today don't know about this kind of cinema. They do not know how one had to strive to get superior visuals without the benefit of advanced technology. Everything is digital now, no film is used.

If I remember right, Neetu conceived Ranbir during this time, when we were picturizing '*Meri kismet mein tu nahin shayad*'. It makes the song even more special for us.

I was at the top of my game when, one evening, R.D. Burman threw a party at his place. He invited all his producers and directors and some of the leading stars that he was working with. My uncle, Shammi Kapoor, was directing the film *Bundelbaaz* (1976) at the time and Pancham was his music director. This was sometime in 1974, when I was a young entrant to the film industry, a brand-new star. At the event, producers and directors who had all been very close to my uncle at one time, made a beeline for me and no one paid much attention to him. A few drinks down, my uncle, with Pancham standing close by, called me and said, '*Yeh log jo aaj tumhare peechhe peechhe hain na, yeh kabhi mujh se aise hi karte thhe, yeh waqt waqt ki baat hai,* Chintu (The people who're running after you today are the same ones who once ran after me. It's all a question of time. A time will come when they'll do the same to you, Chintu).' Truer words have not been spoken.

Rakesh Roshan once told me about a lean period that his father, music composer Roshan, went through while everybody else around him seemed to be churning out mega hits. One day, Roshan sa'ab called Madan Mohan and said to him, '*Aapke gaane bahut achchhe baj rahe hain. Ek kaam kijiye … apni peti zara mere paas bhej dijiye kuchh dinon ke liye. Meri peti se kuchh nikal nahin raha hai* (Your songs are all doing very well. Send your harmonium across to me for a while because nothing special is coming out of mine. Maybe I'll get something out of yours).' This story struck a chord with me. The two men were rivals, but it didn't stop them from admiring each other's talent.

Like friendships, sounds too have changed with time. There was a film called *Naya Daur* (1978), directed by Mahesh Bhatt, with a song written by Anand Bakshi, '*Paani ke badle peekar sharaab, kaanton pe hum tum dhoonde gulab*', to be filmed on Danny Denzongpa and me. R.D. Burman wanted me to record some dialogues and Danny to sing the song. During the music sitting, which I couldn't attend since I was out of town for another shoot, when the song reached the line, '*Botal khaali hone toh do*', Pancham spontaneously started blowing hard into an empty bottle and turned that sound into a rhythm. The film flopped and hardly anybody heard the song but his creativity was memorable. Today, nobody puts in that kind of work. Rhythm dalo, cacophony, rhythm, bas. It's called a rhythm box and everything comes out of it.

Anybody can become a singer these days, because there are voice tuners that automatically bring you into sur even if you go off-key. There are 120, 160, even 200 tracks. So you don't have to bother with a retake or a stray sound, it can all be corrected and mixed by the recordist. But in the early days, even the faintest little untimely 'ting' from an instrument meant the take had to be scrapped and re-recorded. So everyone had to be sharp and alert. And the quality of work, despite all those handicaps, is plain for all to see.

With the arrival of the synthesizer, many of our musical instruments have died an unsung death. I was at Rajkamal Studios in Mumbai once, when Naushad sa'ab told me about a musician who used to play a very quaint instrument. It was from the taar shehnai family, a heritage instrument with roots in the Mughal period. Naushad sa'ab was recording a song when he asked the musician how things were going for him. The answer he got, not surprisingly, was that life was very tough. He got called for a recording barely once in three or four months and could scarcely survive on such sparse work. Synthesizers were all the rage and all the sounds that music directors wanted came out of them. They didn't need live musicians and their instruments anymore. So the musician had got his son to study computer science because there was no question of making a living from music. Naushad sa'ab was greatly saddened because it was certain that the instrument would die with the artiste. I am told that even the sarangi is going out of fashion. It seems to me that all our traditional instruments are dying a slow death.

I love listening to Bismillah Khan's shehnai. But the younger generation doesn't have a taste for it. If we don't value our heritage instruments now, they'll be lost forever. The sitar and the tabla may still garner some attention, but what if we were to lose interest in them too? It would gladden me greatly to see current music directors encourage the use of these instruments in their compositions and honour and preserve this incredible legacy of ours.

There are a couple of other trends that I fear don't augur well for the film industry. I particularly lament the loss of playback singers as a community. We have singers and rock stars but not genuine playback singers. Almost everyone wants to be bigger, richer and more famous, singing their own songs and creating individual identities. How does an actor sing a song like, let's say, '*Dagabaaz re*'? I've no doubt that Rahat Fateh Ali Khan, who sang it, or Sonu Nigam and all these other new boys are accomplished singers. But a true-blue playback singer is one who doesn't have what one might call a personal agenda, who modulates his/her voice to suit the actor. Mohammad Rafi, Kishore Kumar, Manna Dey, Mukesh, Lata Mangeshkar and Asha Bhosle were true playback singers. I was the youthful face of Rafi sa'ab, but he also sang '*Sar jo tera chakraaye*' for Johnny Walker. Perhaps today's music directors don't have the knowledge or the ability to handle singers professionally for playback alone. All of them want an album to run on its own, not pausing to consider that the song being recorded is for a film. A singer must sing to match the actor's character on screen. Unconventional voices, like Shalmali Kholgade's in that song '*Main pareshaan pareshaan pareshaan*' in *Ishaqzaade* (2012), are rampant. How does it get used as a playback voice? How would a hero woo a girl with such a song? How could I woo my girl in Sonu Nigam's voice, singing at such a high pitch?

The lyrics of songs today are even less worthy of comment. I could also pick up a pen, do some tukbandi and pass it off as lyrics. What makes me incredulous is that lyricists today are seeking the implementation of a copyright act that gives them a share of the profits. They are not making private albums, they are writing for a film, which is the whole and sole property of the producer. Also, how do musicians demand a lifelong percentage of royalty from the music they have composed for a film? How do they know that the song they have penned or composed or sung is not popular because of the actor who portrayed it on the screen or the director who filmed it? How are they so certain that the song didn't become a hit because of the actor's charisma and fan following or the director's skill? I find the whole debate illogical.

One cannot compare an Indian film song with songs created in the West. You are doing film music here, not making a private album or composing personal music. It would be certainly justified if the demand was made over a private album. But when you make a song for a film, your source is the situation in the film, your selling point is the actor enacting that song. Those are the strengths that are collectively responsible for the success of that music. I am, therefore, firmly on the side of the producers in this ongoing debate about sharing royalties with writers, lyricists, composers and singers.

There was, however, one long-standing practice that I fought hard to overturn. Previously, when a film did exceptionally well, a shield or a plaque was given to the music team, and never to the actors. My first gripe was with Yash Chopra and HMV over *Kabhi Kabhie*. I argued, 'How are you so sure that the music of this film was not a hit because of my contribution too?' That's when HMV started giving shields to the lead actors as well. I didn't get a shield for the runaway success of the music of *Bobby*, I didn't get a shield for *Hum Kisise Kum Naheen*. But I got it for *Kabhi Kabhie*. And I was thrilled.

There is another achievement I am thrilled about, and it has to do with girls.

7

THE BEAUTIFUL BRIGADE

- Kseniya Ryabinkina (Russian, *Mera Naam Joker*, 1970)
- Dimple Kapadia (*Bobby*, 1973)
- Sulakshana Pandit (*Raaja*, 1975)
- Shoma Anand (*Barood*, 1976)
- Naseem (*Kabhi Kabhie*, 1976)
- Kaajal Kiran (*Hum Kisise Kum Naheen*, 1977)
- Bhavna Bhatt (*Naya Daur*, 1978)
- Ranjeeta Kaur (*Laila Majnu*, 1979)
- Jaya Prada (*Sargam*, 1979, Hindi debut)
- Padmini Kolhapure (*Zamaane Ko Dikhana Hai*, 1981); Padmini had been a child artiste in films like *Satyam Shivam Sundaram* and *Gehrayee*, but this was her debut as a leading lady
- Radhika (*Naseeb Apna Apna*, 1986, Hindi debut)
- Sonam (*Vijay*, 1988)

- Vinita Goel (*Janam Janam*, 1988)
- Sangeeta Bijlani (*Hathyar*, 1989)
- Zeba Bakhtiar (*Henna*, 1991)
- Ashwini Bhave (*Henna*, 1991)
- Rukhsar (*Inteha Pyar Ki*, 1992)
- Varsha Usgaonkar (*Honeymoon*, 1992)
- Tabu (*Pehla Pehla Pyar*, 1994); Tabu had been a child artiste in *Hum Naujawan* and had acted in a Telugu film before this, but this was her debut as a leading lady in Hindi cinema
- Giselli Monteiro (Brazilian, *Love Aaj Kal*, 2009)
- Vaishali Desai (*Kal Kissne Dekha*, 2009)
- Meltem Cumbul (Turkish, *Tell Me O Kkhuda*, 2009)
- Alia Bhatt (*Student of the Year*, 2012)
- Vani Kapoor (*Shuddh Desi Romance*, 2013)
- Pallavi Sharda (*Besharam*, 2013)
- Sasha Agha (*Aurangzeb*, 2013)
- Tapsee Pannu (*Chashme Baddoor*, 2013)
- Mishti (*Kaanchi*, 2014)
- Anushka Ranjan (*Wedding Pullav*, 2015)
- Payal Ghosh (*Patel Ki Punjabi Shaadi*, forthcoming)

The universe works in mysterious ways.

Neetu had worked in films as child artiste Baby Sonia and was a serious contender for the lead role in *Bobby*, but it was Dimple who bagged that role and became my first heroine. Then fate intervened again and it was Neetu who became my co-star in life. Dimple was recommended to my dad by Munni Aunty (character artiste Kishen Dhawan's wife, who was very close to my parents), though I do remember Neetu dropping in with her mother while we were filming the song '*Hum tum ek kamre mein bandh ho*' in *Bobby*.

I was one of the lucky few who didn't have to struggle for stardom or recognition. I have no 'sleeping-on-the-railway-platform-and-skipping-two-square-meals' tales. But I had my own problems. After a debut film that gave me instant stardom, film-makers found there was a dearth of lead actresses to cast opposite a hot new star who was also very young. I was in a quandary. Dimple had got married and opted out even before her first film was released. The others were all older than me and looked it too. Around the time I debuted, Sharmila Tagore and Mumtaz were at the top of their game. Obviously I could not be paired with them. Hema Malini, Zeenat Aman and Rekha had just begun to make their mark and again, given the image I had acquired after *Bobby*, film-makers did not think I paired well with any of them. There were only two bankable actresses, Neetu Singh and Moushumi Chatterjee, who did. But how many films could I do with just the two of them? Out of sheer necessity, film-makers found a third option: of constantly pairing me with fresh faces. In doing so, they made me the only lead actor to have worked with close to thirty new heroines, a record that is unbroken to this day.

There would have been one more name on that list if only Nafisa Ali had said yes to me immediately after *Bobby*. We nearly worked together, not once but twice. However, things didn't work out on either occasion. Long before I actually met her, I had read about Nafisa and seen pictures of her in *Junior Statesman*, a very popular magazine in its time, especially with the young, hip, college-going crowd. She was a swimming champion and was nicknamed 'the Water Baby'. She was also stunningly beautiful.

In the 1970s and '80s, films were not released simultaneously across India. *Bobby* was first released in Mumbai, and sometime later, we went to Kolkata for its premiere. Serendipitously, I met Nafisa at the premiere. Both my father and I were instantly drawn to her and Papa even mentally cast her in his next film after *Bobby*. He had *Henna* on his mind at the time. He immediately dispatched me to talk to her and test the waters, to see if she'd be interested in doing a film with me. So I did. (I have a photograph of the occasion too.) To my delight, Nafisa's response was, 'Of course, I'd love to.' But when she spoke to her father about it, he expressed his reservations about her joining the film business.

After that, whenever Papa met her, he would banter with her and say, '*Achcha, tumne meri* picture *nahin ki* (You never agreed to do a film with me).' But she had her answer ready and would retort, '*Maine aap ke bhai ki* picture *ki* (I did your brother's picture).' At some point, her father relented and Nafisa joined the film industry and she appeared in her first film, *Junoon* (1978), with Shashi uncle.

Around the same time as *Junoon*, Nasir Husain was drawing up a contract for her to work with me in *Zamaane Ko Dikhana Hai*. It was signed, sealed and delivered and everything was in place when, once again, her father threw a spanner in the works. He didn't agree with a few clauses in the contract. Besides, Nasir sa'ab was also keen to cast a fresh face, someone he would introduce to the screen. By then Nafisa had already worked in *Junoon*, so the talks petered off.

So it was back to working with Neetu and Moushumi, or with another newcomer. I made eleven films with Neetu before we got married. It was both a blessing as well as a liability because viewers sometimes yearn for a fresh pair and tire of watching the same faces.

I didn't pair well with most of the reigning queens of the time. Hema Malini was a little older than me and I could only work with her in a non-mainstream film like *Ek Chadar Maili Si* (1986), which was about the old Punjabi custom of a young devar having to marry his older brother's widow. Rekha, Parveen Babi and Zeenat Aman were around the same age but, pitched against my boyish looks, appeared older. Any actor who starts his career very young encounters this difficulty. Shahid Kapur and Imran Khan also found it difficult to pair with a suitable lead actress. It was one of the reasons I made Ranbir wait till he was twenty-six years old before acting in his first film.

The drought of suitable heroines also meant that I could never benefit from being cast with an established lead actress. I did work with Zeenat in *Hum Kisise Kum Naheen*, but the lead actress in the film was Kaajal Kiran, a new girl. Moushumi was married even before she joined the film industry, and she became a mother during the making of *Zehreela Insaan*. She came back to work but couldn't carry off the glamorous, youthful look for long.

Shabana Azmi and Parveen Babi had slipped into the older category by this time, having had their golden years with actors like Shashi uncle and Vinod Khanna. I did star in a few films with Parveen but most of them, like *Rangila Ratan* (1976) and *Gunahgaar* (1981), were utterly forgettable. We had one super hit together, *Amar Akbar Anthony*, in which she was paired with Amitabh.

I first saw Rakhee when she auditioned for *Kal Aaj Aur Kal*. One of my aunts brought her to RK Studios soon after she came to Bombay from Kolkata. I don't know why we didn't cast her. Rakhee became a star with *Sharmeelee* (1971) but she too looked better with older actors than with me. Although she was only about four years older than me, she had acquired the image of an actress far more mature than she actually was. We could only carry off a film like *Doosra Aadmi* convincingly because it was the story of an older woman's obsession with a younger man in whom she saw her dead lover (Shashi Kapoor). There too, it was Neetu, once again, who was cast opposite me. *Doosra Aadmi* won critical acclaim for director Ramesh Talwar, Rakhee, Neetu and me. In many ways, it was a film ahead of its time. Even today, whenever it's telecast, people call or text to say how much they liked it.

Rakhee would cook fish for all of us during the shoot of *Doosra Aadmi*. It's so long ago, but even today I remember her as being temperamental, very moody. I admire her because she was a daring actress. She played mother to Amitabh Bachchan in *Shakti* (1982), though she had played his lover barely six years earlier, in *Kabhi Kabhie*, and in *Barsaat Ki Ek Raat* only a year before *Shakti*. She played my mother in *Kabhi Kabhie* and later in *Yeh Vaada Raha*, though she is just a few years older than me. I still think it was an extremely courageous career move on her part.

In *Yeh Vaada Raha*, I was romantically paired with Tina Munim and Poonam Dhillon, again actors who had just started out. The film was based on Danielle Steel's novel, *The Promise*. Rakhee had a good role in it too, prominent and dramatic. It is sad that *Yeh Vaada Raha* didn't run. When my father saw the film he said, '*Kaash is* film *mein ek hi ladki hoti.*' It was his opinion that the director should have stuck to having either Poonam or Tina. Ramesh Behl had taken the liberty of giving Poonam, whose face is disfigured in an accident, Tina's face. My father felt the audience didn't buy this. Otherwise, the movie would have been very successful. Again, like many of my films from that period, it had some lilting music by Pancham and its songs are still favourites on the radio.

I have enjoyed working with Waheeda Rehman too, though obviously she was not cast opposite me. I had a good streak with her, with three super hits, *Kabhi Kabhie*, *Coolie* and *Chandni*; that unblemished record was broken only with a dud called *Delhi-6*. There is something so aristocratic about Waheeda-ji. She is so elegant. Even now, she sends me biryani every Eid, without fail. She had a bungalow called Waheeda at the foothill of Pali Hill, in which I shot for *Duniya*. The house was later sold and developed into a high-rise, also of the same name.

Saira Banu is another actress I admire. I worked with her in *Duniya* but I didn't have any scenes with her. I also did a couple of songs with Helen. One was in a film called *Phool Khile Hain Gulshan Gulshan*.

I worked with Shashikala in *Sargam* and it was a difficult experience. Perhaps she was carrying a great deal of emotional baggage, because I remember that at some point she had to do an emotional scene, which turned into some kind of catharsis. The director, K. Viswanath, producer N.N. Sippy and I tried our best to console her. But she kept weeping for a long time after the scene was over.

So, by and large, debutantes or newcomers it was for me. Working with newcomers had its advantages, especially if a girl turned out to be lucky and the film was a hit, like *Laila Majnu* with Ranjeeta Kaur, *Sargam* with Jaya Prada and *Hum Kisise Kum Naheen* with Kaajal Kiran. Since the girls were new, I walked away with all the glory, and the films were labelled 'Rishi Kapoor's hits'.

Some of the girls who started their career with me went on to do splendidly well, while a few remained one-film wonders who quickly vanished into oblivion. I don't know what happened to Naseem, Mumtaz's niece, who debuted with me in *Kabhi Kabhie*. Devendra Goel's daughter Vinita also did a film with me, titled *Janam Janam* (1988), but couldn't make much headway as an actress.

Oddly, every time I starred in a film with a new actress and it went on to become a super hit – like *Bobby*, *Sargam*, *Laila Majnu* or *Hum Kisise Kum Naheen* did – I didn't get to work with her again for a very long time. Jaya Prada had worked in four or five Telugu films before she got a break in the Hindi film industry with *Sargam*. But nobody paired us again until *Ghar Ghar Ki Kahani* (1988). I didn't work with Ranjeeta until

Gaal pe gaal chadha hua hain, my family said: I used to be
teased that I was an Iranian kid – I was so plump

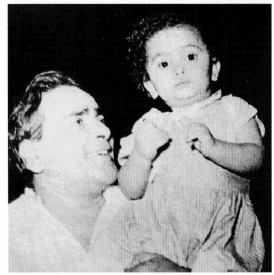

With my grandfather
Prithviraj Kapoor

With Papa

Family fancy
dress party, my
mother holding
my cousin

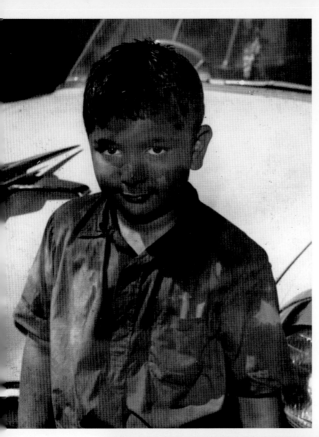

Holy Maverick! Or Holi Mubarak: used to wait for this festival every year

Celebrating Diwali with Dabboo, Ritu, Mummy, Papa and Rima

Courtesy: *The Indian* EXPRESS Archives

Above: Dad won Best
Picture for *Jagte Raho*,
Karlovy Vary, Czech
Republic
Courtesy: *The Indian
EXPRESS* Archives

Left: First trip to Japan
with my parents

Left: We – Raju Nanda, Miheer Chinai, Rahul Rawail – had a band called 'The Nuts'

Bottom: My first time on stage, play at Walsingham High School

One of the most important
days of my life,
22 January 1980

 hrimati Rajee Singh Cordially Invites you to attend the wedding ceremony and reception of Barat of her daughter

Neetu

with

Rishi

Son of Mr. & Mrs. Raj Kapoor

at Bharat Petroleum Co. Ltd.

Sports Club and Staff Colony

Vasi Naka Chembur, Bombay-400074.

on Tuesday the 22nd January 1980 at 7-00 p. m.

Compliments From :

RAMESH BEHL   S. HARBANS SINGH   S. AMRIK SINGH
GULSHAN BAWRA   S. BALWANT SINGH   Relatives & Friends

R. S. V. P.
BILLU
604, Shailja Apartments 50. Pali Hill. Bandra. BOMBAY 400 050.
Phone : 54 16 78

Left: Mr and Mrs Sunil and Nargis Dutt graced our marriage

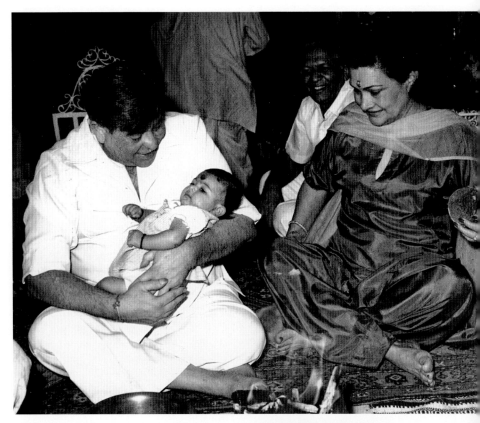

Riddhima's mundan ceremony

With Ranbir

With Karisma

With Neetu and first-born Riddhima

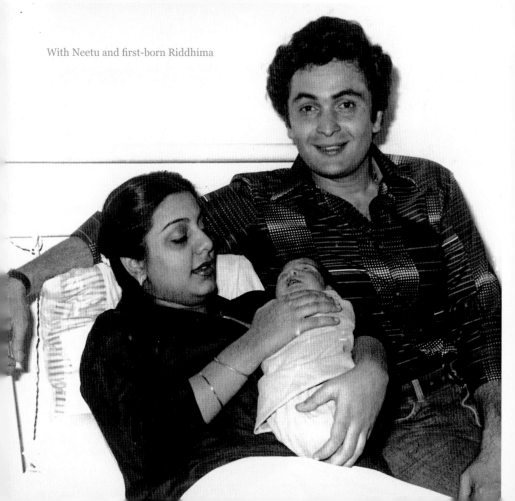

Some quality time
with
the children

My grandfather Prithviraj Kapoor (extreme left) with his grandfather Diwan Keshomal Kapoor (centre)

Family portrait: with Papa, Shammi and Shashi uncle

Waiting for the baaraat at Ritu's wedding: with my grandfather, Papa and Shashi uncle

Right: At the mahurat
for *Bobby*
Courtesy: *The Indian*
EXPRESS Archives

Below: Griha Pravesh
ceremony for
'Krishna Raj',
Dussehra, 1991
Courtesy: *The Indian*
EXPRESS Archives

I have had the privilege
of making the pilgrimage
to Sabarimala and it has
been a fulfilling experience

Right: With Bittu Anand
Below: With Ranbir

With Mom, Papa, Shammi uncle, Dadaji and Dabboo

With Papa, Dabboo and Chimpu

With Papa and Dabboo

Right: Sitting: Mom and Ritu; Standing (L-R): Dabboo, Rima, Chimpu, Manoj and I

Dabboo, Chimpu and I with Mom and Papa

Celebrating Neetu's birthday at Wasabi, Taj Mumbai

In London with Riddhima, Bharat, Samara and Neetu

Right: Christmas at Shashi uncle's is one day in the year the entire Kapoor khandaan gets together

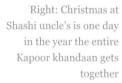

With my siblings Rajeev, Ritu, Rima and Dabboo

With my granddaughter Samara

Celebrating my sixtieth birthday
in Dubai with Bharat, Riddhima,
Ranbir and Neetu

With Neetu and Ranbir

Neetu with my mother-in-law, a
remarkable woman

With my mother

Nikhil Nanda, Dabboo, Nitasha Nanda,
Rima Jain, Manoj Jain, Rajeev Kapoor,
Neetu, Me, Rajan Nanda, Ritu Nanda
and Shweta Nanda

Picture wall at RK
Studios
Courtesy: *The Indian
EXPRESS* Archives

With my oldest friends,
Raju Nanda, Bittu Anand
and Rahul Rawail

Three Musketeers: with my buddies,
Jeetendra and Rakesh Roshan

Those were the days: my oldest gang of friends (from L-R): Ghanshyam Rohera, Rahul
Rawail, Raju Nanda, yours truly, newly-weds Sadiqa and Bunty Peerbhoy, Bittu Anand
and Harvinder Singh Kohli (extreme right)

Right: Revelry with friends: with Nasir Husain, Shammi uncle, Pancham, Dabboo, Ranjeet and Rajendra Nath

With Rajesh Khanna, Vinod Khanna, Jeetendra, Mithun Chakraborty, Satish Shah and Rakesh Roshan

Celebrating New Year's with Rakesh Roshan, Jeetendra, Prem Chopra, Neetu and Sujit Kumar

With Neetu, my life partner: it has been an incredible thirty-seven years of marriage

A still from the immortal song 'Pyaar hua iqraar hua': Dabboo, Ritu and I had a walk-on part in the line '*Main na rahungi, tum na rahoge, phir bhi rehengi nishaaniyan*'

My debut as an actor, *Mera Naam Joker*, which fetched me a National Award

With Simi Garewal and Papa

A still from *Kabhi Kabhie,* a memorable film for me for many reasons

The *Rafoo Chakkar look*

With Dimple, 1972

Test picture for *Bobby*

With Nafisa Ali at the Calcutta premiere of *Bobby*: Nafisa was supposed to make her debut with RK Films, but it did not work out

First-day shoot for *Bobby*:
Pran sa'ab shot for it, I was
still waiting for my turn

At a song recording with
Laxmikant-Pyarelal,
Shailendra, Dimple Kapadia,
Papa and Lata Mangeshkar

At the premiere of *Bobby* in Delhi

The mahurat for *Kal Aaj Aur Kal*

Right: Ranbir giving the
clap for *Prem Granth*
at Loni
Courtesy: *The Indian*
EXPRESS Archives

Donning the director's cap:
on location for
Aa Ab Laut Chalen

My look tests for *Agneepath* convinced me to take on the role of a pimp

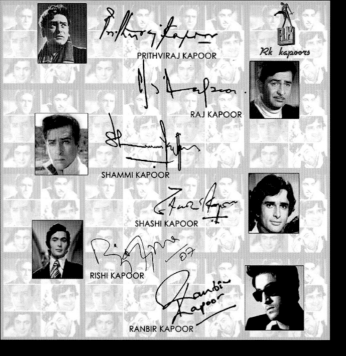

PRITHVIRAJ KAPOOR

Rk kapoors

RAJ KAPOOR

SHAMMI KAPOOR

SHASHI KAPOOR

RISHI KAPOOR

RANBIR KAPOOR

Daflis
Every cool kid had one in the 80s.

A fan sent this image to me: the many daflis I have played in my films

The makeup for *Kapoor & Sons* was a long and arduous process: Greg Cannom did an amazing job with my look

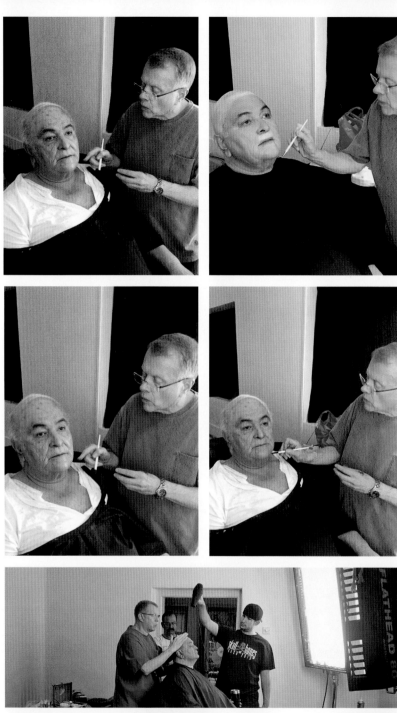
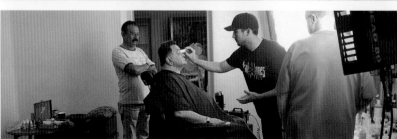

Flying high

Zamana (1985), which happened several years later, or with Dimple until *Saagar,* twelve years after *Bobby*. I never did work with Kaajal Kiran after *Hum Kisise Kum Naheen*.

But the actresses who did their second films with me stayed on to make many more movies with me. Tina Munim co-starred in *Aap Ke Deewane* with me after her debut film *Des Pardes* (1978) with Dev Anand. Randhir Kapoor was Neetu's first co-star in *Rickshawalla* (1973) and her second film, *Zehreela Insaan,* was with me. And so on and so forth.

While on the subject of introducing beautiful new faces, I also happened to be on the panel of judges the year Sushmita Sen was crowned Miss India Universe and Aishwarya Rai, Miss India World. Both Sushmita and Aishwarya returned with the international crowns.

Juhi Chawla and Tina Munim also made a major contribution to my career. After Neetu, the actress I made the maximum number of films with was Tina, and we went on to become good friends. She was discovered by Dev Anand and became a huge star in 1978. Our biggest hits together were *Aap Ke Deewane, Karz* and *Katilon Ke Kaatil*. There were also those that failed to create a ripple at the box-office such as *Bade Dil Wala, Deedar-e-Yaar* and *Yeh Vaada Raha*.

Tina's range as an actor may have been limited, but she exuded an elfin charm on screen that was refreshingly modern for its time and complemented my image beautifully. I had never before worked with a today's-girl like her. People said we looked good together. *Karz*, in which we worked together, will always remain special to me, very close to my heart. I don't know how she feels about it but it's a personal favourite as far as I am concerned, even though it wasn't a huge hit.

Dabboo's acting career ran parallel to mine and we had several leading heroines in common. Two of them were Neetu and Tina Munim. At one point, I was shooting for *Prem Rog* in Stage 1 of RK Studios and with Tina Munim for *Yeh Vaada Raha* in Stage 4, while she was simultaneously working in Ramesh Behl's film *Harjaee* (1981) with Dabboo. *Katilon Ke Kaatil* was another film we did together that ran for twenty-five weeks. Randhir and Rishi Kapoor were Tina's constant heroes and later, Rajesh Khanna, with whom she had a personal equation. With Jeetendra she did barely a film or two, including his own production *Deedar-e-Yaar*, and I co-starred with her in that one too.

Our budding friendship and the string of movies we did together inevitably led to rampant speculation about a secret affair. The media may not have been as powerful back then as it is today, but people made up stories as blithely then too. I was not married at the time and Tina was seeing Sanjay Dutt. One day, Sanju and Gulshan Grover visited Neetu at her apartment in Pali Hill. The rumours had gotten to him. Gulshan later told me that during the filming of *Rocky* (Gulshan was also in the film), Sanju had come to Neetu's house to pick a fight with me. But Neetu handled the situation marvellously. She diffused what could have turned into a very ugly scene by calmly explaining to Sanju that the rumours were baseless. She told him, 'There's nothing going on between Tina and Chintu. They are colleagues and buddies. You have to learn to trust when you're in this industry.' Later, Sanju and I would laugh over the incident. He was heavily addicted to drugs those days, and was high the day he came to Neetu's house too. The truth was established when Neetu and I got married and all my heroines attended the wedding.

Many years into our marriage, Neetu confided in me that the only time she had felt threatened was when I worked with Dimple in *Saagar*. But she needn't have worried. Dimple was a friend, even if she may have been a little more than that during *Bobby*. Ten years had gone by; she was coming out of a marriage with two children of her own and I was also well settled with two kids.

I have never let Neetu down in our marriage. I am a happily married man with a loving and supportive wife. Neetu is not only my wife, she is also a friend. If ever there were any ripples in our relationship, it was because of me, never her. And even then, the reasons had nothing to do with another woman in my life. She has been a rock and stood by me in my weakest moments. If there was an Oscar for the best partner, for being with someone for better or for worse in every sense of the word, she would get it.

When we were shooting for *Bobby*, Dimple would come to work in an Impala, the ultimate car of the era. Amitabh Bachchan, who was filming *Bandhe Haath* (1973) at the time, drove to RK Studios in a Fiat. Dimple was the daughter of a rich industrialist, Chunibhai Kapadia, and she made sure everyone knew it. She would brag to me that even if *Bobby* didn't do well, she would still be well off, whereas I'd have to struggle to make a name and living for myself. She was outspoken, bratty and bindaas. She used to play cricket with the guys but she wouldn't bowl or field, only bat, and the others would let her.

After *Bobby*, though, she became Mrs Rajesh Khanna and quit acting. We did *Saagar* exactly ten years later, when she made a comeback.

Dimple and I met socially a few times while she was still married to Rajesh Khanna. But it was a rocky marriage and by the time she returned to films we were both different people. She was stunning even then, but had lost her flamboyance and confidence. She also felt the need to assert that she was a great actress. I could see her trying too hard to live up to her image in *Bobby*, but it wasn't necessary. She was only twenty-five and very beautiful. Here, I must mention how much a source of strength her sister Simple was to her at this point. She constantly motivated Dimple and helped her emerge from this phase.

Many years later, we did another film, *Pyaar Mein Twist* (2005), where we were shown as young lovers who break up, get married to different partners, become parents and then fall in love again. I wish that film had been made well. There was so much promise in the story and the casting.

Rumours of a link-up were back again when Juhi Chawla and I had a successful run at the box-office. *Chandni* had been a hit, and she had a guest appearance in it. *Bol Radha Bol* was a commercial success. *Eena Meena Deeka* didn't do well but *Saajan Ka Ghar* (1994), a very regressive film, made a lot of money. And once again, there was nothing there.

As the years progressed, the girls who were cast with me got younger and younger. In the 1990s, leading ladies cast opposite me included Manisha Koirala (*Anmol*), Urmila Matondkar (*Shreemaan Aashique*) and Meenakshi Seshadri, with whom I did a few ghar-parivaar kind of films – family socials, as they were called – and the landmark *Damini*. With the age difference between me and the ladies growing, even the thought of an affair became more and more absurd.

While I didn't have a close friendship or a relationship with my leading ladies, barring Tina Munim and Dimple Kapadia, I respected them tremendously and credit them for much of my success. There could have been no singing-dancing-romancing star Rishi Kapoor without the great chemistry we shared on screen. I was never an action hero and for a romantic hero to work well, the heroine has to play a major role. It's nothing if not teamwork; you are not going to make box-office history all by yourself. Shah Rukh Khan, Aamir Khan, Salman Khan or even Ranbir, all romantic heroes, owe much of their success to the actresses who help them sizzle on screen.

There was only one heroine who was a little reluctant to work with me, very likely because she was the bigger star at the time. Sridevi was making waves and I had hit a plateau when we worked together in *Nagina*. She was also very reclusive. I was later told that she was an extremely shy person and very inhibited.

One of our most embarrassing moments together happened when we were shooting a song for *Nagina* at RK Studios. When you are in the midst of a 'take' and the assistant cameraman suddenly says the magazine has run out (when the camera needs a new roll of film), it's a very awkward moment for actors. The lights are on, you are in position, and you have to hold it, looking odd and static, while new film is loaded. During *Nagina*, Sridevi and I found ourselves in that awkward situation, just standing there, waiting, when she suddenly spoke to me and said, 'Sir, I have seen *Khel Khel Mein* four times.' I was so taken aback, I could only mumble something about a film of hers that I had seen, and that was it. That was the only conversation I had with Sridevi all through the filming of *Nagina*. Otherwise it was always 'Namasteji' and 'Good nightji'.

It was during the making of *Chandni* that we became friendly. She opened up to me, and the new level of comfort also improved our performance. Yash-ji gave us a free hand in the film, leaving a lot of room for improvisation. It worked well since I like to be spontaneous and improvise on set, and so does Sridevi. She contributed a great deal towards making scenes work. The 'Cognac *sharab nahin hoti*' sequence, for instance, was entirely improvised. It was not in the original script. It was made up on the spot by Yash-ji, Sridevi and me.

Sridevi is a terrific actor who balances method acting (which she picked up from Kamal Haasan) with spontaneity. She has also evolved over the years. When I saw her in *English Vinglish* (2012), I was floored. She has flowered into a highly intelligent actor.

I was probably one of the first people to know that Sridevi was in a relationship with Boney Kapoor. The first time I had an inkling of it was when we were shooting a song for a film in

Goa. Sridevi had left the location before me and I was heading back to the Taj for lunch when I saw someone who looked like Boney from afar. But I wasn't sure. Fortunately, the general manager of the hotel, Joe, was a classmate of mine. I called him up and asked, 'Is Boney here?' He said, 'Who Boney?' I replied, 'Boney Kapoor.' He looked up the name on the computer and reported that he wasn't. It occurred to me then that he may have used an alias, so I asked Joe, 'Has an Achal Kapoor checked in?' And the answer was 'yes'. Achal Kapoor is Boney's real name, and that's when I guessed what was brewing between the two. Three or four months later, after they had got married, there were whispers that she was carrying his baby. The dress man of our film revealed that all her clothes were being altered, her trousers were being loosened. The director was also told not to take shots below the waist. But for the most part, Sridevi kept her personal life away from public scrutiny, and professionally, she was wonderful to work with, a fabulous actor. I had two huge successes with her, *Nagina* and *Chandni*. We also did *Banjaran* (1991), which was an average film.

Poonam Dhillon was another actress with whom I did a lot of work. Poonam was always very easy to work with, and a pretty girl. We did films like *Yeh Vaada Raha, Ek Chadar Maili Si* and *Sitamgar* (1985). I was also very happy to work with Madhuri Dixit, although none of our films together were successful. I would definitely want to correct that record someday. We made four films together, all turkeys. Madhuri is a lovely girl, very straightforward, great fun, and a fine actor.

I remember Padmini Kolhapure as being very childish

during the making of *Prem Rog*. I loved to see her cry on screen, she did it so effectively. Padmini was the only heroine who looked good when she cried. And she had the most expressive voice ever. As an actor, she used her voice to superb effect.

Tabu has blossomed over the years. She was awkward right through the making of the first film we did together, *Pehla Pehla Pyar* (1994). Director Manmohan Singh had to keep scolding her to stand properly. She was very self-conscious about being taller than me, and ended up slouching to compensate for the difference in our heights. I had to wear shoes with high heels to look right with her or even a little taller, while she wore flats. When I met her some time ago, she reminded me about those days. 'Remember how you would keep shouting at me to stand like this, or stand like that?' And I said to her, 'All that shouting has worked for you, hasn't it? You are standing tall in your career today.' We did two more films together, both insignificant. I ended up making not one successful film with Tabu, Madhuri or Manisha Koirala.

Almost all the films that I made with Meenakshi Seshadri were only moderately successful. The one outstanding film was *Damini*. It was the role of her career, while I, as her husband, had one of the most complex characters I have played.

Meenakshi was a technically correct actor. What she lacked was emotion. When she danced, every move was executed perfectly, not one step would be out of place, in fact she was one of the best dancers around, but there was no jaan, no life in her. I would say the same for Urmila Matondkar, with whom I did films like *Tehzeeb* (2003) and *Shreemaan*

Aashique (1993). According to me, Urmila was the finest dancer of our times, a better dancer than even Sridevi and Madhuri. I used to think, whoa, what's this girl all about? But she was missing fire and spunk, that something special. She was at her best in *Rangeela* (1995).

I only ever did one film paired with Rekha: *Azaad Desh Ke Ghulam*. But we had no chemistry at all. We did other films like *Sheshnaag* (1990) and *Amiri Garibi* (1990) but she was not cast opposite me in them. Rekha always got along better with Neetu than with me. Whenever they met, they got on like a house on fire. They would gab in Tamil because Neetu had picked up a bit of the language when she made films in Madras as a child artiste.

Strange as it may seem today, I was even cast in a film with Jaya Bachchan. It was very early in my career but it was aborted because she had just got married and many people felt I looked far too young beside her.

When I became a character actor, one of the first actresses from the younger generation that I worked with was Kajol, although obviously not in a romantically paired role. Kajol is unique. She can work with anyone in any film and make it believable. She can work even with someone younger, like Ranbir, and look good with him. *Fanaa*, a film in which Kirron Kher and I played her parents, was a hit. *Raju Chacha* (2000) and *Kuch Khatti Kuch Meethi* (2001) were the other films in which we worked together. I will never forget the compliment she paid me after a particularly difficult shot. 'What a pleasure it is to work with you as an actor. You don't know how much you inspire me,' she said.

It was with Kajol that I eased into the second innings of my acting career – one of the most gratifying periods of my life, a phase where privilege, honour and unique roles have come my way.

8

NEETU, MY LEADING LADY

I first met Neetu briefly when she visited the sets of *Bobby* with her mother. After *Zehreela Insaan*, she became a near constant in my filmography and a very busy actress in her own right. We began to see each other at some point and got seriously involved around the time that I finished work on *Amar Akbar Anthony*. In those days, seeing a girl meant going to a party, holding hands and doing a slow dance with her. Nothing more.

I was considered an eligible bachelor in our circles. I had become a household name at the age of twenty-one. I was making unimaginable amounts of money and I was a legendary film-maker's son as well. Which means, of course, that there was no dearth of smitten fans.

I remember Jo (Jyoti) in particular, a lively young girl who was about fifteen or sixteen years old. My father had spotted her at a restaurant in Connaught Place, Delhi. Forever on the lookout for a pretty girl to cast in his films, he asked her if she'd like to work with him. This was soon after *Bobby*. Jo was excited and game to give it a try, so Papa invited her to Bombay for a screen test. But what the naked eye sees and what the camera lens registers can sometimes be vastly different and it didn't work out. However, I met her many times. She was a huge fan of mine and would often come to watch me shoot. She was stunning to look at and I was quite fascinated by her. But since I wasn't thinking about a long-term commitment at the time, nothing ever blossomed between us and soon she went off and got married. I never saw her after that. Neetu used to rag me about Jo and say that I was in a relationship with her. But she was wrong. I only remember Jo with a sense of nostalgia, as part of my early years as an actor.

Until the time I finally got married, my parents continued to receive proposals for me, many from very distinguished families. When I started dating Neetu, I didn't formally speak to them about it but they sensed where I was headed. My father tactfully fended off all proposals by telling the families that I was seeing someone and that they presumed I would be marrying her. Even though I was silent about my relationship with Neetu, my family knew about it and quietly and wholeheartedly accepted it.

There was never any doubt that I was madly in love. But if it seemed like Neetu was the one head over heels in love with me and not the other way around, there were good reasons for it. When I was going steady with Yasmin, I used to be petrified that my father would find out. That fear of being caught out remained with me as I grew older. Even when I started dating Neetu, I couldn't muster up the courage to tell my parents that I wanted to marry her. For some reason, I was terrified that my father would find out I was spending time with a girl. I was so full of doubts and complexes that if I spotted my parents while walking with a girl, I would instantly abandon her and walk away. I had no sense of chivalry whatsoever. Looking back, I wonder if I should have turned to a psychiatrist for help to work out my feelings.

Although my brothers knew, my parents knew, and pretty much the whole world knew, I could never voice my intentions to Neetu or to them. I wasn't even sure if I was ready for marriage. I was twenty-seven years old and still living with my parents in Chembur. Today this may seem like a very young age to get married, especially for a man, but in the 1980s, few men remained single past their mid-twenties. Still, I couldn't make up my mind.

Given how committed we were to each other, nobody could fathom why I wasn't popping the question. How could they know that I was battling a million demons in my head? I had serious misgivings about the effect of marriage on an actor's longevity, given how Rajesh Khanna's career went on a downward spiral post marriage. What if his story repeated itself with me, since I was also a romantic hero and was marrying an actress?

I often think I may never have married Neetu, or we may have got married much later than we did, if it weren't for my sister Ritu. Left to myself, I may never have taken our relationship to the next level.

But we made headlines when I went to Delhi for an engagement in my sister's family and came back to Mumbai with a ring on my own finger. I hadn't a clue that Ritu had been plotting and planning along with my friends Gogi (film-maker Ramesh Behl) and Ravi Malhotra (father of Karan Malhotra, the young director of Karan Johar's 2012 film *Agneepath*). At the airport in Mumbai, as I waited to board my flight, I met Saira Banu and Dilip Kumar, who asked me where I was going. When I told him I was headed for Delhi to attend an engagement, Dilip sa'ab joked, 'Don't pull a fast one on me. Aren't you going there to get engaged yourself?' How prophetic Dilip sa'ab's words turned out to be.

I was completely in the dark about my sister's plans to bring Neetu and her mother to Delhi too. And I was caught entirely off-guard when my parents and close friends got Neetu and me to sit on a mandap meant for somebody else's engagement and made us exchange rings. They had decided that it was time for me to get hitched. But since it was all so unplanned, we didn't have any rings to exchange. Ultimately the ring that Neetu gave me was Ravi Malhotra's with an 'R' (for Ravi) on it.

My father loved and heartily gathered Neetu into the family, which was a huge relief for me. I really don't know why I had feared otherwise.

When I started dating Neetu, her mother allowed her to go out with me only if Lovely, her cousin, came along. The date would begin with the three of us sitting in a car and driving around. But, of course, we had our own little ways to work around this little hurdle. As soon as we were out of sight of her house, Lovely would go off to meet his girlfriend while Neetu and I would continue on our own.

When Neetu and I first met, I was in love with Yasmin. During the *Zehreela Insaan* shoot in Chitradurga, I would be in total panic if I couldn't get through to her and would ask Neetu to talk to her on my behalf. Over time, as we worked together, Neetu and I began to be drawn towards each other. In the early years, I was a flamboyant brat who'd annoy her and tease her, even ruffle her makeup. Neetu was always a good, well-brought-up girl. We were doing two shifts a day and were constantly thrown together. It was a glorious period for us – we were totally in love. Before we got married, she and I had made eleven films together. Most of them fared well, so we were considered a very successful screen couple.

Neetu's mother Raji Singh was a sweetheart and I got along famously with her. She was a simple Jat woman, not highly educated but all heart. Neetu was a child star who became a leading actress at a very young age. When she worked with me in *Zehreela Insaan* and *Rafoo Chakkar*, she was barely fifteen years old and was chaperoned by her mother or her mama. There was always a family member with her because she was a kid and not aware of a lot of the things happening around her. I had little to do with her then. Our relationship began much later. When I started growing fond of her, my mother-in-law saw it first and so I took her into confidence. I told her that I liked Neetu very much and would like to marry her someday.

She was equally clear that we shouldn't see each other unless I intended to marry her.

I would go over to Neetu's place every evening after the day's shoot, and her mother was always welcoming. The whole industry knew that I was seeing Neetu. Wherever she was and whoever she was shooting with, she would try to wrap up by 8 p.m. and rush back home to be with me. My colleagues and friends, including Jeetendra and Amitabh Bachchan, would tease me about the fact that the moment the clock struck eight, she would start saying she had to leave. I too would work only until 8 p.m., so that we could be together by 8.30 p.m. We were both very busy actors, she more than me because I used to work on only one film at a time while she did double shifts. Winding up work by eight was the only way we could make time for each other.

We didn't have colour television then, or cable or video. We had black-and-white TV sets telecasting only state-sponsored Doordarshan programmes. So watching TV was never on the agenda. Neither were there many options for going out. When we met, we'd simply talk about our day. Sometimes we would go out for a drive or for dinner. There was no fear of being exposed or creating a scandal because the media was not the monster it is today. There was no paparazzi culture either. Everything was smaller in scale, there were fewer journalists, and most of them were our friends.

It was in 1975, during the shooting of *Kabhi Kabhie* in Kashmir, that our love affair blossomed. I went to Paris for a shoot soon after and sent her a telegram: '*Sikhni bahut yaad aati hai* (I really miss the Sikhni).' She was overjoyed when she received it and showed it off to everyone on the set saying, 'See? He's missing me.'

Kashmir played a huge part in our romance. We shot in different parts of the state for different films umpteen times.

It was while we were dating that Neetu and I started calling each other 'Baba', which soon got shortened to 'Bob'. To this day, she calls me Bob, never by my name. I like to think it's in keeping with the age-old tradition of Indian women addressing their husbands as ayeji or suniyeji, never by name.

My mother, for instance, always addressed my father as ayeji, suniyeji. It was unimaginable for women in her time to even try to get around it. Even after he passed away, Mom was still very uncomfortable taking his name. But when talking about him to the press or anybody else, she'd refer to him as 'Raj–ji'.

Neetu and I were always very professional on the set. We may have been dating, but there was no question of playing hooky. When she decided she didn't want to work in films after we got married, she handled her exit with characteristic grace and professionalism and gave ample notice to all her producers. She finished all her assignments before we got married on 22 January 1980.

Like most couples, we've had our ups and downs and our share of fights and misunderstandings. Adjusting to married life was difficult for me to start with, because I'd never been answerable to anybody before. But we have spent an incredible thirty-seven years together as husband and wife and I feel blessed to have her in my life.

In the beginning we lived with my parents in Chembur. That's where Riddhima was born on 15 September 1980. By the time Ranbir came along two years later, on 28 September 1982, we had shifted to Kesar Villa in Pali Hill, which was my mother-in-law's house.

Insecurities surrounding my fate as a romantic hero continued to linger after my marriage. And the doubts that had plagued me became very real when *Karz*, a film I had high hopes for, was released in the same year as my marriage and didn't perform to expectations at the box-office, followed soon after by the debacle of *Zamaane Ko Dikhana Hai*. I blamed Neetu for it, believing marriage had robbed me of my charm. I went into a depression and could not bring myself to face either the public or the camera. I've already written in some detail about this phase in my life but I must make a passing reference to it again to spotlight Neetu's role in it. Naturally, she was worried and so were my parents, who took me off to our farm and to Shirdi afterwards. Papa would quote from the *Bhagavad Gita* to get me to understand and accept the situation, but I was traumatized and not very receptive. Neetu was pregnant with Riddhima and had to endure my breakdown in that fragile condition. I finally came through it with the help of supportive colleagues, family and friends, but I can only imagine how agonizing the experience must have been for her.

The truth is that I would never have made it through that spell had it not been for Neetu's staunch loyalty. She has been my pillar of strength throughout our life together. I am a difficult man, I have many quirks and fears. My sisters and my mother have always said that Neetu deserves a medal for staying married to me, and I have to agree with them. Incredibly, she has done it without nagging me to change, and patiently puts up with my whims and moods.

Through all these years, though, whatever our problems, I have never stepped outside the bounds of our marriage, nor has she. We have a wonderful time together and have two lovely children we dote on. We have never been separated, we have always lived under the same roof and have shouldered all our problems together, as a couple.

Many of our friends, who have seen us over the years, label us the ideal couple and are upset if they sense any trouble in paradise. But a little turbulence is inevitable. Neetu and I have had prolonged 'super-fights'. We are both supremely egotistic and have had quarrels that resulted in us not speaking to each other for six months at a stretch. In most of our fights, I am the one to blame because I sulk and don't talk to her even when I know I am in the wrong. We communicate with each other through a third person, and it is only after we have both got it out of our systems that normalcy returns to the household.

Before we were married, we had plenty of lovers' tiffs. Right through the shooting of the song '*Jeevan ke har mod pe*' for *Jhoota Kahin Ka*, we were not talking to each other. She would sit sobbing in her makeup room with her mother and I would do something to distract myself. Even recently, we were not on talking terms while filming our romantic guest appearance for Yash-ji's *Jab Tak Hai Jaan* (2012).

Our fights are mostly because of our differing views on

various issues. Sometimes we fight about our friends. Neetu has often said that I'm immature, which of course I don't agree with. I remember Dabboo describing one particularly rough patch in our lives as our midlife crisis. It was during the time that my career as a lead actor was coming to an end. It was also the time when I was about to direct *Aa Ab Laut Chalen*. And there I was, having problems with Neetu as well. It was a boiling cauldron that was bound to bubble over.

Despite everything, we've remained totally in love and can't do without each other. The fact that it was our thirty-fifth wedding anniversary in January 2015 speaks for itself. We couldn't celebrate it, though, because I was shooting with Paresh Rawal for *Patel Ki Punjabi Shaadi*. And I didn't take Neetu out for dinner or do anything special the next day either, because we'd had a fight and were giving each other the silent treatment!

But I'm not only about quirks and tantrums. And Neetu knows and appreciates those other aspects of my life. She likes the fact that I have great faith in God, that I believe in karma and like visiting temples and holy places. *Mujhe bahut sukoon milta hai, shraddha bhi meri bahut hai*, I like the peace and tranquillity of these places and my faith is also very intense. I do a small puja every day, and on Mondays I perform a half-hour puja for Lord Shiva. I have been doing this ever since my *Bobby* days, since I was twenty-one years old. All this is thanks to my mother's influence. I have also made the annual pilgrimage to Sabarimala in Kerala twice. I have kept the forty-one-day vrat, abstaining from eating meat and drinking alcohol. I washed my own clothes and walked all the way from Pamba to the temple on the hill. I felt cleansed and ready to take on the world by the end of the pilgrimage.

But one thing I do not do is mix my food with my religion. I am a beef-eating Hindu. I also have a bit of the Christian in me because of my studying in Jesuit schools. I find it comforting to have crosses and figurines of angels around me. I pick them up from all over the world, sometimes close friends gift them to me. They have a special place on one of the walls in my home.

I went to a Catholic school, so I still say my 'Hail Marys' and make a sign of the cross every time I pass a church, and I pray in English. Every time I visit New York, I go to St. Patrick's Cathedral on 5th Avenue. I also once joined forces with my friend and legendary batsman Sunil Gavaskar to save a temple in London. The temple had been established in a manor gifted to the Hare Rama Hare Krishna Sanstha by George Harrison. But there were problems with the local precinct and they didn't have the money to fight their case. So Sunny and I undertook a walk to raise funds. They ultimately won the case and the right to stay on there. The trustees were so pleased with our efforts that they bestowed honorary memberships upon us and our names are inscribed on a wall inside the temple.

I could dedicate several chapters to Neetu in this book because there are so many memories and shared moments with her that I hold dear. But I remember one particular instance when Papa decided to take us to Amsterdam to shoot a song for *Prem Rog*, amidst the world-famous tulips. He took a skeletal unit along, and Neetu and my mother accompanied us. Since there were no spot boys or dress men, Mum used to make tea for everyone and Neetu would serve it. Every evening, after pack-up, she would diligently wash my white shirt and Padmini Kolhapure's white sari because we were required to wear them for the entire duration of the song.

When Neetu gave up her flourishing career at the age of twenty-one, she was one of the top actresses of her time. To put this in perspective, today girls begin their careers at that age. It was, as I have said often, her decision to wind up her career after marriage. I can say with a clear conscience that I did not force it upon her. We did agree before we got married that once we had children, one of us would be the earning partner and the other would be the nurturing parent. But to be honest, I didn't try to convince her to keep working either. There was a chauvinist in me that didn't want his wife to go out to work. I wanted Neetu to finish all her commitments before we got married. All I can say in my defence is that my views have changed since then.

Neetu's sacrifice didn't go unnoticed, and she earned the admiration of one and all, including the media. I think her mother deserves a lot of the credit too, for supporting her in that difficult decision.

Shortly after we began our married life, major repairs had to be carried out in our Chembur house, which resulted in my parents moving into a friend's bungalow in Union Park, Chembur, while Neetu and I shifted to Kesar Villa, my mother-in-law's house in Pali Hill, Bandra. I can tell you that caused a lot of amusement. It became a big joke in the film industry, with Prem Chopra and my other friends teasing me about the two great actors who lived in Pali Hill, both as ghar jamais. The other great actor being referred to was Dilip Kumar, who lived in his mother-in-law Naseem Banu's house.

While we were staying at Kesar Villa, Neetu and I bought a plot of land close by and started building Krishna Raj, our own bungalow, in Pali Hill. Meanwhile, we lived with her mother for close to ten years. Ranbir was born there in 1982 and it was also while living there that I lost my father. We shifted into Krishna Raj much later.

During the years spent living with my mother-in-law, I tried to help out around the house in every way I could. I didn't live off her, only with her. When we finally moved into our own bungalow, she moved in with us. She was a great support because I travelled a lot and it was comforting to know that there was someone to watch over Neetu and the kids in my absence. Mummy (as I called her) shared the responsibility of looking after the children. She and I would also share a drink in the evenings, until she had to give up alcohol altogether for medical reasons.

Neetu's second innings in films began with *Love Aaj Kal* (2009) in which she had a couple of shots at the end. She was so nervous about acting after such a long hiatus that I had to cajole her into doing it. My sister Rima and her family had to come to London for the shoot just to boost her morale. Neetu went on to do a full-length role in *Do Dooni Chaar* (2010) because the original choice, Juhi Chawla, did not want to play a mother's role. I was really keen to work with Neetu but had to coax her to do it. I explained to her that now that the kids were settled in their respective lives, she had time on her hands and could do the occasional film. Besides, the role suited her. It would give her an opportunity to showcase her acting skills. She said no, but agreed to meet Habib Faisal, the director, for a quick twenty-minute chat. I was immensely relieved when the chat stretched to include a full narration of the story and she loved the role enough to agree to work in the film.

On the first day of the shoot, however, I wondered if she was up to it when she kept forgetting her lines. Neetu had been known for her ability to memorize her dialogues and would finish dubbing faster than her co-stars. Had she lost her touch after all these years? A little later, she took me aside and told me she was finding it difficult to read and remember her dialogues because she was reluctant to wear her reading glasses. I told her to pick up her spectacles at once and get going with her lines. Once she did that, she easily slipped back into being the quick learner she always was.

I constantly encourage Neetu to undertake more projects, but she tells me that she's no longer cut out for the grind. She insists that she has lost touch with acting, it's been thirty-seven years since she gave it up. The only films she has done in recent times are *Do Dooni Chaar* and a guest appearance in *Jab Tak Hai Jaan*, both of which were with me, and *Besharam* (2013), because she got to work with her husband and her son. She did it to spend time with us and for no other reason. She says to me, 'I'm not dependent on films for a living, I don't want to do it, I don't want to work. I'm happy in my own space. I don't want the responsibility of getting up and going to work.'

On a normal day, Neetu gets up around 9–9.30 a.m. and enjoys not having to rush to work. 'I can't get up early and I can't shoot till late because you're home at that time and I want to be with you. So working with other people doesn't work for me.' She gets so many offers but she's clear that until something excites her, she won't take it up. However, once Neetu makes up her mind about something, we all know she'll see it through. Recently, when Ranbir, she and I co-starred in the immensely forgettable *Besharam*, she worked very hard to pick up the Haryanvi accent. That's Neetu for you. Whatever she does, she does it with unmatched sincerity.

She did that with our marriage too, and became a great mother, wife and cook. She didn't know how to cook to begin with, but she learned from scratch and became one of the best cooks in the family. In the first few years of our marriage, she would make exotic food – she made the best lobster thermidor in town – and would pamper me with her cooking. She, on her part, gives me credit for teaching her table etiquette and how to serve food with elegance and style.

Neetu has looked after our home, our family, our kids and me with loving care. She is a disciplinarian and has been rather strict with me about my eating habits. She doesn't relent even if I throw a tantrum. There's only brown bread, brown rice and whole-wheat grain in our house, which works well for my diabetes. You'll never find white rice on the table unless we're having a party. We also avoid processed food. But every time my parents came over for dinner, Neetu would cook to their taste, knowing they liked the rich fatty food that she was trying to wean me away from. And knowing that I love Peshawari food, she allows me to binge once in a while when I am in Chembur.

I don't belong to the gym generation. I also know that I'm no Hrithik Roshan, I'm never going to have a body like him. My doctors have told me I don't need to lose much weight at this age, fifteen-odd kilos would be fine. I think it's doable if I give up alcohol. Unfortunately, I don't see myself doing that in the near future, unless of course I am offered a special role that requires me to lose weight.

One thing I have discovered over the years is that Neetu has incredible willpower. She likes to have a drink but will never binge. Ranbir has inherited the best traits of his mother. He loves to eat but is strict with himself. Riddhima too doesn't eat much. When it comes to food and drink, I'm the quintessential Kapoor who can't control himself. I guess I make up for all three of them, particularly when Neetu is not looking.

9

BUDDIES, BAD MEN, PEERS AND CONTEMPORARIES

I have always been an insular person, comfortable with my own fraternity. This means that almost all my close friends are from the world of Hindi cinema. However, stardom has given me glimpses of what lies beyond the film industry and acquainted me with an interesting array of people from different walks of life, providing me the opportunity to forge friendships outside the studios.

Apart from cinema, the one everlasting passion of my life has been cricket. I am an ardent fan of the game and follow it closely. It is this fascination that brought me close to cricketing legend Sunil Gavaskar. Our paths crossed when he was the toast of the cricketing world and I was a budding actor. Crowds jostled for his attention, but being Raj Kapoor's son helped me stand out from them.

Papa had once sent Gavaskar a telegram: 'A pat for your bat'. In the days before mobile phones, telegrams were the only way to swiftly convey personal messages. Sunny cherished Papa's telegram and it paved the way for a new friendship in my life. Sunny, his wife Marshneil and I soon became very good friends.

Sunny is a wonderfully articulate and courageous man, unafraid to speak his mind. He is well travelled and is a treasure trove of exciting experiences and stories. It's always a pleasure to spend time with him and we are close enough to be able to discuss anything. He sends me birthday wishes every year and tells me that wherever he may be, he raises a toast to me with a glass of red wine.

Through Sunny, I met a number of Pakistani cricketers too. At one time I was very friendly with Wasim Bari, who was then the wicketkeeper of the Pakistan team. He is now with the Pakistan Cricket Board. I also met Wasim Akram in London and got to know Shoaib Akhtar, among others. When Wasim lost his wife Huma in 2009, I called him to offer my condolences and I know he was touched by the gesture.

But it wasn't always bonhomie and brotherhood. I remember having a showdown with Javed Miandad once. He and I had started our respective careers around the same time. He had come to Mumbai to play a cricket match soon after *Bobby* was released in 1973. At that time, for no good reason at all, I used to find all the Pakistanis annoying and Miandad would speak in such a squeaky voice that it got on my nerves. Then one year, when they were in Bombay around the time of my dad's annual birthday celebration, he decided to host the whole

Pakistan team. Naturally, I had to be on my best behaviour. Nevertheless, my hackles were up and, as the evening wore on, I began to lose my inhibitions. Soon, Miandad and I got into a silly argument over something innocuous. Today I can laugh off the incident as inane and trivial, a result of the brashness of my youth, but I remember that it got rather ugly that day.

Miandad, Mudassar Nazar and Zaheer Abbas would visit India frequently. Zaheer Abbas was a regular in Delhi because he was seeing a girl who lived there. I think he later married her. I remember snatches of my interactions with all of them because they were a big part of my life back then.

During the filming of *Patiala House* (2011), a cricket-themed drama, I also got friendly with Australian cricketer Andrew Symonds, who had a role in it. I remember how different his habits were from ours. He would have dinner by 7.30 p.m. and when we had wrapped up for the day, he would join us for drinks from 8 p.m. until midnight. We did just the opposite. We'd drink from 7.30 to 10 p.m. and then have dinner. I admired his discipline, not surprising in a career sportsman, even if I didn't follow suit.

Patiala House saw a lot of cricketers walking on and off the sets. Balwinder Singh Sandhu, who was a couple of years younger than me, was the bowling coach on the film. He had been a member of the Indian cricket team that won the World Cup in 1983 and would regale us with stories of that time.

I first met Kapil Dev, who led us to that historic World Cup victory, at an event, and found him immensely likeable. It was his refreshing candour that taught the nation that it was not imperative to speak impeccable English or have a great education to make an impression. He is a man who speaks from the heart and he remains the quintessential good-hearted Jat.

Along with the good, fame has also brought me in contact with people of dubious character.

One of them was Dawood Ibrahim.

The year was 1988, a time when mobile phones were unknown to us in India. I had landed in Dubai with my closest friend, Bittu Anand, for an Asha Bhosle–R.D. Burman night. Shailendra Singh was to perform. Asrani and I were the only two actors on the show. Dawood always had a man at the airport to keep him posted on VIP movement in and out of the UAE. In those days, there were very few flights between Mumbai and Dubai and if I remember correctly, Gulf Air and Air India were the only two airlines plying the route.

When I was leaving the airport, a stranger walked up to me and handed me a phone. He said, 'Dawood sa'ab *baat karenge* (Dawood sa'ab would like to talk to you).' Obviously, this was before the 1993 blasts in Mumbai and I didn't think of Dawood as a fugitive on the run. He wasn't an enemy of the state yet. Or, at least, that was the impression I had. Dawood welcomed me to Dubai and said, 'If there is anything you need, just let me know.' He also invited me to his house. I was taken aback but assured him that I'd definitely think about it.

I was staying at the Hyatt Regency in Dubai on that trip and Dawood's airport man would regularly drop in to use the gym there. Then I was introduced to a fair, pudgy guy who looked British. This was Baba, the second-in-command in

Dawood's hierarchy, the don's right-hand man. He said to me, 'Dawood sa'ab wishes to have tea with you.' I didn't see any harm in that and accepted the invitation. That evening, Bittu and I were picked up from our hotel in a gleaming Rolls Royce. While we were being driven to his home, a conversation went on around us, in Kutchi. I don't understand Kutchi but my friend did, and he realized that instead of being taken straight to Dawood's residence, we were being driven around in circles, so we wouldn't know the exact location of his house. There was a car phone over which those who had come to fetch us were receiving instructions, and they had to keep up the drill till they were told that it was all right to head for the house.

As we were entering the house, I caught a glimpse of someone peeping through a window. It was Dawood. Immaculately dressed in an Italian ensemble that wasn't exactly a suit, he greeted us warmly and apologetically explained, 'I called you to tea because I don't drink or serve alcohol.'

So, we had a tea-and-biscuits session for four hours. He spoke of a number of things, including some of his criminal activities for which he had no regrets. 'I have carried out petty thefts but I have never killed anyone, though I have got someone killed,' he revealed. He claimed to have had someone shot in a Mumbai court for lying. I can't remember exactly what he said, but it was about someone going against Allah's word and so they had to do it. He claimed, 'I was Allah's messenger, so we shot him through his tongue and then through his brain.' Director Rahul Rawail later used this real-life incident as the basis of a courtroom murder scene in his film *Arjun* (1985).

Dawood also told me he'd loved me in the film *Tawaif* because my name in it was Dawood. I resurrect the life of a downtrodden woman in *Tawaif* and Dawood was pleased that through the film I had (unwittingly) glorified his name. Years later, in Nikhil Advani's *D-Day*, I once again played Dawood on screen.

Over tea and biscuits Dawood spoke of his fondness for my father, my uncles, Dilip Kumar, Mehmood, Mukri and other actors. I remember feeling rather fearful when I first arrived there, but as the evening progressed my anxiety melted away and I relaxed, and we shared innumerable cups of tea over four hours. He asked me again if I needed anything, including money. His exact words were, 'If you need anything at all, any money, anything, just feel free to ask me.' I thanked him and said that we were already well taken care of.

That meeting with Dawood was in March 1988 and on 2 June my father passed away in Delhi. We returned to Mumbai from Delhi on 3 June and the next day, Baba, Dawood's guy in Dubai, landed up at our home in Chembur at 6.30 a.m. Dabboo and I were woken up by one of the staff, who announced, '*Koi aapse milne aaya hai* Dubai *se*.'

Baba had come as Dawood's representative to offer his condolences on my father's death. He said, 'I had to come surreptitiously and I'll have to fly back right away.'

I met Dawood only once after that, in Dubai. I love buying shoes and I was with Neetu at a sprawling Lebanese store called Red Shoe Company. Dawood was there too. He had a mobile phone in his hand and was surrounded by eight or ten bodyguards, all flaunting mobiles. As on our previous encounter, when he had offered to take care of me, this time too he said, 'Let me buy you whatever you want.' I politely declined and said, 'Please don't embarrass me. I appreciate your gesture but I'd like to do my own shopping.' He gave me his mobile number, but I couldn't offer one in return because this was in 1989 when we didn't have mobile phones in India. Finally Dawood said, 'I am a fugitive because I will not get justice in India. There are a lot of people there who are against me. There are also many in India I have bought. I pay several politicians who are in my pocket.' I said to him, 'Dawood, please leave me out of all this, yaar. I am an actor and I really don't wish to get involved.' He understood. He was always extremely nice to me and showed me a lot of warmth.

But everything changed soon after. I don't know what made him go after my country the way he did. I have had no interaction with him at all after that chance meeting at the shoe shop. But there have been some more encounters with members of his family. I made a film called *Shreemaan Aashique* which had music composed by Nadeem–Shravan and lyrics by Noora, Dawood's brother, who had a flair for writing. I heard that Dawood's cronies would wake Nadeem up at 2 a.m. and say, 'Noora wants to speak to you.'

Noora was also part of a group that felicitated us in 1991 for *Henna*. They hosted Zeba Bakhtiar and the entire crew of the film and gave the team of *Henna* one million dirhams as a token of appreciation. Dabboo refused to take it and said, 'We have not come here for your money, we are here for your love.

This is the first film made on Indo-Pak friendship. It was Raj Kapoor's dream that our two countries should become one.' I remember that Noora spent most of that evening chatting with Kiran Kumar, who was very friendly with him.

Another dubious character I used to know is Rattan Khatri, once referred to as Mumbai's matka king. He produced a film called *Rangila Ratan* that had Parveen Babi and me in the lead with Ashok Kumar in a supporting role. Matka ruled the lives of Bombay's working class back then and Rattan Khatri was the don who ran all the gambling dens. I recall we were shooting at RK Studios. In the evening, he would ask either Dadamoni (Ashok Kumar) or me to pick a card, the number of which was flashed all over Mumbai within minutes. That was the lucky number for the day.

I remember hearing about an episode when Rattan Khatri was on a plane from Bangalore to Mumbai. The flight got delayed and he wouldn't have made it in time to announce the matka number for the day. So he actually got the pilot to connect with the control tower and announce the number because if there was a delay in putting it out, there would be chaos. Even the police were okay with this because they didn't want a law and order situation on their hands. I believe Mr Khatri is still somewhere out there. It has been decades since I bumped into him. He was a simple, unassuming sort of guy, who always wore a pajama–kurta with a scarf.

I have been, and always will be, most at home with my circle of male friends from the film industry. Among them, I count Guddu (Rakesh Roshan) and Shambu (Jeetendra) as real buddies with whom I've partied, holidayed and shared a bond that goes way beyond our work. Prem Chopra is a part of this circle too, but I've already dwelt on that at length.

It was during a stretch of shooting on location at Pahalgam for *Khel Khel Mein* that Guddu and I became really close. There was no television in those days and few avenues of entertainment were available to us. We didn't want to sit around and drink ourselves silly, so we were always on the lookout for something to do. I remember that one evening, soon after Manoj Kumar's *Roti, Kapada Aur Makaan* was released, we drove from Pahalgam to Srinagar to see it.

Guddu and I worked in quite a few films and, as our bond strengthened, our wives got drawn into the circle as well and we became a close-knit group.

I met Jeetendra sometime around 1969 when I was in London. I had dropped out of school and Papa wanted me to supervise the post-production of *Mera Naam Joker*, for which I ended up spending around eight months there. I first met Jeetendra's brother Prasan Kapoor through some common friends and then got to know him as well. There's a difference of ten years between us, unlike with Guddu, who is about the same age as I am, so I always treated him with respect. I don't ever call him by his name. It's always either 'Jeetu-ji' or 'Shambu!'

Jeetendra has often reminded me of how formal I was with him initially, when I'd bow and greet him with, 'How are you, sir?' That is what came naturally to me because he was older, but he soon bridged that distance with his warmth and friendship.

Jeetendra also helped me chalk out a roadmap for my career. Although the final decisions were always mine, he guided me through some difficult turns along the way. It's not as if I blindly looked up to him. I had my reservations about the way he did certain things, for example, the kind of films he did in the south. Though he became very successful with these films, I could never see myself a part of this school of film-making. I remember Rajesh Khanna telling me once, about how they had wrapped up a film – I think it was *Maqsad* (1984), which starred him with Jeetendra, Sridevi and Jaya Prada, the customary stars for all south films of the era – in eighteen days! But there were some areas in which I followed his lead, especially when we were both working as lead actors. I thoroughly admired his preparedness and his discipline. He loved being a star and I loved watching his enthusiasm, whether he was acting in a film or producing one.

Jeetendra enjoyed a great deal of success, especially in the south, where he was for a while the first choice for all film-makers. There was a long period when he was shooting more often in the south than in Mumbai. Whenever he returned to Mumbai from Chennai or some other southern city, he would ask his wife Shobha to call us over, along with our wives, for a drink. We had some really memorable evenings sitting around his bar in Gautam Apartments, Pali Hill. When we were younger, we worked hard and partied hard too. We also had some great holidays together. Shobha and Jeetendra were always a lovely, hospitable and down-to-earth couple, despite their great success.

Many years ago, I remember, when my closest buddy Bittu Anand fell on hard times and needed to be bailed out, I did a couple of films for him, but they were all flops. Jeetendra was a very big star at the start of the 1980s, getting second billing after Amitabh Bachchan. When Amitabh met with an accident on the sets of *Coolie*, Bittu and his brother Tinnu Anand, who were to make *Shahenshah* (1988) with Amitabh, were in a fix. So I took them to Shambu. However, he refused their offer, saying it didn't feel right. Perhaps he didn't feel comfortable taking on a project meant for another actor, especially when that actor was ailing. And that is one of the things I grew to admire about Shambu. He always stuck to his principles. There was one brief spell, however, when some unpleasantness transpired between him and me. I don't blame him for it, but it wasn't my fault either.

It all started with *Kucch To Hai* (2003), a film I did with Jeetu's daughter Ekta Kapoor. It required a ten-day stint at the most, a sort of guest appearance. My role was similar to that of Dev Kumar in *Khel Khel Mein*, where audiences believe the character to be the bad guy only to find out that he is a cop. I didn't have much work then, so I agreed to do the film.

The production and filming turned out to be one big mess. They overshot the film and then reshot it. They even changed the director, Anurag Basu, midway through the filming. Soon afterwards, they changed the cameraman and then they changed my character too. They turned me into the villain and kept going up and down, re-sketching the characters and the script like they do in television. I spoke up and advised Ekta that this was not how films were made. In a film you can't keep fiddling with the characters and changing the plot according to the mood of the day. I pointed out to her that there was no discipline on the sets and no clear line to follow. The actors were all in the dark and hadn't a clue where we were headed. By the time I came to grips with what I'd done in a scene, I was told that my character had turned into a villain, that they had junked what had already been shot and thought up something new. I was completely at sea, I didn't know what was going on. I am a responsible actor. My approach to work has always been that, no matter how the film shapes up, I must be consistently good. Acting is the only job I am good at and the last thing I wanted to do was to mess with my performance. So all the confusion on the set was unsettling.

Then came the incident of the wedding of Rahul Rawail's nephew, Rajat Rawail (Gongli). I was shooting for Ekta's film in Mehboob Studios, which is also in Bandra and close to my house. The shoot was to go on till 6.30 or 7 p.m., giving me enough time to go home, get ready and head for the reception. Everybody in the industry knows how close I have always been to the Rawails. I had to be at the wedding. The whole industry was also familiar with the way I work, that when we're shooting in Mumbai, I report to the studio at 10.30 a.m. and I don't shoot after 8.30 p.m. But on the set that day, I was suddenly told that I was required for a night shoot at faraway Madh Island and that it would go on till 2 a.m. This was sprung on me despite my having told them that I had to attend Gongli's wedding reception. I learnt that apparently Sunita Menon, Ekta's astrologer friend, had told her that the film had to be released on a particular day, so they were rushing to make all kinds of last-minute changes. When I protested this new development, Jeetendra intervened and insisted that I finish the shoot and go to the reception directly from there since Punjabi wedding functions tend to go on all night. I couldn't disobey him.

But I wasn't happy. I felt it was unethical on Jeetendra's part to intervene. Friendship and work should not mix. Although I didn't like it, I drove to Madh Island. When I arrived there, I found to my great annoyance that everything was in disarray. The first shot did not happen until 11 p.m. and I had to continue filming until almost 2.30 a.m. I did throw a tantrum saying, 'I have to leave,' but nobody was listening. So finally it was only after 2.30 a.m. that I could shower (in the vanity van) and race to the reception. But by the time I got there, the event was over. The Rawails felt let down that I had arrived so late and I was truly annoyed with Jeetendra for his role in it. And in the end, the scene we shot that night at Madh Island was edited out!

When the film flopped, someone asked me during an interview why I, who was known to be a responsible actor, had agreed to play such an ill-conceived role. I replied, 'I totally agree with you, I don't know how I did this inconceivably negative role.' I also mentioned to the journalist that it was never meant to be that way. That when the role had first been explained to me, it had been a positive one, but it underwent a number of revisions and became completely different. I was honest in the interview and did not hold anything back – I stated that it was a confused script, that the director had been thrown out, and that I didn't get proper instructions from anybody. I also clarified that everyone associated with the making of *Kucch To Hai* had walked over from the television industry and that I could not adapt to the new director because his vision was suitable only for television.

When the interview was published, Jeetendra was furious. He shouted at me over the phone: 'How could you talk about Ekta like that? If she reads it, do you know how hurt she'll be?' I contended that I had only stated facts and I had a duty to defend myself as an actor. I couldn't possibly have kept quiet; I had to let the public know why I had done such a role at this stage of my life and what had transpired during the making of the film.

I don't blame Jeetendra for being mad at me because he was standing up for his daughter. And I can't blame myself because I had only disclosed facts. I was especially upset when, in the course of the conversation, he taunted me and said, '*Kya bada* hero *bann gaya hai tu* (Now you have started thinking you are a big hero). What is wrong with you?' Apart from the fact that he should not have mixed friendship and work, I felt it was unbecoming of him to talk to a friend like that. Still, as hurt as I was, I refrained from retaliating in a similar fashion.

The tension kept building, though, and took its toll on our friendship. One day I let it all tumble out before Guddu, who agreed with me that Jeetendra should not have behaved the way he did. The whole industry knew that Ekta had thrown out first Anurag Basu, then the cameraman and countless chief assistants. She was riding high those days. But the young Ekta of thirteen years ago was different, very unreasonable, not the confident, mature woman we see today.

Today, when Jeetendra and I meet, there is no ill feeling between us. He still hosts Neetu and me. But we don't meet as often as we once did. Our worlds have become different. I am a drinking man while Jeetendra doesn't drink anymore. He has turned vegetarian and a teetotaller. Also, twelve years ago, he moved to his bungalow in Juhu, while I continue to live in Bandra. When I'm not shooting someplace, I go to my office at RK Studios which is in Chembur, and both places are far from where he is. But he still remains in my heart.

Unlike with Jeetendra, Amitabh and I didn't start off on the best of terms. Initially we had a rather uncomfortable, blow hot, blow cold relationship. I was immature and defiant back in the 1970s. He was ten years older than me but like an idiot I used to call him Amitabh, never Amit-ji. Thankfully, I was able to overcome my differences and replace them with a warm camaraderie, which later turned into a family relationship (his daughter Shweta is married to my nephew Nikhil, Ritu's son).

During the making of *Kabhi Kabhie*, there was every indication of a cold war between us. He never spoke to me and I didn't speak to him.

I think that Amitabh was sulking because I had won the best actor award for *Bobby*, given by the leading film magazine

of the era. I am sure he felt the award was rightfully his for
Zanjeer, which released the same year. I am ashamed to say it,
but I actually 'bought' that award. I was so naïve. There was this
PRO, Taraknath Gandhi, who said to me, 'Sir, *tees hazaar de do,
toh aap ko main* award *dila doonga.*' I am not the manipulative
sort but I admit that I gave him the money without thinking.
My secretary, Ghanshyam, also said, 'Sir, *dete hain, mil jayega*
award, *isme kya hai.*' Amitabh probably learnt from someone
that I had paid for the award. I can only say it was 1974, I
was twenty-two years old, and incredibly naïve and bratty. I
was flush with money and was not wise or mature enough to
understand what I was doing. Only later did I realize my folly.

I have another theory about why Amitabh didn't warm
up to me during *Kabhi Kabhie*. He was playing the role of a
rather serious, unsmiling man in the film and his character was
not supposed to like mine. Perhaps he just wanted to stay in
character and that was one of the reasons why he was aloof
throughout the filming. Or perhaps the truth is that my guilt
over having bought that award made me read too much into
everything.

Amitabh and I went on to do several films together, including
Amar Akbar Anthony, *Coolie* and *Naseeb*. And gradually the ice
thawed. During *AAA* our equation was easy-going. It was a
Manmohan Desai film and we had to do all sorts of outrageous
things. I remember that both of us would pull Pran sa'ab's leg
by asking him for acting tips. We were not adversaries in any of
the films we worked on together. We didn't fight for the same
woman. Bachchan's professional adversaries were always Vinod

Khanna, Shatrughan Sinha, Shashi Kapoor or Dharmendra. I was much younger and mostly played his younger brother. The song '*Lambuji Tinguji*' (*Coolie*) summed up our screen equation beautifully.

Talking about *Coolie* takes me back to 26 July 1982, a bad day for both him and me. As it happened, we were both shooting for the film in Bangalore, with two separate units. In the morning I was required to do an action scene where I had to jump from a height. Some boxes and a tarpaulin were spread out down below to break my fall, as is the usual practice. Just before my shot, Amitabh came to where I was standing and checked out the scene. Somehow he was not convinced that the precautions that had been taken were adequate. He asked me whether I had checked everything and I told him that all was well. Then one of the stuntmen whispered to me that instead of doing a regular jump, I should attempt a dive. It would make the scene more dramatic.

I don't know what I was thinking, but I went for the dive. I landed safely on the boxes but got badly grazed on the face and hands. Amitabh fired me for my carelessness, telling me that if I wanted to do my stunts I should be better prepared and that I should have stuck to a jump. He was genuinely concerned and I was touched. This is an advice I would like to give to all aspiring actors: prepare well if you intend to do your own stunts. I was nursing my wounds when I heard about Amitabh's fight sequence with Puneet Issar. Apparently, he stood up after the shot and walked away. Then he went out and lay down on the ground, wincing in pain. At first, everyone thought it was a minor injury. People were rubbing Iodex on his abdomen. I had a tube of Bengay that I sent over. Pack-up was announced and a doctor was called. No one could gauge the extent of his pain. After he had spent a restless night, Jaya-ji was summoned. When the doctors in Bangalore realized that they couldn't do much for him and that he was seriously injured, it was decided to move him to Mumbai's Breach Candy Hospital.

One got a sense of Amitabh's star power when, within a day, the biggest names in the film industry had arrived in Bangalore. I remember seeing Yash Johar, Yash Chopra, Vijay Anand, Prakash Mehra and so many others. Yash Johar actually got six rows of seating dismantled on an Indian Airlines flight so Amitabh's stretcher could fit in. The pilot was asked to ensure he steered the plane away from turbulent pockets so the patient wouldn't be discomfited. And before you knew it, Amitabh was at Breach Candy, being attended to by the best medical teams from India and overseas. The whole country, including me, prayed fervently for his speedy recovery.

He returned to shoot six months later and Manmohan Desai arranged for an outdoor stint at Reclamation Ground. Over one lakh people turned up for the shoot and local dadas had to be requisitioned for the bandobast as it was beyond the means of the police. I still remember the charged atmosphere every time Amitabh stepped out into the open and the crowd let out a roar, the likes of which I hadn't heard before. More than thirty years later, it still rings in my ear. It only reaffirmed what a huge star he was.

With Rajesh Khanna, the other phenomenon of that time, I had a strange, inexplicable equation. When I came on the scene in 1973, I had heard stories of his superstardom. I didn't witness it directly.

Kaka-ji married Dimple Kapadia in March 1973. He was the reigning superstar, but his stardom needed a fillip. When he married Dimple, who was fifteen years younger to him, Kaka-ji once again made headlines. I remember taunting Dimple, who was still shooting for *Bobby* after her marriage, that Kaka-ji wasn't the man of the moment. It was Amitabh's *Zanjeer* that had worked. Amitabh was the one to look out for. Of course, I did this just to bug Dimple. The fact is that both *Daag* and *Namak Haraam* released in 1973 and got Kaka-ji the required notices. And J. Om Prakash's *Aap Ki Kasam* (1974) – that had Mumtaz, Rajesh Khanna and Sanjeev Kumar and had been shot around the same time as *Bobby* but released a year later – was also a stupendous hit.

I had tremendous respect for Kaka-ji but never felt close to him. I did go to his wedding with Dimple. There is a photograph of Ghanshyam and me with the newly married couple. A fan of mine sent it to me. Later, I heard that Kaka-ji himself told someone that he wasn't afraid of the competition from Bachchan because the latter was the angry young man while he (Kaka-ji) still ruled as the biggest romantic icon of the era. Apparently, he was more worried about me because I was the new 'romantic' kid on the block. Someone who was also ten years younger!

If you think about it, Kaka-ji couldn't have done the

teenybopper roles that I was doing around that time in movies like *Kabhi Kabhie* and *Khel Khel Mein*. He was more suited to *Daag* and *Aap Ki Kasam* because he was much older – and married – by then.

Anyway, as I mentioned before, I keep wondering whether it was because he married Dimple, my first leading lady, that there was stress between us. Again, just like I saw too much into Bachchan not liking me because I had bought the best actor award, I think I also made too much of Kaka-ji not liking me. Perhaps I was too small and insignificant and he didn't even spare a thought for me. All I know is that I was peeved because he had married Dimple and I had no heroine to work with. I was so full of contradictory emotions and feelings.

But I am sure there wasn't any major animosity between Kaka-ji and me because I had no qualms about approaching him for my maiden directorial venture *Aa Ab Laut Chalen*. And he would not have agreed to be in it if he was still nursing a grouse against me.

No matter what he thought of me, Rajesh Khanna was a Raj Kapoor bhakt. He used to come to all our parties. When Papa first conceived of the idea of making *Satyam Shivam Sundaram*, he wanted to cast Kaka-ji in it but, as I said before, I was among those who didn't allow that to happen. Later, Papa himself felt Shashi uncle was a better bet.

Everybody expected that Papa's follow-up to *Bobby* would bring in the same collections. When that didn't happen, they labelled it a washout, which is not true. It may not have been the hit people expected it to be, but it was not a flop either.

Personally, I think *SSS* was Papa's poorest film, script-wise. It made the least sense. I remember telling him that I didn't buy the concept of a man sleeping with a woman but not seeing her face. Likewise, when Chimpu directed me in *Prem Granth*, I told him that I found the subject odd. It dealt with the subject of caste but somehow the script went around in circles.

Going back to Kaka-ji, I did have some initial reservations about doing *Saagar*. I was going to reunite with my *Bobby* heroine and I was hesitant. I sent a message to Kaka-ji, asking him whether it was okay for me to do a film with Dimple. If I remember right, he got back to me saying that if I didn't do the film, someone else would.

In any case, I was more worried about what Neetu would think of my working with Dimple after all these years. The talk of an affair between Dimple and me were long dead. However, in 1984, when *Saagar* was being made, I was just four years into my marriage. Dimple had separated from Kaka-ji in 1983, exactly ten years after her marriage. Neetu must have had some reservations, but she was very dignified about the whole thing. It is to her credit that she didn't put her foot down and allowed me to do *Saagar*.

Like the unfortunate misunderstanding with Jeetendra, an episode involving my other close friend, Rakesh Roshan, also caught me off-guard. Guddu wanted me to do a guest appearance in his film *Koi Mil Gaya* (2003) as Hrithik's father.

It would have involved a two-day stint but I told him that I didn't want to do it because I truly felt it would be a bad career move on my part. I was just being frank and was totally unprepared for his sharp reaction. I was left reeling when he retorted, 'Bloody idiot, at this age what career are you talking about? You don't have a career. You can only do small roles here and there.' His remark offended me greatly, though I am sure he did not mean for that to happen. He could have simply been pointing out the fact that after a certain age it is tough to make an impression in an industry that's obsessed with youth.

In hindsight, I can't help but feel that his hurtful retort was just the push I needed to jump into the fray once more and create a new and distinct space for myself in my second innings, this time as a character artiste. I refused Guddu's offer but itched to rise to his challenge and prove to him that I could still have a successful career. I told myself that one day I would make him admit it too.

Today I am glad to be in a comfortable place. I get the roles I want, I get the money I want, and I work in as many films as I want. A few years ago, senior actors found it difficult to come by substantial roles. Not anymore. Look at the films Amitabh has been doing of late. If I have been jobless for the last six months, it's because after being spoilt with an array of roles like Duggal (*Do Dooni Chaar*), Rauf Lala (*Agneepath*), Dawood (*D-Day*) and Dadaji (*Kapoor & Sons*), roles that challenged the actor in me, it is hard to play a regular daddy to a hero or heroine. I am proud to say I have reinvented myself. If there is no meat for me to sink my teeth into, I cannot be tempted.

Guddu is still a good friend, we still meet. But once again, our worlds have diverged. I am busy and enjoying the opportunity to play a variety of roles, Guddu is busy making films. He spends more time with Jeetendra these days. They live in Juhu and are practically neighbours, so they're always together.

When I think of my co-stars and friends, I realize that I have a special affinity for the evil men of the Hindi screen. I've loved Prem Chopra as a co-star, a family member and a friend. The other baddies I have enjoyed working with are Amjad Khan, Danny Denzongpa and Ranjeet (Goli to us). They were great buddies of mine and I really miss working with them.

Goli calls me up once in a while, always complaining, '*Milta nahin hai* (You hardly meet me these days).' Danny Denzongpa and I made many films together, including big hits like *Laila Majnu*. The screen presence that Ranjeet, Danny, Amjad and Prem Chopra had can never be replicated by any of the new generation of villains.

Amjad used to call himself an RK product because he was introduced as a child artiste along with Jagdeep, Mohan Choti and others in our home production *Ab Dilli Dur Nahin* (1957). He and I worked together for the first time in *Hum Kisise Kum Naheen*. Amjad was older than me and would often remind me that his father, Jayant sa'ab, also resided in Punjabi Galli, where my grandfather and half the industry once lived. He was proud of the fact that we were all Pathans – his father, my father, Dilip Kumar. He was a Muslim Pathan and I was a Hindu Pathan from the same region, Peshawar. Amjad was a polyglot who spoke a number of languages, including Pashto, Gujarati, Urdu, English, Punjabi and Marathi. He was also a 'tea-totaller': he would drink thirty to forty cups of tea every day.

Amjad was very fond of me. Perhaps he and I connected because I was one of the few boys around with a modern outlook and he was also progressive in his worldview. Maybe he couldn't share a similar rapport with other co-actors because not many of his contemporaries could converse on a variety of topics. He and I spoke about music, about cinema, we had much in common to discuss. We did quite a few films together, including *Hum Kisise Kum Naheen, Katilon Ke Kaatil, Bade Dil Wala, Phool Khile Hain Gulshan Gulshan* and *Naseeb*, and he had an imposing presence in every one of those.

Amjad was very protective of Neetu. He used to say that she was his little sister and she would say in turn, 'You're the brother I don't have.' But there was another side to him too, a nasty side. I remember the way he behaved when he didn't like someone.

We were in the midst of shooting *Hum Kisise Kum Naheen* when Amjad met with a grave road accident that almost took his life. Nasir sa'ab waited for him to recover before resuming filming and you could see the change in Amjad: he was much thinner and a deep scar ran from his throat to his chest, where he was operated upon.

The industry is connected in innumerable ways, with our

paths crossing and re-crossing at different points and different times. Amjad's second son, Seemaab, was an AD with Sajid Khan when I worked in *Housefull 2*. I told Seemaab that he should lose weight and try his hand at acting. I have carried Amjad's first son, Shadaab, on my shoulders in the jungles of Masinagudi near Ooty, where we shot the climax of *Hum Kisise Kum Naheen*. Amjad had come with Shehla, his wife, and Shadaab to the shoot. Twenty years after he passed away, I attended his daughter's wedding and I know Shehla was moved to see me there.

Amrish Puri was a busy villain in the years that I was a lead actor. He was never a friend, more of an uncle. He knew me as a young boy from Punjabi Galli in Matunga because his brother Madan Puri, whom I called Maddi uncle, used to live there. Amrish Puri wanted to, but never got to work with my father. He was to do *Ram Teri Ganga Maili*, it was offered to him, but his dates were already committed to Steven Spielberg's *Indiana Jones: Temple of Doom*.

Sanjeev Kumar was a very senior actor when I entered the film industry. He was a friendly man and often played cards with us at Jeetendra's place. He lived close to me, in Pali Hill, but he was never a close friend like Jeetendra, Guddu or Prem-ji. We used to meet socially. He was a good actor with a wicked sense of humour, he could bitch a lot. It's sad that he passed away so young. But however short his life and career, Sanjeev managed to do one RK film, *Biwi O Biwi* (1981). He was very friendly with my uncle Shammi and my brother Dabboo. He and I also worked on a film together, which is still in the cans.

It was called *Maang Sajado Meri* and starred Asha Parekh and Ranjeeta alongside us. A well-made social romance, it was written by Manmohan Desai and directed by Prayag Raj. The film was complete and ready for release when a problem erupted between the producer and the financier. The financier decided that it was better for him to scrap the film and not release it, so he could write off the entire cost and gain some tax relief.

The other actor who was a contemporary but with whom I had little interaction was Vinod Mehra. When he insisted that I should star in his first directorial venture, *Gurudev* (1993), I agreed. It was around the time that Anil Kapoor was making his mark and Vinod must have thought, Rishi Kapoor *ke saath achchhi jodi banegi*, the two men would make an impressive new team on screen. Unfortunately, Vinod passed away before he could complete work on the film.

Speaking of Anil, he and I were first cast together in *Vijay* but it didn't work at the box office. After *Gurudev*, we also did *Karobaar* (2000), which took so long to make that it simply fizzled out when it was finally released.

I must say that Anil is one of the most hard-working men I have ever met. He is one of our better actors and I thought he was brilliant in *Dil Dhadakne Do* (2015). I have never seen anyone so sincere and dedicated. He is sixty years old, but you can't tell. I think it's the result of a tremendous amount of discipline. But sometimes there can be too much of a good thing, and I do believe there are times when it shows that he is trying too hard. For me, acting is about 'putting in effort to show effortlessness'. It's something B.R. Chopra once said to me. And I have tried to live by it.

Anil's sincerity has brought him the success he so richly deserves. I've worked with his daughter Sonam too, in films like *Delhi-6* and *Bewakoofiyaan* (2014). She's a sweet girl. Having worked with her and seen them together, my guess is that Anil is surrounded by women at home and all of them bully him. Bully him out of love.

All these colleagues and contemporaries have been an integral part of my life in films. I look back at my association with each of them with fondness and nostalgia. As the immortal song in Papa's film *Mera Naam Joker* goes: '*Jaane kahan gaye woh din*'.

10

FIGHTS, FLARE-UPS AND FANS

I've been involved in my share of scrapes over the years. The Khans of Juhu (Feroz and Sanjay in particular) and the Kapoors have always shared a close bond. Both equally flamboyant and fearless, we've had some pretty heated run-ins too. One evening in the 1980s, at a party hosted by socialite and entrepreneur Parmeshwar Godrej at China Garden, Sanjay Khan and I had a really ugly argument which could have ended in a police case.

I can't remember what triggered it. I have a vague memory of it being either because I spoke up for my friend Jeetendra, who was Sanjay's contemporary and rival, or because I behaved obnoxiously. Whatever the reason, Sanjay flung a glass full of liquor at my face. It narrowly missed striking my eye and I escaped with only a cut. But I was furious. He was an actor himself and knew the extent to which our faces are our fortune.

But he still threw a glass at me from a very short distance. It could have damaged my eye permanently or disfigured my face.

The next day, Sanjay apologized profusely to me. His wife Zarine apologized too, so I decided not to take it any further. I just dismissed it saying, 'It's okay, everybody gets drunk.' It's a fact that we were all drunk that evening. However, it is hard for me to entirely put the incident out of my mind. No matter who was in the wrong, you don't just fling a glass at someone's face. Most definitely not at a fellow actor because, for us, our physical appearance is our rozi-roti.

Since then, though, Sanjay has always met me with great love and affection. There has never been any trace of animosity between us.

But it was a brawl that greatly upset both families, including Feroz Khan, my dad, my brothers and my uncles. My mother, who has seen plenty of drunken brawls, thought that Sanjay's behaviour was unacceptable. It was also dangerous. If I had lodged a police complaint, he would have been arrested on the spot.

Over the years, I have had some minor skirmishes with Salim and Javed too. In 1973, they had delivered a super hit with *Zanjeer*, the same year in which I had my blockbuster, *Bobby*. I was strutting around like an emperor and they weren't behaving any differently.

In the 1970s, video piracy had not yet reared its head. Films were sold leisurely and released on different dates in different territories. *Bobby* was released on 28 September in Mumbai, a month later in Delhi, and at the end of the year in Bangalore.

The film was a massive hit everywhere and I became an overnight sensation. No Hindi film had done as much business until then. In the euphoria that followed, I remember one fan unbuttoning her shirt and asking me to autograph her bra!

Talking of fans, in the wake of the new selfie culture, a fan once wanted to take a picture with me in the washroom, when I was peeing. I was outraged to say the least. There was another fan, a married woman from a well-to-do family, who stood outside my bungalow for weeks on end with her two children, claiming she was my wife. I didn't want to register a police complaint because I could see that the lady was mentally unsound. But it got awkward. Neetu had to go out a couple of times and explain to her that she (Neetu) was my wife. But the lady kept insisting that the romantic songs I sang on television were meant for her.

Though fans can often get unreasonable and irksome, one of the greatest joys of this profession is the adulation we get and the sheer joy of interacting with such a wide variety of people. This often makes for amusing encounters.

There is a Russian fan who sends me photographs of the places where I have shot for my films. She watches my films and dutifully visits these locations. She even made a pilgrimage to Shirdi, in the mistaken belief that the qawwali in *Amar Akbar Anthony* was shot there. I had to tell her that we shot the song in a set. Another fan puts together a collage of the many daflis I have played in my films!

I remember shooting for *Henna* in Austria, filming the song '*Bedardi tere pyaar mein*' with Zeba. I was pitching in as production head. Neetu used to make tea for the unit. We had an Austrian crew. One day a crew member came up to Dabboo and asked, 'Mr Director, we see heroine, where is hero?' Dabboo pointed at me. The guy was astonished. 'Mr Production Manager is hero?' When Dabboo nodded, the guy said, 'You will now say that Mrs Kapoor is big heroine.' Dabboo nodded again. No longer sure we were not pulling his leg, the man asked Dabboo: 'You will say you are hero too?' How could we tell him that this was one big family of film stars!

Another time, during the shoot of *Aa Ab Laut Chalen*, my friend Raju Nanda was handling production. After a tiring day, he suggested we go out for drinks and dinner. As we settled down at this restaurant for a quiet evening, a waitress took our order for drinks. By this time a few Bangladeshi waiters had spotted us. There was some hullaballoo in the kitchen. The waiters came and started asking for photos and autographs. I was feeling quite chuffed about all the attention when the waitress came over with our drinks and asked me: 'Hey, you guys know each other? Did you work here before?'

Coming back to Salim–Javed, I was in Bangalore for the release of *Bobby* and was free one evening with nothing to do. Someone mentioned to me that a film called *Sholay* was being shot near Bangalore and that the crew was staying at Bangalore International Hotel, so I went across. The hotel had a well-known nightclub with a famous singer who would perform every night. I didn't know anyone as I was still new to films. I ordered a cola – I wasn't into alcohol back then – and looked around with interest. The first person I noticed was a strange man sitting at the bar and looking at me with what seemed like disdain. I didn't quite understand what he wanted from me.

A little later, he came up to me and asked, 'Are you Rishi Kapoor?'

'Yes,' I replied.

He introduced himself as Javed Akhtar. He could have been the king of England for all I cared. Besides, Salim–Javed had not yet become *the* Salim–Javed. I knew they had written a few films like *Zanjeer* and *Yaadon Ki Baaraat* (1973) but I wasn't in awe of them.

Javed continued, 'You must be very happy that *Bobby* is such a huge hit.'

I replied, 'Yakeenan, I am.'

'*Mubarak ho*,' he said, congratulating me. '*Bobby bahut kamaal ki* hit *hai* (*Bobby* is a great hit). *Par yaad rakhiyega* (Please remember) that we're in 1973. In the year 1972, we had *Yaadon Ki Baaraat*, in '73 we wrote *Zanjeer*, in '74 we will present *Haath Ki Safaai* (it starred Vinod Khanna, Randhir Kapoor and Simi Garewal and turned out to be another huge success) and in 1975 we will release such a film that if it makes a profit of even a rupee less than *Bobby*, I will break the nib of my pen. I will never again write in my life.'

The man was drunk to the gills but his confidence was phenomenal. *Bobby* had done unprecedented business and to predict that an unreleased film would break its record or else he would quit his profession was brave, if not foolhardy.

A few years later, Salim–Javed wanted me to work in *Trishul*, directed by Yash Chopra. They offered me the role that eventually went to Sachin, but I said no. I must be the first and only actor in the history of Hindi cinema to have refused Salim–Javed at their peak. *Kabhi Kabhie* had been released by then. Ramesh Talwar (erstwhile AD to Yash Chopra) had become a friend; I was already doing his film *Doosra Aadmi*, which Yash-ji was producing. And I was on excellent terms with Yash-ji too. But I turned down *Trishul* because I didn't like the way the role had shaped up. Salim and Javed bristled at my rejection and the animosity bubbled to the surface when I encountered Salim Khan at Playmate Club (which used to be in Hotel Sea Rock in Mumbai) a few days later. The hotel itself was later pulled down, but those days many of us, including Salim sa'ab, would go to Playmate to play billiards.

I was playing a game of snooker when Salim sa'ab walked over and asked me, 'How did you have the guts to refuse Salim–Javed?'

Not one to be intimidated, I shot back, 'I didn't like the role.'

Salim sa'ab boasted to me, 'Do you know that to this day nobody has said no to us? We can destroy your career.'

'What can you do to finish me?' I demanded.

He said, 'Who will work with you? You know, we had offered *Zanjeer* to Rajesh Khanna and he turned us down. We didn't do anything to him but we created an alternative to him, a hero called Amitabh Bachchan, who destroyed Rajesh Khanna. We will do the same to you.'

I shrugged. 'Go ahead and show me,' I said. I don't remember if I was drinking that day but I refused to be bullied by anybody. Thankfully, it didn't turn into anything serious. I'd only hurt their ego by turning them down when every other actor thought it was an honour to work with them.

Later, I starred in *Amar Akbar Anthony*, which broke many box-office records while a film called *Imaan Dharam*, written by Salim–Javed and directed by Desh Mukherjee, bit the dust at the box-office. It was such a dud that people started saying, 'Salim–Javed *ki* film flop *ho gayi*.' It was the first time that a Salim–Javed film had failed so badly, and that too despite boasting a star cast that included Amitabh Bachchan, Shashi Kapoor and Sanjeev Kumar.

Manmohan Desai used to have a chief assistant, a mischievous, fun-loving guy who said to me, '*Saala*, Javed *sabki bajaata hai* (Javed makes fun of all us), let's go and needle him over *Imaan Dharam*.'

Javed had an apartment somewhere in Bandstand and we headed over immediately. Javed sa'ab was welcoming. He brought out glasses and poured us all drinks. After a few rounds, we began taunting him. '*Sarkar*, Imaan Dharam *toh* flop *ho gayi*,' we said. I drove the point home by repeating it a few times. I must give credit to Javed sa'ab for handling it well. He turned around and observed, '*Sarkar, hamari to ek film* flop *hui hai, tum ne to granth likhi hai flopon ki* (We've had only one failure while you have a whole saga of setbacks).'

In the years that followed, Salim sa'ab became a great morale booster for me. He thought of me as a good actor and as someone who could keep Raj Kapoor's legacy alive. Javed sa'ab and Shabana and I have also admired each other's work. Later, I did work for films written by them. While *Zamana* was a Salim–Javed script, *Saagar* and *Duniya* were written by Javed. Unfortunately, none of these films worked.

Despite all the goodwill, Javed managed to hurt me very deeply a while ago. In a programme on some television channel, during an episode dedicated to lyricist Shailendra, who was a member of my father's core group until his dying day, Javed blamed my father for the lyricist's untimely death. I cannot fathom why. Perhaps it was to spice up the episode. Quite a few people have told me that he has always had a hang-up about my father. I am hurt and upset about it to this day, and I have let him know that I do not appreciate his baseless, irresponsible and false accusation. He did say that he did not mean it the way it came across, so I let sleeping dogs lie.

Javed had claimed that Shailendra died because of the debts that piled up during the making of his film *Teesri Kasam* (1966), a film my dad worked in. He alleged that Papa had delayed the film with the result that Shailendra had run up those debts. I wonder what debts he was referring to because my father paid for everything and he was not paid for the film either. He even completed the film with his own funds.

The truth is that my father kept telling Shailendra not to make the film. Shailendra died because his own brother-in-law cheated him. My father took it upon himself to pay Shailendra's hospital bills and cleared all his debts. I have checked this with all the senior people who worked with RK, I have asked my mother about it, I have interrogated everyone who was around at that time. I think Javed should publicly apologize for his defamatory statement or furnish substantial proof that my father had anything to do with Shailendra's death. Having made such an accusation, he should have the courage to back it up with evidence or admit that it was a mistake.

I am extremely fond of Shabana, so I didn't allow the situation to get out of hand. But I did tell Farhan Akhtar at a party that Anil Ambani had hosted for Steven Spielberg that I was extremely upset, and that one day my patience would wear out and it wouldn't be pleasant. I am a patient man, but I have never been afraid of anyone and I don't mean to start now.

With the dawn of the digital age, some of these skirmishes have moved online. I am as forthright and frank in my Twitter avatar as I am offline. I say what I feel should be said, without fear or favour. Isn't that the way it should be? Neetu has often asked me to hold back. But what's the point of it all if you cannot voice your opinion? I don't say anything that can hurt anybody. I do not do it for the sake of sensationalizing anything.

Some of my most controversial tweets pertained to those I made about the Gandhi family. In May 2016, I commented on the issue of national assets being named after the Gandhis. What I highlighted was the politics of dynastic identity at play. I also wanted to know on what grounds Rahul Gandhi was being promoted as Congress president. Just because he is the son of Rajiv Gandhi and Sonia Gandhi? Does he have a vision for the country? Has he carved an identity for himself without the crutch of the 'Gandhi' name? I haven't been a successful star just because I am Raj Kapoor's son. Ranbir isn't there just because of me. You have to have something to prove yourself.

Of course, this raised the hackles of many sycophants of the Gandhi family. There were threats of violence and mobs were hired to pelt stones at my house. I was accused of being pro-BJP. I categorically deny that. I have opposed the beef ban and also the appointment of Gajendra Chauhan as the chairman of Film and Television Institute of India. I also spoke up against prohibition in Bihar. I'm a tax-paying citizen and I have a right to say what I feel. I may be right or wrong, it is open to debate.

I have nothing against the Nehru–Gandhi family. They have made immense contributions and sacrifices for the country. We have always supported the party. I have been secular in my beliefs and approach all my life. I'm only talking about the sycophants who are trying to exploit the family and fool the common man. But we aren't illiterate anymore. The youth is more aware. I believe in calling a spade a spade.

But I have now started holding back. I didn't do this to get a Rajya Sabha seat or a Padma award. I have been working in the film industry for forty-four years non-stop and you think I will do this to get a Padma award? I am still a student of cinema. I don't have any aspirations to be a politician. Of the hundred-odd years of cinema in India, the Kapoors have had a presence for eighty-eight. We have been entertaining people. I am not a politician. I would rather be an actor.

11

A PRIVILEGED
SECOND INNINGS

There's a huge difference between what I was and what I am, and I'm not talking about my weight. In my former avatar as Rishi Kapoor the romantic hero, I never had to do any homework. For the first twenty-five years of my career, I got by without having to do any preparation whatsoever for a role. And it wasn't just me, none of the leading men in the 1970s and '80s had to, or ever did. So when I hear that Ranbir is attending a workshop before starting a film or flying off to New York for acting lessons before he can play a hearing- and speech-impaired man in a film, it's an alien concept for me. I'm not against it, I'm just not used to it.

But what I didn't do as a lead actor, I have had to do as a character artiste and I have to confess I thoroughly enjoyed it.

My life as a character actor began as I was completing the only film I ever directed – *Aa Ab Laut Chalen*. It didn't do too well. Directing a film is a thankless job and for a person like me, a perfectionist, I find it very tiring. In times to come, I will definitely direct again but I am at my best in front of the camera. So I said yes to Veeru Devgan's offer to do a character role in *Raju Chacha* and then my friend Rahul Rawail's *Kuch Khatti Kuch Meethi*. A steady stream of extremely interesting characters came my way after that, and all the films did well.

Audiences in my youth were fiercely loyal to their stars, generous with their praise and forgiving of all limitations. We didn't have to put in much effort to court them. The themes, stories, plots, scenes and climaxes were repetitive: a happy family is suddenly disrupted and gets separated. A villain must be bashed to a pulp and a heroine must be wooed with song, dance and cheesy lines before all the family members miraculously unite again. At any given point of time, every male lead had about four films on hand with astonishingly similar lost-and-found themes. But our patrons went home happy and satisfied, and were willing to come back for more of the same, seeking little change in what was being dished out to them Friday after Friday.

I have worked in several films with the same premise and so have all other actors of the era. A sprinkling of five to six melodious numbers compensated for the lack of originality or experimentation in mainstream cinema. As long as the audience could go out humming the ditties, they went home happy, as did the film-makers. The only exception to this was the realistic or parallel cinema championed by a handful of fringe actors, which required meticulous preparation. The concept of prepping for a role was alien for the rest of us.

It's on this front that I find a real change. Ranbir prepares for his roles. Good, bad or indifferent, he works on every character he plays. He does only one film at a time, with complete focus on the character, and goes into the studio totally in the zone and ready. Cinema itself has evolved over the years. Today you can't repeat the lost-and-found theme, the audience will put a whip to your backside and demand that you think afresh. Tastes have changed and exposure to the big wide world has much to do with it. Television and the internet provide so much information free of charge that the audience is spoilt for choice. You need to really give them your best and the newer the theme, the more receptive they are. They will not settle for recycled stories because they have alternate avenues of amusement which they will switch to in a trice. Restless attention spans win out over brand loyalty.

One of the first roles I had to prepare for was that of Rauf Lala in *Agneepath*, a dark, evil character mired in the drug and prostitution business. I was, and still remain, humbled by the faith that producer Karan Johar and his young director Karan Malhotra had in me, the quintessential singing-dancing romantic hero. Needless to say, I was totally unprepared for it when they approached me. It took a lot of coaxing for me to agree to do the role. It was beyond anything I had ever imagined I would be asked to do. To even associate Rishi Kapoor with a baddie required a fertile imagination. Casting me as the uncouth

Rauf, and pitting me against Sanjay Dutt who played the central villain, Kancha Cheena, was a masterstroke by the two Karans. There was no Rauf Lala in the original screenplay, it was a later addition, and with no reference points it was a real challenge for me. But it gave a sparkling new dimension to the film. My look, with kohl-rimmed eyes, helped me immensely in playing a crude man in the slave trade. The karakul cap and traditional kurta-pyjama were touches my director and I conceived together. I worked hard to transform my former soft image, including my body language and acting style. I even injured myself quite badly during the fight scenes, but I was so caught up in my character, I barely noticed and continued without breaking for first aid. I had to convince the audience that this was one evil bloke and it gave me a lot of satisfaction to know that I pulled it off.

I also played a baddie, a corrupt-to-the-core cop, in *Aurangzeb*, which I count as one of my finer performances. It remains a greatly underrated film, a gritty and realistic cop-and-mafia drama set in Gurgaon, which deserves a wider audience. Since the film failed at the box-office, few saw my work in it.

Another role that was a sharp variant from my popular image as a romantic hero was my character in *Do Dooni Chaar*. It wasn't just that I had to play someone older in years but the look of the character was completely novel for me too. My initial thought was that I looked too well-fed and *khaate-peete ghar se* to pull off the role of a middle-class person who had to struggle to buy even a small car. However, Habib Faisal was confident of my abilities as an actor and that paid off. My characters in

Do Dooni Char, where I played a middle-class schoolteacher, *D-Day*, where I played an underworld don (rather like Dawood Ibrahim), and *Kapoor & Sons* also tested my mettle as an actor. A lot of homework went into each of these roles, including multiple discussions with my directors on the character, and they have caused me to change my approach to my work. I also dubbed differently when I played these roles.

In *Kapoor & Sons*, I played a ninety-year-old grandpa who is a bit of a pervert but the heart and soul of the film. It took me four to five hours every day for the makeup alone. Karan Johar spared no expense and engaged American makeup artist Greg Cannom, whose credits include his incredible work on Brad Pitt in *The Curious Case of Benjamin Button*, along with Logan Long and my personal makeup man Pappu Gondane and the makeup team of Dharma Productions. My makeup alone cost a whopping ₹2 crore.

Shooting for the film, which took place in Coonoor, wasn't an easy task. I completed my work in it in approximately twenty-six days and there wasn't a single day when I didn't argue and fight with my director Shakun Batra. We argued because I couldn't agree with his method of working.

You see, I'm a drinking man. And yet every morning, I was up at 5.30 a.m. From 6 a.m. I was in the makeup chair with Greg working on my face. Once the prosthetics were done, I could scarcely recognize myself. At 12 p.m. I would report for work. And then the actual drill would begin. Shakun wanted to cover every shot from many different angles. But I am an old-school actor. I respect all schools of acting but my strength is spontaneity. I couldn't recreate the same expression for all the shots. In fact, with every successive shot I lost my verve. I found myself getting restless as the same shot was taken from different angles. This new practice of capturing a single shot from several different angles has gained acceptance because, in the digital era, there is no fear of raw stock being wasted. But I could not shake off the feeling that it turned actors into robots. However, once the film was released and the accolades poured in – the latest being the Screen award and the Stardust award for best supporting actor – I had to concede that my anger was misplaced and there was merit in what Shakun did. I admitted as much to both Karan Johar and Shakun.

Curiously, as I got older, the offers kept getting better. Many of the films didn't fare well but I began to enjoy an unexpected benefit of being a character actor – I no longer had to shoulder the responsibility for making a film work at the box-office. That was the leading man's burden. Instead, I could simply enjoy working in the film and the appreciation that came my way for the performance.

The biggest compliment I received at this stage was a call that came through when I was in Moscow, where I had gone to receive an award. I thought Yash Chopra was calling to talk about Ranbir, whose *Rocket Singh* was due for release. Also, he had just delivered a fantastic performance in *Ajab Prem Ki Ghazab Kahani*. But all Yash-ji wanted to talk about was my film *Do Dooni Chaar*. He'd seen a few rushes and was gushing. 'I can't believe that you can look like a common man and can turn in this kind of work,' he said over and over again.

As a lead actor, the characters written for me were always wealthy lover boys and I insisted on scenic locations and good-looking lead actresses. Nobody ever offered me any poverty-stricken roles. Stories revolving around poverty and distress were meant for film-makers who made art-house cinema. I belonged to the glitzy world of mainstream, commercially viable cinema where everything was lavish and beautiful. In the popular cinema of my time, it was Amitabh Bachchan who got to play the downtrodden common man, not I. I was always the rich man you could fantasize about. And even in films where I didn't play a rich person, I always got to wear fancy clothes and woo the heroine in style. Film-makers in my era did not set much store by realism.

Happily, the second wave of films I worked in did well commercially and people began to believe that I was a lucky mascot for them. I don't come cheap, I have a hefty price tag as a character actor too, but film-makers have been more than willing to pay it. In return they get a very sincere actor who is professional and gives them what they want before the camera. I've always played with a straight bat and producers have appreciated this quality in me.

When I was offered *Hum Tum*, Aditya Chopra told me that he wouldn't make the film if I did not act in it though I was required only for ten days. He said that he could think of no other actor who could impart the life lessons to Saif as convincingly as I could. It was a high for me when he said that he would be hard-pressed to find a replacement for me. That's the sort of comment that makes me feel I've handled my work in the right spirit.

For decades, I had breezed through a steady line-up of romantic roles. It came so naturally to me that except for choosing a new jersey, there was little pre-shoot work to do. We made either action or romantic films with music being the common thread and we sauntered through our shoots. Just look at the painstaking groundwork that actors do today. I give a lot of credit to Ranveer Singh – you can see how much effort went into his portrayal of Peshwa Bajirao in the romantic period drama *Bajirao Mastani* (2015). Similarly, Ranbir too had to work hard on his look for *Rocket Singh* and *Rockstar*.

Some of the older actors do it too. Aamir Khan underwent an inspiring transformation when he put on twenty-three-odd kilos and then lost the extra kilos to play a wrestler in the upcoming *Dangal*. Salman Khan prepped vigorously for *Sultan* (2016). I fully endorse this new trend, this is how an actor should go about his work. Back in the day, we were so caught up in our image that we were comfortable working only within its restrictive parameters. You had to excel within your chosen genre and then became famous for it. Actors such as Jeetendra, Rajesh Khanna, Amitabh Bachchan, Dharmendra, Mithun Chakraborty and myself were all typecast. The few who chose to venture off the beaten path were Sanjeev Kumar, Pankaj Kapur, Om Puri and Naseeruddin Shah. They definitely needed to prep for the kind of roles they did.

The rest of us didn't do anything dramatically different each time we were cast in a new role. Amitabh Bachchan didn't have to prep to play Anthony, nor I to play Akbar. A Prakash Mehra or Manmohan Desai film didn't require you to get into the mood or train for a role. It was Amitabh Bachchan's inborn talent that allowed him to embody each new character effortlessly and entertain his audience. They weren't earth-shatteringly unique characters.

However, even in our time, there were some scenes that demanded an extra effort from the actor. Discussions were required to ensure that everyone was aligned with the director's interpretation of the scene. Sometimes an actor's interpretation of it would be different. If the director was malleable and ready to consider another viewpoint, we would reach a happy compromise. In the absence of specific instructions from a director, I would do what came most spontaneously to me. But I have also worked with a few directors who wanted everything done only one way. When you encounter such a person, you have to adjust your mindset to work in sync.

Action sequences, in particular, require a lot of preparation. As in a dance sequence, the footwork and movements have to be precise and fluid. Good actors do it well and make it seem realistic. People enjoyed watching Amitabh Bachchan's fight scenes. He excelled in them, he was prepared for them, he knew how to time each action.

When it comes to acting, one of the best lines I've come across, perhaps apocryphal, is Laurence Olivier's comment to Dustin Hoffman during the making of *Marathon Man*. One of method acting's most earnest exponents, Hoffman had to enact a scene in which his character had supposedly stayed up for three days and nights. Upon being asked by his co-star how he did the scene, Hoffman admitted that he too had not slept for seventy-two hours to bring some realism to it. 'My dear boy,' replied Olivier smoothly, 'why don't you just try acting?'

Speaking of Dustin Hoffman, on one of my several trips to Moscow, I travelled via London. When I was there I heard that Dustin Hoffman would be playing Shylock in Shakespeare's *The Merchant of Venice* at the West End. I'm a huge fan of his, so I booked myself a ticket and also a Rolls Royce to get me there. I went to the theatre, saw the play and even got a chance to meet Hoffman backstage.

When he was leaving, I saw him call for his Ford Escort. I was so embarrassed. I thought to myself, he is Dustin Hoffman and he is travelling in a Ford Escort. And I'm an upstart with not half as many achievements to my name and I arrived in a Rolls Royce. Believe me, I was ashamed of my vanity that night.

There are two life lessons I've given Ranbir as far as this profession goes. One is to put in the effort required to translate into ease on screen and the second is to never let success go to the head or failure to the heart. Success and failure are a part and parcel of cinema. You cannot succeed in every role or every film. But what needs to be consistent is your effort and your work. I can safely claim that my work has always been beyond reproach, I have stayed afloat all this while only because of my consistent work.

To reach this place, I have had two very different but equally critical and productive phases. My second phase as a character artiste is particularly gratifying because I could disprove certain misconceptions that people have about senior actors.

So much has changed over the years. Today films are made on generous budgets, actors are paid handsomely, even technicians are well paid. I don't see film-makers and producers cutting corners or trying to save a rupee here and there. Even medium-budget films are made on a grand scale. There's substantial food and drink for everybody, all sourced from well-known restaurants. There's mineral water for everybody. It's no longer tap water for most and water from home only for actors. I used to carry my own boiled drinking water and buttermilk. Today, spot boys and stars drink the same water. Life on the sets has changed for the better and I'm not complaining.

But there are a few other changes that are not so welcome. It's wonderful that sound and camera have become technologically advanced, but there's also something called sync sound now, and I hate it. I throw tantrums when it comes to sync sound because I like to re-create the scene in front of a mike in the sound studio. I like to dub a film. That's my method, and I say to my producers, 'What do you lose if I dub for my films? I'm the one putting in an extra effort while dubbing by enacting my scene all over again in the studio. You're getting two performances for the price of one. And you have the option to check which sound you want to keep.' Ninety-nine per cent of the time, producers have retained my dubbed track because I improvise a lot during dubbing. My only plea to them is to respect what I bring to the table once they have signed me on. I am supposed to deliver my best and this is how I give my best. Some of them agree with my view and respect me for it.

Modernization has been a boon to the film industry. Like

vanity vans, which are so welcome. We don't have to do our makeup in the open anymore and be embarrassed by people gaping at us. Vanity vans are especially useful for actresses when they have a costume change. These vans are fitted with good air-conditioning, decent washrooms and television sets.

Film-making has also become much safer than it used to be. At one time we performed our own stunts, but actors don't have to do that anymore. We had stunt doubles then, but now because of the green mat technology, life has become easier for everyone. The stuntman doesn't have to risk his life either.

However, being overly reliant on technology has also robbed cinema of some of its flesh-and-blood realism. That's why a film like *Argo* (2012) got as much attention at the Oscars as *Life of Pi* (2012). The latter had so obviously used green mat technology, all the effects were done on the computer. You end up with a renewed respect for older films like *The Old Man and the Sea*, when you think of how patiently they must have waited to shoot their scenes, as opposed to *Life of Pi* where everything was so synthetic. Even if these films do very well at the box-office, award committees see through them. They know these were designed safely and antiseptically in the studio. Without a doubt, they make for great viewing. But you also know they are not real.

Another radical change is that celluloid film has vanished and we have entered the digital era. In the old style of film-making, with a reel of film in the camera, a director would have a picture in his mind of how to design a scene. He would know if the shot was to be a trolley shot, a close-up, or a long shot.

Today directors have it easy because they don't have to worry about the expense of film. Everything is drawn on a digital card. They're going back to the theatre and television style of film-making where the whole scene is covered from all angles. But actors like me find it very difficult to work with this technique because I cannot recreate an emotion on demand. Time and again I have told them, 'I'm not doing theatre, I'm not doing television, I cannot memorize so many lines because I'm not used to it.' Later, with the help of AVID, the editing software, they decide which scene has worked better. I can only describe this as sheer laziness. And, whether they like it or not, I can say with surety that some of the biggest film-makers I have worked with over the last five years are guilty of this. They are never sure of how to design a scene, which is very, very sad.

I dislike retakes. And I never watch the monitor during or after a shot. An actor should be sure of his work, of his performance.

A change of a different kind that I struggle with is the level of comfort between actors and actresses on set. They are more like chaddi buddies. There was an era when the arrival of a star was an event in itself. There would be a buzz and some excitement, whispers and shouts of 'Hero *aa raha hai*'. Today everything is too casual, including relationships. If they want to have an affair, they have it; if they want to stay over in each other's homes, they do it. There's nothing like seeking a soulmate. Everything is so open. Or maybe I am just too old-fashioned.

I also marvel at the level of confidence young actors possess these days. I've worked with a whole bunch of them, including Arjun Kapoor, Sushant Singh Rajput, Ayushmann Khurrana and Karthik (who was in Subhash Ghai's *Kaanchi*). They are so well informed and so knowledgeable about a variety of subjects. They have access to the internet, television, cable TV. There is so much to see and imbibe. We had none of that when we were becoming actors.

Today, the lines between a star and an actor are also blurring. An actor can also become a star. Irrfan Khan, who spent so many years on television, is a star at the age of forty-seven. Not only is he doing exceptionally well in India, but he's feted and felicitated in the West too. There were the rare exceptions earlier, such as Amrish Puri, who found stardom when he was almost fifty years old. But it happens more frequently now. Today, Irrfan shares honours with the glamorous young crop of actors at an awards night. That's finding stardom. What else does stardom mean? Throwing your weight around like Rajesh Khanna did? Is stardom only defined by popularity, such as Salman Khan or Shah Rukh enjoy? Whatever the definition of stardom, I've always believed that if an actor works hard, he will earn it. I know that I am not the right candidate for stardom – I'm not thin and I'm not young – but I want to do good work, and will never stop wanting recognition for it. I am passionate about cinema, I am passionate about acting. Every time I interact with directors and producers, I feel like a child playing with a new toy.

There's a remark Naseeruddin Shah made to me when we were working in a film called *Khoj*. He said, 'Why don't actors, male and female, understand that hands have been given to us by God as a biological part of the human body? Why do they have to do all kinds of weird things with their hands when they don't know what to do in a scene?' Naseer was bang on. Experience has taught me to distinguish between a good actor and a bad actor by what he does with his hands in a scene. You can instantly spot an insecure actor when you see his hands jammed in his pockets. Even a great actor like Ashok Kumar admitted that often he did not know what to do with his hands. That is why he always had a cigarette, pipe or lighter, anything to keep his hands busy. Many yesteryear actresses would play with their sari pallu. They too were ill at ease with their hands. Nowadays, everyone is striving to look confident and super natural. But I still know of actors who put their hands in their pockets or keep them folded.

Those who feel that I am where I am only because I am Raj Kapoor's son are way off the mark. It is a myth that actor *ka beta hai toh chalega*. No actor can make it on the strength of his lineage alone. There are many star sons who have failed to make it big. There is a saying that nothing grows under a banyan tree because the sun never penetrates through its dense foliage, making it inhospitable for any other plant to take root. This analogy may well have been the story of my life, but I didn't allow it to happen. I worked hard, very hard for my success. I've also had dips in my graph but I fought back each time and came out on top again.

I pride myself on my ability to be objective. I know my strengths and weaknesses as an actor. I am a natural actor who needs to fathom the entire scene. I like the director to flow with me and when he doesn't, it's difficult for me to perform. I become an impediment, a rock against which the tide crashes and is forced to reverse its flow. Habib Faisal, with whom I've done only one film, *Do Dooni Chaar*, understood this and consequently I delivered one of my best performances for him.

I accept that the director is the captain of the ship and I must follow his lead. But as the actor who is going to essay the role, I too have a certain mental picture and a plan for how to convey it. The lines that are written for you are not always paramount. A writer does not enact the scenes. There are certain directors who are very rigid about following the script, it is like a *patthar ki lakeer*. But I'm not an actor who should be forced to do something he doesn't want to do. I am a disciplined actor, I am paid for doing what the director wants, so I acquiesce. But it stifles me. I'm happiest and at my best when I get a free hand. However, I am careful not to go beyond the parameters of my character. I like to improvise but only within the framework of the character and the story.

My attitude towards wooing the West has also changed. Today I would be happy to make Indian films that can be pitched in an international arena. An aesthetically made film with something new to say, something like *Do Dooni Chaar*, works well for me. I would be proud to be a part of a film that makes a statement. I would like to do that kind of cinema and show my wares outside the country.

I have never been offered a Hollywood film, however. I can't claim to the contrary or sneer that I wouldn't want to do one. In the 1980s, the BBC offered me *Tandoori Nights*, a television serial. But I couldn't do it because I was too busy to fly to and from London every week to film for it. I have never been made an offer since. I'm told that you can hire an agent, go there and audition. I have never done anything like that in my entire life. I have never ever pitched for a role. I have done what has come my way, because of what people thought of me and wanted from me. This has also meant that I have lost a lot of roles along the way due to other people's manipulations, which I am aware of, but I don't want to take names.

Perhaps it is a shortcoming of mine that I have never pursued international projects. It could be my laziness or my akkad, my ego, that got the better of me. I know that my arrogance is a big problem, but I have never been able to conquer it.

Among the many welcome changes I have been witness to in the industry is the transformation in the movie-watching experience. There was a time when we used to go to the movies as youngsters, when rats scurried around inside the theatre, fans whirred loudly and, forget about stereo, you could barely hear the sound. Theatres were not air-conditioned, the seats were uncomfortable, badly maintained, and the toilets were a disaster. Theatres today are a pleasure to go to. Well air-conditioned, with plush seats, great sound and projection, an array of snacks at the food counter. There was nothing like this in the 1970s and yet films were being made, and films which did great business too. We watched films in theatres with a thousand other people, in pitch darkness, not caring about who was sitting next to us.

I've always been an inveterate theatre-goer. We'd go to cinema halls like Vijay Talkies, Natraj, Roxy or Liberty to get a whiff of the audience's reaction to our films. We'd go in after the film had started, sit quietly in the last row and slip out before it ended. It was no big deal. There was no ego – at least, I had none. We also used to have something called a 'premiere', which would be a gala event. It's a dead concept now.

I love going to the multiplexes today. I love going to PVR Juhu to watch a new release, usually with Neetu, although she refuses to see the new movies.

While I'm fortunate to still get work on my own terms, I also get offered a whole lot of junk. Sometime ago, a director offered me the role of a brigadier in the army. I asked him, 'From which angle do I look like a brigadier to you?' I notice that often film-makers sign up a new boy and a new girl and come to me with a character role. Only then do they want to pitch the project to a studio for financing. I say no to them because I don't want the responsibility of being the only bankable name in the film. I am not a big star and I'm done with carrying a film on my shoulders. I occupy a privileged position where I have the option of saying no to an offer and I do say no very often. I don't want to come off as a fool, trying to carry a film on my shoulders. I did *Chintu Ji* (2009), which flopped miserably. When I did *Do Dooni Chaar*, I had nothing to lose. Even when it got stalled for a while, it didn't affect me. But that film put me on a pedestal. Important, pivotal roles began to be offered to me.

I don't live in a fool's paradise. A film with only Rishi Kapoor wouldn't get enough funds. If it can't be marketed, how will it reach the theatres and who would come to watch it? I consider all these aspects when an offer comes to me. I have no reservations about working as a character actor but the role must have some meat in it. I'm happy to be doing *Patel Ki Punjabi Shaadi* with Paresh Rawal. I'm game to share honours with another actor. What I don't need to do is a film where there's a lead actor, actress and three character actors.

There is a tendency for actors of my age to accept all that's offered to them because they're not worried whether the picture flops or runs. If money were my sole goal, I would be doing every film that came my way. But I am conscious that I get paid for my hard work, my talent and my passion, and I am not prepared to compromise merely to inflate my bank balance. This is not to say that I have not erred in my choices. Frankly, I think I made a mistake when I did Abhinav Kashyap's *Besharam*. But at that time the idea of Ranbir, Neetu and me being in a project together excited me. Today, Abhinav and I are in talks for another project and I'm excited about the script. When I did *Housefull 2*, I was aware that it was hardly going to be memorable cinema. But I also knew that I would never get another chance to work with Dabboo. It's only brainless cinema like that which could throw us together. So I did it. If I'd been in it only for the money, I would have said yes to all of Sajid's other films. He was keen to have me on board for *Himmatwala* (2013) and also for *Humshakals* (2014).

I believe senior actors such as Om Puri, Paresh Rawal, Boman Irani and I have an advantage because two generations of audiences are familiar with us – our peers as well as moviegoers of Ranbir's generation. TV has kept us alive in their memory. But having said that, I also hear a lot of '*Arre yaar, yeh* Ranbir *ka baap hai.*' I often get introduced as 'Ranbir's daddy'. For me, there could be no better accolade.

My attitude towards my work is one of utmost dedication. I'm in it for the passion, not the money. It's very important to me that I be recognized and remembered as a competent actor who adds value to a film. I ask myself, 'If I hadn't done it, who else could have done that role better?' The answer to that is important to me. The honest answer should be, I was the best for it.

I am a hard-core commercial actor and I hate it when people remark that what we do is not art. Is fighting and dancing not an art? How many actors can enact singing a qawwali like me? Or dance like Mithun Chakraborty? Or do a '*Khaike paan Banaraswala*' like Amitabh Bachchan? It's very easy to sneer at us and say that 'serious' cinema is superior to what we do. Unfortunately, there has been a longstanding tendency to look down on actors in commercial cinema. I do understand that no actor can have only aces in his career. Even if you are Amitabh Bachchan or Dilip Kumar, you will be remembered for three or four performances at best. All of Amitabh's films could not be *Deewaar* and Dilip Kumar could not keep repeating *Ganga*

Jumna. Every film that Robert De Niro did could not be a *Raging Bull* or *Taxi Driver*. I for one cannot decide which my best films are. I have been frequently asked this question on several forums. But to me it is like choosing which of my five fingers I like best.

At one time I was fond of other forms of gambling but today my biggest gamble is my work. I am constantly putting myself to the test. I don't know how my film is going to fare, how my performance is going to be received. Isn't that a big gamble? I have no alternate avenues of work, I'm not qualified to do anything else. I am not a well-educated man. I barely got out of school, or rather, barely failed out of school. So it's really luck that has carried me this far. But I have to keep doing it. I want to be remembered as an actor who did his job with utmost sincerity.

In the context of the creative arts, I am sure no artist is immune to the need for awards and recognition for his work. I am no exception, though I must say this is one aspect where good fortune has often eluded me. My luck with awards has been so rotten that the one time I did actually win an award, for *Do Dooni Chaar*, the organizers forgot to call me on stage! They later filmed me receiving the award against a blue screen in a hotel for the telecast. I often think it is just deserts for my original mistake of having bought my first award for *Bobby*. Of course, the awards have now started pouring in and one feels vindicated about one's work.

What actually riles me is the way awards work in our country. One can list any number of glaring omissions and inconsistencies in the way both private organizers and the state bestow awards. Pancham, for example, never received a state award all his life. And it was as late as 1982 that he got his first Filmfare award. Imagine, his contribution to Hindi film music going unrecognized all his life! My uncle Shammi Kapoor too passed away without any honour bestowed on him by the state. One does not begrudge the many talented younger artistes who have been given the Padma awards, but surely a legend like Shammi Kapoor deserved one? And now that Rajesh Khanna has been given a Padma Bhushan posthumously, why not consider Shammi uncle for the same? I am sure there are others like him who have been similarly overlooked.

It is, however, a great consolation for me that I am one of the two or three senior actors who are still approached for prominent roles. It thrills me to know that I continue to work at the same time as my son.

My ultimate goal is to get the Dadasaheb Phalke Award. I hope that it will be my work, and my work alone, that will be the determining factor. It is only if I get the Dadasaheb Phalke Award that I will feel truly rewarded and recognized. I would be the third generation in my family to receive it after my grandfather and father and it would be a dream come true. I am overjoyed that my uncle Shashi Kapoor has also got it. God willing, if Ranbir is worthy of it, he will keep the legacy alive.

12

ON FATHERHOOD

This book would be incomplete without a chapter on my children, Riddhima and Ranbir. They have made me a very proud father. I may have never acknowledged as much to them in person, but I'd like them to know how impressed I am that they have both decided to walk the path of their choice, each in their own way.

When Riddhima was born in 1980, Neetu and I were over the moon. And no, neither of us was disappointed that our first-born was a girl. The arrival of Ranbir made our family complete.

My father was delighted when Ranbir was born, his first and only 'proper' grandson (my sisters' sons are not Kapoors and Dabboo has two daughters). In his will, he left a family heirloom specially for Ranbir: a beautiful old gold coin with an inscription in Afghani or Peshawari script. He did not will it to me, but directly to his grandson. Ranbir, in turn, has to leave it to his grandson. There's also a necklace of gold coins that he bequeathed to Ranbir. Several years from now, that too will be inherited by his grandson.

Although I was busy with work when the kids were little, I always made sure we had time together as a family. I had the Sundays off, and every year I would take them abroad for a full month. They would also accompany me on my outdoor shoots. I gave them all the time and attention I could manage in an otherwise packed schedule.

Whenever we travelled, we were accompanied by a whole retinue of people, including a cook and a maid. We would also cart along a video camera, a video player and a television set so that our daughter could watch cartoons while she ate her meals. In the early days, whether I was filming in Kashmir or Mysore, or in the US for stage shows, I used to have a special cook for Riddhima, so she could get the kind of food she wanted. Bahadur and Amma from our domestic staff travelled everywhere with us. My whole crew stayed with me for the comfort and safety of my wife and kids.

I have often danced to my daughter's tunes, like most fathers tend to do. I used to be a heavy smoker but I gave up cigarettes when she told me, 'Papa, I won't kiss you in the morning because you smell.'

When Riddhima grew up and decided to get married, I was, quite frankly, pleased. Over the years, we have grown close to each other and I take every opportunity to dash to Delhi to see her and spend time with my granddaughter.

Ranbir was also always clear about what he wanted to do, though he would only talk to his mother about it, never to me. He wasn't fixated on acting or being a star. He was ready to be a cameraman or a director or a set designer or an editor, as long as it had to do with films.

That's why, when he went to America, he did not join an acting school. He wanted to enrol at the School of Visual Arts in New York. But he didn't do well enough in his SAT to get admission to the school of his choice. When the late Ismail Merchant, who made films such as *The Householder* (1963) and *Bombay Talkie* (1970) with my uncle Shashi Kapoor, heard of this, he spoke to the faculty and told them that Ranbir was the grandson of one of India's greatest film-makers. How could they deny him admission? The school then took him on for his family background in the creative arts.

Ranbir wanted to learn all the facets of film-making. He stayed there for four years, after which he did a crash course in acting at the Lee Strasberg Theatre and Film Institute for nine months. I was not happy about it, but I said, it's your call, and let him study what he wanted. I was against the course at Lee Strasberg because they teach you method acting. But I also felt that Ranbir should decide for himself what kind of actor he wanted to be. I now think he has picked up the best of both schools of acting.

After coming back to India, Ranbir worked as an assistant director to Sanjay Leela Bhansali on *Black* (2005) for a while. Neetu and I will forever be indebted to Sanjay for the spectacular manner in which he launched Ranbir's career as an actor with *Saawariya* (2007). However, I do have a bone to pick with him.

As it happens, Ranbir ended up starting his career with a film based on the same story that inspired a film my father had once worked in. The film was called *Chhalia* (1960) and it was based on Fyodor Dostoyevsky's story *White Nights*, the same fantastical premise that Bhansali's *Saawariya* is based on.

I was keen to know what my son was doing in his debut film, I wanted to know what the story was. But whenever I asked Sanjay, he would be evasive and promise, 'Sir, I'll come back to you.' He didn't give me a straight answer for a few months, and I began to wonder if he was avoiding me. One day, he called up Neetu and told her, 'Sir keeps asking me, "What are you making, what are you making?" Now you tell me, what story could I have narrated to Amitabh for *Black*, what could I have told Shah Rukh about *Devdas*?'

Neetu told me what he had said and I agreed to back off, thinking to myself that if he is a good director, it must be all in his head. Since he was a responsible film-maker, I decided that Ranbir was in safe hands. Neetu and I had both loved *Devdas*, we were mesmerized by the opulence of his cinema. He would come by sometimes and play the music he had recorded for *Saawariya* and I thought they were excellent compositions.

But then the film was released and it bombed. When we saw it for the first time, I was aghast. I immediately recalled my father's film, *Chhalia*, which was Manmohan Desai's first film. It didn't run for even two shows. That story could never be made into a film. If only Bhansali had told me, I would have dissuaded him. *Saawariya* had Salman Khan, in *Chhalia* it was Pran sa'ab. Bhansali had Ranbir, Manmohan Desai had Raj Kapoor. Here it was Sonam, there it was Nutan. *Saawariya* had great music, so did *Chhalia*. *Chhalia* was set in the context of Indo-Pak relations. *Saawariya* had, I don't know how to describe it, a spaced-out blue or green background. People uncharitably called it a 'blue film'. Neither film worked commercially.

The failure of *Saawariya* didn't upset me because Ranbir was appreciated for his work and he moved from strength to strength. Sometimes, when an artiste thinks he is making great cinema, he is often not open to accepting anybody else's inputs. He is running with his vision. Not my father, though. When he made films, he would shoot one schedule and invite the whole town to see it. He used to value people's opinions. Today, I am told that film-makers like Aamir Khan and Rakesh Roshan show their product to people as the film progresses. I gather that the Yash Chopra family doesn't show its films before their release to anybody. But when *Rocket Singh: Salesman of the Year* (2009) was ready, they called us to see it on a Tuesday, three days before its release. When you see a film, even if you dislike it, it's only polite to say, 'All the best for Friday.' That's what I did when I saw *Rocket Singh*.

Jaideep Saini, the writer of the film and a friend, and director Shimit Amin wanted to know what I thought of it. I said to them, 'If you ask for my opinion three days before its release, how does it matter? You have already made the overseas delivery. If you had asked me two months back, I would have given you my frank opinion.' I added, 'You don't feel satisfied if the lead actor does not succeed at what he's doing.' They replied, 'That would be the usual ending, we wanted to do something different.' I retorted, 'Then why ask anybody for his opinion?'

I believe that a film-maker's primary objective is to entertain the audiences. And nobody is God, no one can predict things or get it absolutely right. A wise man once said, 'If anybody knew how to grow hair on a bald head or predict the success of a film, he would be the richest man in the world.'

I remember my father being cocksure that people would sit for over four hours to watch *Mera Naam Joker*. He was wrong. He reshot the climax of *Ram Teri Ganga Maili* because he listened to people. He did something similar during *Bobby* too. After *Joker* and *Kal Aaj Aur Kal*, he could not afford to have another failure, he had to make sure that *Bobby* was a super hit. That's why he changed the original ending written by Khwaja Ahmed Abbas, in which the two young people die. He also introduced Prem Chopra's character and added a commercial angle to the film. In the West too, they have screenings where they solicit public opinion.

I believe Ranbir has had it tougher than I did, because the acting scene is far more competitive today than when I entered it, making his success that much sweeter. There is such an abundance of talent and so many options out there that to come out on top each time is truly a feat.

Of course, he is only about ten years old in the industry, having started his career in 2006. When he made films like *Rocket Singh* and *Rockstar* (2011), my friends, my family, even some of my producers, wondered what he was up to. *Kabhi lambe baal, kabhi Sardar bana hai*, what's he doing? Everyone expected him to go down the traditional path and establish himself as a star before proving himself as an actor.

I do not have a say in Ranbir's creative choices, I have never attempted to interfere in his career. Of course I must admit that as a father I felt uncertain at times because deep down I felt the objections were valid. People around us meant well. Indeed, what was Ranbir doing in movies like *Rockstar*? Or *Wake up Sid* (2009)? In *Raajneeti* (2010) he shared the screen with five other lead actors and then he played a hearing- and speech-impaired person in *Barfi* (2012). His unconventional choices used to scare me.

But everything changed for Ranbir after *Barfi*. The film was at once a vindication of his stand and a massive blow to all his critics who had denounced his choices. As an actor he proved himself in *Barfi, Rocket Singh, Rockstar, Wake up Sid*, while *Ajab Prem Ki Ghazab Kahani, Yeh Jawani Hai Deewani* (2013) and *Ae Dil Hai Mushkil* (2016) sealed his commercial appeal.

After the success of *Barfi*, people clamoured for him and eagerly looked forward to a Ranbir film. That's why he fell so hard with *Besharam*. It was the kind of 'entertainer' that some other actors would have pulled off well. But coming from Ranbir, it tanked. He had built up such an enviable body of work, nobody quite took to him in this kind of cinema. But even the flop film managed to rake in ₹60 crore and had a knockout first-day box-office collection. There is an audience out there that wants to go into a theatre and see him in any film he stars in, which is a great achievement at his age.

Now everybody expects Ranbir to experiment. His choices failed again with *Bombay Velvet* (2015) and to some extent with *Tamasha* (2015). I didn't see these films but Neetu did. She felt that the film-makers had gotten ahead of themselves by repackaging a tried-and-tested formula in a non-commercial style. Of course, it is never only the actor who can be blamed for the failure of a film. There are times when a script fails, the execution fails, the mammoth cost of film-making causes it to fail, or it could be a combination of all these and more. Ranbir himself, I am told, got some flattering reviews.

I think Ranbir has the right attitude towards his work. He does only one film at a time. He takes his work seriously, he slogs over his character, he works closely with his director and is completely involved with the film. That's what matters. The rest, including the eventual result, hit or flop, is secondary.

Growing up, when Ranbir talked about wanting to become an actor, he used to tell his mother that he didn't want to work in films wearing a baseball cap worn back-to-front, a basketball in his hand and balancing on a skateboard. Nor did he want to have forty backup dancers flouncing around behind him. He didn't say this to me directly but he told Neetu, 'I don't want to do such films, I'd rather not work in films at all.' He had his game plan worked out in his head right from the start. His focus was on films outside the commercial sphere, films that were risky but gave him a kick as an actor. He is an intelligent actor. Even if he did *Raajneeti* with a host of other actors, he didn't let anyone encroach on his space. He stood out despite all the heavyweights around him.

His commitment to his craft, in my view, is faultless. In January 2014, social media and print publications were agog with the news that he had gone to New York to ring in the New Year with Katrina Kaif. What nobody knew was that he had gone to New York to enrol himself back in school to learn how to stammer for a role in a forthcoming film. My sister Ritu was overwhelmed when she heard this. She said, 'He is such a huge star, he doesn't have to go to a school to learn any kind of acting.' But that's how true Ranbir is to his passion. I also remember the time he was prepping to play a boxer in *Bombay Velvet*, there were weights all over the house.

Frankly I am not the right person to judge Ranbir's work. I see his films but I don't like any of them. I am always analysing them as an actor and not as a father and always end up being overcritical. Neetu is far more perceptive. She knows which film will work and which won't. Thankfully, I have been proved wrong time and again. I didn't like *Barfi* or *Yeh Jawani Hai Deewani*, but both of them were super hits. I didn't think much of *Raajneeti*. I watched it only because of Ranbir. And that too was a successful film.

I once said, 'I always knew I was a big father's son but I didn't know that I was a big son's father too.' It was an honest statement. I am Raj Kapoor's son but I am also immensely proud to be Ranbir Kapoor's father. On my Twitter handle I call myself the hyphen in the middle!

However, there has always been a thin barrier that stands between my son and me. He is part of a new generation and I'm uncomfortable with some of the things he does. When he was younger and I noticed something that I didn't like, I used to tell my daughter, 'Tell your brother to take it easy, man, to have some respect for the elders in the house.' At the same time, I realized that if I came down too heavily on him, he had the option of moving out of our house. He could afford to, many times over.

Ranbir has strange likes and dislikes. When he's home, he loves to start his day with scrambled eggs and caviar. I marvel at his indulgence. I grew up as Raj Kapoor's son, but we never had scrambled eggs and caviar. I tell Ranbir that caviar isn't good for him but he's extremely fond of it. And then, for someone who starts off his day with such a flourish, he starves the rest of the time. He is not fond of liquor, but it would be good if he gave up smoking. I managed to finally give up cigarettes in my second attempt. It's been years since I smoked. Ranbir went to some spa overseas and now I hear he doesn't smoke. That is good. He never smoked in front of me, anyway. When he turned eighteen, I gave him a beer and said he could drink in my company. So he has a drink with me once in a while but he is not a heavy drinker.

The distance that exists between us is similar to the one between my father and me. Ranbir and I see each other through this space but can't feel each other. At least, I can't. There are times when I feel I've missed out on being a friend to my son. I was a strict father because I was brought up to believe that's how a father should be. In one of his interviews, Ranbir said, 'My father is not a friend. He is a father. I can't backslap him and joke around with him.' He is a friend to Neetu but not to me, and that's something I deeply regret.

Maybe I should have reached out to him. But there's also a part of me that innately dislikes too much familiarity. Perhaps I like that distance in a father–son relationship. Backslapping each other, sharing a cigarette and saying, let's have a drink – these are things I would not be comfortable doing with my son. It goes against the traditions that I believe in.

After her marriage, Riddhima and I have become very close. She is the mother of a five-year-old girl, my first grandchild, and becoming a parent seems to have helped her understand her own parents better and appreciate them more, or so I like to think. Ranbir is close to me too, but in a different way. I help him with the nitty-gritty of business deals because I have much more experience than him in such matters and he is in a vulnerable position where people could take advantage of him. So while his focus is on his work, I handle all the other aspects of his career, especially the finances. We also have a very good trustworthy chartered accountant in Bimal Parekh, who is like family to us.

When I started out, I remember, I used to be nonplussed by anything to do with finance. This trait seems to run in the family. My father had no head for business either. He always said, 'God has given me the talent to act and to make films but he hasn't given me the brains to handle money matters. I have no business sense at all.' Papa managed to set up a studio but he was taken for a ride all his life. His films earned big money but his accounts were never in order.

I don't know what the future holds for us as a family. Ranbir has reached the age where he wants to settle down, maybe get married and raise a family. When I fell in love with Neetu, my parents didn't stand in the way of my happiness. We feel the same about Ranbir today. Whoever my son falls in love with and brings home will be welcomed warmly by both Neetu and me.

I never talk about Ranbir and his personal life to anyone if I can help it. I run away from the media on this count or I bully them and say, 'You will not ask me any questions on anything other than what I'm here for.' But sometimes there's no escaping it. Once, I remember, I'd been invited to inaugurate the new branch of my bank at Bandra Kurla Complex. A few media people were covering the event. It was not related to films in any way, yet one of them asked me, 'What do you have to say about Katrina and Ranbir?' My expression obviously changed as I turned around and silently headed for my car. When I later saw the footage on TV, I realized that they had even zoomed in on my expression as I sat in the car. They managed to make a story out of my silence too.

Will the bond between me and Ranbir, or indeed, all four of us last forever? Will my brothers' families and mine continue to share our lives the way we do now? I don't know. I can't vouch for tomorrow's generation, I can't foresee what our kids will do. I have no idea how Dabboo's kids and mine will behave in the future, with the RK banner, the RK legacy, or RK Studios.

The way I see it, I loved my grandfather Prithviraj Kapoor because I knew him. But what does Ranbir have to do with Prithviraj Kapoor, whom he has never met? He only knows that he was his great-grandfather and he'll respect his memory like anyone in his place would. But there's no love. That's the law of nature. It's said that memory exists only for three generations. Ranbir may remember Raj Kapoor, but how can one expect his kids to feel anything special for their great-grandfather?

Maybe there will be battles over property, family disputes and litigation. Such things happen between brothers too, but Dabboo, Chimpu and I have tried to keep it all intact. We run RK Studios together. We go to the office and look after the business interests of RK as a team. This also means that we get to meet at least once in a while.

When we hand everything over to our kids, it will be up to them to decide how they want to handle the legacy of Raj Kapoor. I can't run away from the fact that RK is an inactive banner, in hibernation, and I am partly responsible for this. If my brothers haven't done anything about keeping the RK banner flying, I haven't either. I've always been preoccupied with my career as an actor. Tomorrow, if Ranbir wants to make a film, I don't see him making it under the RK banner. He may make it in his name, he could start his own banner. Why would he make a film with my brothers under RK? When my father started making films, he didn't start a company with his brothers or his father. We are all individuals in the film business.

For me, it's different. It will always be RK. I know that the goodwill earned by the banner is enormous and intact. The audience will come to see an RK film even if it's made after a gap of fifteen years. We may have not done much with it, but it's still a strong banner because we have not compromised it either, by producing rubbish just to make money.

To be honest, I don't see myself or my brothers making

another film. I am busy as an actor and that is my passion, not film-making. I wouldn't be surprised, though, if Ranbir goes on to make movies while also being an actor, like my father did. Who knows, maybe he will prove to be the true inheritor of the RK legacy.

AFTERWORD

Decoding Rishi: Actor, Son, Husband and Father

NEETU KAPOOR

First, a checklist:

Is Rishi Kapoor a grouch? Guilty as charged.

Is he loud, gregarious, and prone to wound with words? Check all three please.

Is he suspicious of people, stiflingly possessive, difficult to live with? You seem to know my husband well.

Is he generous with gifts? Not really.

Does he sulk? Do we fight? Have I ever thought of leaving him? Yes, yes, yes. I've entertained the thought of walking away every single day of our life together.

So why am I still Mrs Rishi Kapoor, thirty-seven years after saying 'I do'?

Because thirty-seven years is a long time. And I cannot, would not, live with any other.

Because once you get to know my husband, he's the most straightforward man there is. Though, admittedly, it's not easy to 'get to know him'.

Because I truly believe that I couldn't have asked for a better man, or indeed a better life, than what I've had with him.

Because, as the years roll by, I appreciate him a little more each day.

Because his good qualities far outnumber his annoying habits.

Because this list of 'because' only gets longer.

Do I look like a bechari? It certainly seems to be a common refrain when people speak of me and of the perceived 'sacrifices' I have made as Mrs Rishi Kapoor. The truth is: my life has played out exactly the way I wanted it to, and sacrifices were neither made nor required. In fact, the best thing that ever happened to me thirty-seven years ago was that I got married to a man called Rishi Kapoor.

Rishi is a difficult man … until you know him. He has an aggressive disposition that scares people. He is brash, he is prone to getting worked up and hyper-animated during conversations and can be brutal in his 'tell it as it is' frankness. To top it all, Bob doesn't trust people too easily. In fact, he's downright suspicious and is constantly looking to unearth people's real motives. Which means not too many people venture close and it's tough for him to make friends. Perhaps that explains why there are hardly any new faces around him and why the few friends he has, have been with him for a long, long time. They are the ones who have seen the nicer side of Rishi Kapoor;

they are privy to the knowledge that his overbearing, grouchy exterior is simply a façade.

Today, Bob and I have arrived at a place of comfort and understanding that wasn't there fifteen years ago. One glance, one little gesture, and I know what's on his mind. He has begun to value my opinion on movies and other matters. His dependence on me has grown too. Maybe it's because some of his old friends are not around anymore.

Along with his deeply suspicious nature, Bob has a jealous streak in him, mostly where I'm concerned. Suspicion and jealousy can be a corrosive combination, but we've dealt with it well. To maintain equanimity in the relationship, I have made him my top priority and I know that I cannot be too friendly with anybody else, over him. And 'anybody' includes our son Ranbir. I'm not suggesting that Bob is jealous of Ranbir, but I know him well enough to sense the envy he feels when motherly love pushes him to second place.

Bob has to know and be comfortable with a person before he can truly befriend him or her. Earlier, I found it irksome and wondered why he had an issue with every friend I made. But gradually, all of us have understood and accepted this trait. So my friends take the trouble to first put him at ease and only when he's comfortable with them do I breathe easy. Otherwise he can get terribly cranky.

I dated Bob for five years before our marriage, so I have actually been with him for forty-two years. I don't for a moment claim that it has been a bed of roses all the way. There have been moments of concern in our marriage. What has helped us weather the storms is that I am blessed with a sea of patience and he is blessed with endearing qualities that more than make up for his quirks.

One quality that I particularly admire is his passion. He is passionate about movies, he is passionate about his family, and he goes crazy when any of us is travelling. One rule that is non-negotiable is that we always have to text him and say 'Jai Mata Di' when taking off and landing anywhere. He's fidgety until he gets the message.

Once, Ranbir messaged him after boarding a flight but there was a delay in the actual take-off. Meanwhile, Bob had mentally calculated the time of arrival based on when the message had been sent, and when he didn't hear from Ranbir at the estimated time, he went berserk. Eventually, when Ranbir did land and text, he got his ear chewed off. His father's point was, 'Why did you message me when it wasn't yet time for take-off? I timed your landing in my head and I was worried sick.'

Bob cares immensely for all of us, so he worries in the same measure. His world is his family – Riddhima, Ranbir, Bharat (Riddhima's husband) and now our granddaughter, Samara.

During the promotion of *Besharam*, when all three of us flew together, Ranbir said much to my amusement, 'Thank God both of you are here. Now I don't have to message and say, "Jai Mata Di." It's such pressure on me that if I slip up, Papa will go mad.'

My family is, without a doubt, my world too, the world that I always aspired to have. I had no other dreams or goals. That's why there was never any dilemma over having to choose between my work and my marriage. I was never ambitious, and at no point in my life did I think I wanted to be an actress forever.

I was only thirteen when I began to work and by the time I quit at twenty-one, I had done some seventy-odd movies. I'd just entered my teens when I encountered fame and fortune, so to speak, and it followed me for the rest of my life. But it was only the fame that I personally experienced. I was oblivious to the fortune that came with it. My mother handled what I earned, she made the financial decisions and investments, and when I got married, I simply moved from her house to my husband's. Earlier, my mother used to take care of our expenses and give me money whenever I wanted any. Then my husband started taking care of the finances. So when I wound up my career to get married, I didn't think I was giving up my independence or indeed, anything of consequence. I was just excited to be getting the life I had yearned for.

Movie-making was not my lifeblood. I acted as instructed and I was so young that I'd wear the clothes I was given and mouth the lines that were handed to me without question. On set I did not think about the trajectory of my character or anything like that. I simply did whatever I was told to do by the director. At home, my mother handled everything while my boyfriend ruled my emotional life.

Perhaps because I was so young, I simply went with my heart. I knew Rishi Kapoor well, I wanted to live with him and raise a family with him. I wanted this despite the fact that he was the most troublesome boyfriend in town. He made me cry almost daily but I still wanted to see him every day. He imposed impossible, stressful conditions on my work schedule, including the ground rule that I had to pack up at 8.30 p.m. and no later than that. His decision became a nightmare for me whenever I had a late-night schedule. The songs *'Dhoom mache dhoom...'* and *'Maiya main toh...'* in *Kaala Patthar* were both shot outdoors, at night. Yash-ji had erected a set below Raj Kamal Studios, where the rest of the cast, Amitabh Bachchan, Rakhee, Shatrughan Sinha, Parveen Babi and Shashi Kapoor, had to stand around doing nothing while I did all the singing and dancing. We would start work at 7 p.m., after sundown, and continue filming till about 2 or 3 a.m. Bob had relaxed his rule a bit for *Kaala Patthar* and given me a grace period of one extra hour, which meant I could shoot till 9.30 p.m. Everyone on the set knew that Neetu Singh was madly in love with her demanding boyfriend and would be unmanageable after 9.30 p.m., so they would all start work sharp at 7 p.m. Yash-ji had a harrowing time, knowing that he only had two hours and then I'd vanish. But I was so paranoid about my boyfriend's diktat that nothing else mattered.

One evening, while filming *'Dhoom mache dhoom...'* we worked later than usual and one shot was still to be canned. Fortunately, there were no mobile phones then. So I called my house and told the maid, 'Phone *uthake niche rakh dena. Sa'ab will call, I don't want him to get through. I'll tell him I got stuck in traffic.*' While I meant her to keep the receiver off the hook, the maid followed my instructions literally, took the phone off the table and put it on the floor! Luckily, Rishi didn't call that evening, but you can imagine the kind of stress I was under. Our dating days were filled with so much tension that it was a relief to finally get married.

Before I got married, my daily routine was fixed. I would shoot until 8.30 p.m., pack up and go out for a drive or dinner with my possessive boyfriend. Marriage was a way out of this routine for me. I wanted to relax, not have to report for work or have meetings. I got exactly what I wanted – a husband, a home, a family. I made the right choice in every way because Rishi Kapoor the husband was infinitely better than Rishi Kapoor the boyfriend. As my boyfriend, he was so brash and incorrigible that my colleagues would feel sorry for me. For instance, I had no makeup man and enjoyed doing my own makeup. While I was getting ready, he would barge into my room, ruin my makeup with an eyeliner pencil, and stand there laughing. Or he'd grab my bag and empty its contents on the road. They were silly, bratty little ways of troubling me. And he'd constantly crib about my clothes.

Fortunately, he has calmed down a lot after marriage, though he's still very stingy with his compliments. It takes a lot for him to say 'you're looking good' and in all these decades, I think he has complimented me only twice. Each time, I was convinced that the outfits I wore must be terrific to draw such praise. So I've kept them aside as must-wear for very special occasions.

He doesn't compliment Ranbir either and my son really waits for his father to say something nice to him. Instead, he's always criticizing him or lecturing him on what not to do. I constantly tell Bob to back off and talk to his son as a friend. But he says, 'That's the way I am.' Perhaps that was the kind of relationship he had with his father.

In the past few years, I have counselled him frequently on how to communicate with Ranbir. Our son is now a young man and it's time my husband spoke to him man-to-man, rather than bully him like a child. The good thing about Bob is that, somewhere, my constant pep talks register. I now find him more relaxed with Ranbir, discussing his work and trying to understand what's happening.

Unlike when he was a boyfriend, as a husband Rishi has never given me cause for concern about our relationship. I don't know why he thinks I was insecure when he worked with Dimple in *Saagar*. I don't entertain feelings of jealousy or pettiness, and I've always been confident about the special relationship we share. He comes home to me every day, except when he is travelling on work. He has done that every single day of our married life together.

My husband was really anxious when we went to the first trial show of *Saagar*. He had filmed a few kissing scenes with Dimple and was convinced I'd pounce on him as soon as the screening was over. So he waited nervously for my reaction while I sat through the film quietly and afterwards, got into the car without a word. Then I turned to him and said, 'Bob, I'm so ashamed of you. How could you have been such a bad kisser? I expected you to be cooler, more with it.' I could see him almost pass out with relief.

An actor's wife needs to have a large heart, you cannot get

worked up over minor incidents. If you take them to heart, you'll either slash your wrist, sink into depression, or leave your husband and be miserable forever.

I'm sure Bob hasn't been squeaky clean, there must have been a couple of trespasses. I won't name anybody but I always put it down to a passing attraction. Such things happen in most men's lives, and they did happen, but I chose not to give them any importance. They were just fleeting distractions that came and went.

It's funny how I would get to know when he liked an actress a little more than he needed to. He used to drink his whisky and get high every evening. In that state he always got a lot of things off his chest. Without realizing that it was his wife he was confiding in and not a male buddy, he would disclose everything about the girl he was interested in. When I'd ask him about it the next morning, he'd wonder how I got to know his little secret. It happened so many times that he soon grew nervous about what he'd be spilling before me the next time he was drunk.

While he's very proud of Ranbir, Riddhima grew up knowing that if she ever told her father she wanted to be an actress, he'd kill himself. She is a wonderfully talented and beautiful girl. She's a fabulous mimic and would have given any actress a run for her money. But even as a child she knew how much it would upset her father if she decided to become an actress. He doesn't think badly of actresses or feel that girls shouldn't work in movies. But he's zealously overprotective of his wife and children.

Riddhima understood her father well. For the sake of his peace of mind, she never attempted to pursue acting as a career. Instead she said, 'I want to design clothes,' and Bob happily sent her to London to study.

My own feeling is that he couldn't have taken the garbage that people write or say about actors, especially on television. There have been so many stories about Ranbir, who sometimes tells me, 'Mom, I haven't even met these girls and they link me with them.' I haven't been introduced to any of the girls he's supposed to have seriously dated. The only person I knew about and met was Deepika. And, more recently, Katrina. This ugly side of stardom scared my husband and he didn't want to see his daughter entangled in that mess. It was something that worried him all through her growing-up years until she got married to Bharat. Once she settled down, Bob was a much-relieved man and his relationship with Riddhima grew stronger and more open.

Riddhima has also become more confident around her father. As kids, Ranbir and she were very scared of him. His brusqueness instilled fear in them, like when he told them to come home on time or sleep on time. 'Eat your vegetables' was another bugbear, especially for Ranbir, who hates vegetables with a passion. Once, we were at dinner and my husband was saying, 'Come on, move the food, finish the vegetables.' I felt really sorry for Ranbir as I watched tears rolling down his cheeks and falling on the plate, but he kept eating out of sheer fright.

With the fear receding, both my children have a healthier and happier relationship with their father. In fact, now I have to forbid him from calling Riddhima too frequently. She is married, has a husband and a house of her own to run, and we can't keep interrupting them, especially on a Sunday. But Bob can be obdurate on this score too. He argues, 'But I call Bharat too on Sundays.'

He's on Facetime all the time with Riddhima and Samara and all my attempts to caution him against it have failed. I tell him to text her, asking her to call him when she's free. But when he wants to talk, he will. He is simply not sensitive about these little things.

I do think he should be more careful about other people's feelings. I have often had to pull him up for saying something that wasn't very nice and tell him outright, 'That was out of line.' He listens to me and tries to make amends. I make sure he apologizes to his mother, or his sister, or anyone else he has hurt.

Over the years, I have forged my own equations with everyone in the family. Before my marriage I worked in several films with Dabboo, so there is a mutual fondness. However, because he is my husband's older brother, I respect him and can't call him my buddy. Chimpu is the youngest and I know my husband is upset and angry about the way things have turned out in his brother's life. But he doesn't know how to deal with it. He doesn't know how to show his concern for him. They end up not talking to each other properly and it appears that they don't see eye to eye. But Bob is actually very worried about Chimpu. Perhaps because I am far more compassionate and patient, I can openly say, 'Forget it, Chimpu.' Most times my husband and he talk to each other through me. There is a distance between them. Chimpu has settled down in Pune but I am in constant touch with him.

My husband is not a friendly person. He's not the sort to network and keep in touch with people. The onus is on everyone else. He is happy with his routine of getting up in the morning, having his breakfast, going to RK Studios or to a shoot, coming back home, having a drink, eating and going to bed. If somebody calls him, he'll respond, but he won't take the initiative. And then he'll complain that people have forgotten him. It doesn't strike him that he hasn't called his friends either. Most of his old friends know what he's all about, so they make the effort. But left to himself, he won't connect with anyone. He is very content in his own world.

The relationship between a daughter-in-law and a mother-in-law is a very delicate one, with each feeling a sense of claim over one man. I think the man plays a huge part in bringing the two women together, on an equal plane, and giving them both the love and respect they deserve. In this respect, Bob has maintained a fantastic balance. He holds his mother in very high regard and he keeps me close and at that level too. He has always told his mother how important I am to him and he has told me that his mother is important to him. It speaks very well of him that he wrought such a good relationship between his mother and me where both of us respect each other wholeheartedly. My mother-in-law is someone the whole family loves and worships and that includes me.

I sometimes tell Ranbir, 'I don't know why I love my mother-in-law so much.' But I have begun to realize that I take my cue from my husband, his unstinting concern and love for her. Whether we're at home or travelling, he'll ask me, 'Have you phoned Mummy?' After all these years, he knows the kind of relationship I share with her and that I don't need to be reminded to call her. But he still feels the need to ask me. I tell Ranbir, 'You have to show your wife or girlfriend how important I am to you. If you don't give me respect, she will not respect me either. Even today, after all these years, your father asks me, "Mummy *ko* phone *kiya?*" I may have spoken to her a dozen times but he still wants to ensure that I am in constant touch with her.'

I have been lucky because everyone in my husband's family is big-hearted and full of love. They expect nothing from you in return. It's not the kind of family where you have to call them day and night, take gifts for them or put them on a pedestal. Even before we were married, his sister Rima was my closest friend and she would slip me updates on her brother. Which girl he had called, who he had sent flowers to, which girls he was flirting with.

I loved his father too. Bob was petrified of him. He was so scared of him that he would shiver in his presence. But I had a warm relationship with him. When he was into his drink, nobody wanted to be near him. But I would sit with him in his room and I learnt a lot from him because he'd talk about philosophy, relationships, people, and lots of other things.

In these three decades and more that Bob and I have been married, most of our arguments have been over food. His insatiable appetite and unhealthy relationship with food, a

Kapoor family trait, has been a major source of contention in the house. He was a romantic hero and every time we went to a trial show of one of his films, people would pick on me and say, 'What are you doing? Your husband is so fat.' I used to dread going to a screening because I knew I'd be admonished as if I was the guilty party. Those were the days when the wife was blamed for everything, she was held responsible for all her husband's follies. I was always fighting him, saying, eat this, don't eat that. And he would get angry with me because he is such a foodie. I used to put him on diets that he would never follow and each time, I'd stop talking to him for at least a month. I used to feel bad about it, but then he would finally relent and say, '*Achchha theek hai yaar, kya karoon, baat to kar mere se.* At least talk to me.' He would lose some weight then, but it always came back. The classic yo-yo phenomenon. Gain weight, lose weight, gain weight again. Ever since I met him, his weight has been my personal struggle. But all the haranguing has finally paid off because today he has become conscious of what's on his plate.

My kids are diet conscious too. They know exactly what to eat. Metabolism also plays its part and Ranbir is very fortunate in this regard. He has such a high rate of metabolism that he just doesn't gain weight. But he is also a poor eater. He has a bad habit of always leaving some food on his plate. He never seems to finish what has been served to him. If I give him juice, he will leave some in the glass. If I give him two eggs, he will eat only one. That's just the way he is.

I don't have Ranbir's metabolism. I have to work at losing weight. Riddhima is slender but that's because she is so rigid about her intake. When I look at her, I feel ashamed of my indulgences. I have never seen her touch dessert. Never. She has breakfast, lunch, coffee at 5 p.m. and dinner at 8 p.m. Two rotis, chicken, a vegetable and dal. She will eat a full meal, but that's it and not a morsel more. She eats nothing that's fried. She has two Marie biscuits for breakfast and never more than that. She is happy with her regimented eating, but I sometimes get angry with her for being so unrelenting.

My husband is not a lavish spender, nor is he generous with gifts. He is very cautious and wise with his money. I've never heard him say, 'Hey, just go ahead and buy it.' He takes his time to gauge if an expense is worth it. When Ranbir was fifteen or sixteen years old and wanted a car, Bob told him, 'No, this is not the age to have a car of your own.' He didn't like spoiling his children. Growing up, Ranbir and Riddhima always flew economy. He also never gave either of them extra money for shopping. I used to spoil them a bit. But that's the way we maintained a balance and I think the effort was well worth it, because both Riddhima and Ranbir are humble and understand the value of money. People tend to give me a lot of credit for bringing up the children right, but some of it must go to their father too.

When Ranbir turned eighteen, the Honda CRV had just been launched and I really wanted him to have one. So I told Bob that I wanted it. His response was not unexpected: I already had a car and there was no need for another. I told him, 'Bob, I really want it, please buy it for me.' He turned me down. I kept at it for six months, until he finally relented. As soon as I got it, I handed over the keys to Ranbir and he was thrilled. But I had to really push my husband for it. When we go abroad, he will not tell me to go and buy myself a bag or a designer outfit. On the contrary, he calls it a waste of money. When I really want to buy something, I have to save for it because I know my husband isn't going to surprise me.

But when it comes to food, Rishi Kapoor is a different man. When we go to New York, he will take me to the fanciest restaurants, where he will merrily spend hundreds of dollars on a single meal. And then he will turn a real scrooge over spending money on something really insignificant. On one occasion in New York, while returning to the apartment we were staying in, after we'd just splurged on a rather fancy meal, we remembered that we needed to buy milk for the morning tea. It was close to midnight, but he wanted to walk two blocks to a place where the milk was 30 cents cheaper.

If I remember right, the only 'big' gift he ever bought me was when I turned fifty. My mother-in-law says that his father was also like him, it's a Peshawari trait. They will not give you anything easily. If you really want something, you have to keep asking them for it. You'll get it eventually but they won't give it to you instantly.

Finally, what are my thoughts on my husband as an actor? I consider him to be among the best in the business. He is unmatched as an artiste. I have worked with him and I can tell you that the difference between a scene as it was narrated to him and what you see on screen is tremendous and that is because of what he brings to it. It is irrefutable proof of his passion as an actor and his deep understanding of his craft. Even at the height of Amitabh Bachchan's superstardom, I think my husband held his own. Many younger actors say that they've been awed by his performances in films such as *Laila Majnu*, *Karz* and *Sargam*.

We were seeing each other when he was working in *Sargam*. One day, while I was shooting with Mr Bachchan for another film, he said to me, '*Mera dimaag kaam nahin kar raha hai*, I'm flabbergasted, he has blown my mind. How could Chintu dance, play an instrument and sing at the same time?' Rishi Kapoor could enact playing any instrument like he knew how to. He went above and beyond the basic requirements for every role. For *Laila Majnu*, he went to Los Angeles and bought his own makeup. He wanted to show Majnu bleeding, with peeling skin and cracked lips, when he was in the desert. Today, makeup artists take care of your look in every scene, but he did everything himself for *Laila Majnu*. He went to Los Angeles to pick up special effects makeup for a number of other films too.

Rishi and I made a great on-screen couple, very fresh and youthful, and starred in some fun films, full of song and dance and romance. Today, many of Ranbir's fans and youngsters tell us, 'You were my mother's favourite pair. My parents were great fans of yours.'

It has been a fulfilling life with Rishi Kapoor, as a co-star and as his wife. Other lead actresses like Dimple Kapadia and Tina Munim may have paired well with him on screen, with some amount of success, but I can safely say that I have been his best partner – on screen and off.

FILMOGRAPHY

2016	Kapoor & Sons; Sanam Re; Chalk N Duster (Special Appearance)
2015	Wedding Pullav; All Is Well
2014	Kaanchi; Bewakoofiyaan
2013	Besharam; Shuddh Desi Romance; D-Day; Aurangzeb; Chashme Baddoor
2012	Jab Tak Hai Jaan; Student of the Year; Housefull 2; Agneepath
2011	Tell Me O Kkhuda; Patiala House
2010	Do Dooni Chaar; Sadiyaan: Boundaries Divide … Love Unites

2009	Chintu Ji; Love Aaj Kal; Kal Kissne Dekha; Delhi-6; Luck by Chance
2008	Thoda Pyaar Thoda Magic; Halla Bol (as himself)
2007	Sambar Salsa; Namastey London; Don't Stop Dreaming
2006	Love Ke Chakkar Mein; Fanaa
2005	Pyaar Mein Twist
2004	Hum Tum
2003	Tehzeeb; Love at Times Square; Kucch To Hai
2002	Yeh Hai Jalwa
2001	Kuch Khatti Kuch Meethi
2000	Raju Chacha; Karobaar: The Business of Love
1999	Jai Hind
1997	Kaun Sachcha Kaun Jhootha
1996	Daraar; Prem Granth
1995	Yaraana; Hum Dono; Saajan Ki Baahon Mein

1994	Ghar Ki Izzat; Prem Yog; Eena Meena Deeka; Mohabbat Ki Arzoo; Pehla Pehla Pyar; Saajan Ka Ghar
1993	Sahibaan; Gurudev; Anmol; Dhartiputra; Izzat Ki Roti; Damini; Shreemaan Aashique; Sadhna
1992	Kasak; Honeymoon; Bol Radha Bol; Deewana; Inteha Pyar Ki
1991	Garajna; Ghar Parivaar; Banjaran; Ranbhoomi; Henna; Ajooba
1990	Azaad Desh Ke Ghulam; Sheshnaag; Sher Dil; Amiri Garibi; Naya Andaz
1989	Gharana; Hathyar; Naqab; Chandni; Khoj; Paraya Ghar; Bade Ghar Ki Beti
1988	Hamara Khandaan; Janam Janam; Vijay; Ghar Ghar Ki Kahani; Dharam Yuddh (TV Series)
1987	Khudgarz (Guest Appearance); Sindoor (Guest Appearance); Hawalaat; Pyar Ke Kabil; Khazana (Special Appearance)
1986	Nagina; Naseeb Apna Apna; Dosti Dushmani; Ek Chadar Maili Si; Pahunchey Huwe Log (Guest Appearance)

1985	Saagar; Sitamgar; Rahi Badal Gaye; Tawaif; Zamana
1984	Aan Aur Shaan; Yeh Ishq Nahin Aasaan; Duniya
1983	Coolie; Bade Dil Wala
1982	Deedar-E-Yaar; Prem Rog; Yeh Vaada Raha
1981	Katilon Ke Kaatil; Zamaane Ko Dikhana Hai; Biwi O Biwi (uncredited); Naseeb
1980	Gunehgaar; Karz; Aap Ke Deewane; Dhan Daulat; Do Premee
1979	Salaam Memsaab (Special Appearance); Laila Majnu; Duniya Meri Jeb Mein; Jhoota Kahin Ka; Sargam
1978	Phool Khile Hain Gulshan Gulshan; Pati Patni Aur Woh (Guest Appearance); Anjane Mein; Badaltey Rishtey; Naya Daur
1977	Doosra Aadmi; Hum Kisise Kum Naheen; Amar Akbar Anthony; Chala Murari Hero Banne (as himself)
1976	Barood; Ginny Aur Johnny (Special Appearance); Rangila Ratan; Kabhi Kabhie

1975	Zehreela Insaan; Rafoo Chakkar; Zinda Dil; Raaja; Khel Khel Mein
1973	Bobby
1970	Mera Naam Joker
1955	Shree 420 (uncredited)

INDEX

Index

Index

Index

Index

Index

Index

ACKNOWLEDGEMENTS

I would like to thank all my friends, fans and well-wishers for the love and support they have given me all my life. I also remember and thank my friends who are no more: Bittu Anand, Raju Nanda, Ghanshyam Rohera, Harvinder Singh Kohli, Salim Al-Midfa, Ravi Malhotra and Suresh Kohli. Suresh actually got this autobiography rolling a few years ago and put me in touch with HarperCollins. They have been my lifeline and have seen me through many ups and downs in my life and career. A big hug to each of them, wherever they are.

I have dedicated an entire chapter to her. But I would still like to thank Neetu for being the best support system I could ever have. I would also like a special mention for my two children, Riddhima and Ranbir, who have made me happy and proud.

I would like to thank my publishers, HarperCollins, and editors V.K. Karthika and Shantanu Ray Chaudhuri for giving me this opportunity to recapture my memories through this

Acknowledgements

book. Most of our lunch sessions, at times lasting five hours, were animated ones, with me speaking myself hoarse.

I would like to thank my co-author Meena Iyer for listening patiently to me (I'm an impatient man), jogging my memory when needed and penning my thoughts with precision.

And last but not the least, I would like to thank my siblings, uncles, cousins, actually the entire Kapoor family. I wouldn't be who I am had it not been for them.

CO-AUTHOR'S ACKNOWLEDGEMENTS

My parents (Krishnan and Alamelu) and my sister Lalitha. They've been gone long but I often feel they never actually left.

D-Day

Pyaar Mein Twist

Patiala House

Student of the Year

Sanam Re

Aurangzeb

Kapoor & Sons